Making Sense of Science

Physics

Also in the *Making Sense of Science* series

Biology Jackie Hardie and Chris Avery
Chemistry John Groves and David Mansfield
Human Biology Jackie Hardie, Chris Avery and Graham Wells

MAKING SENSE OF SCIENCE
PHYSICS

David Lucas
Physics Master, Bosworth College, Desford, Leicester

Mike Bowker
Principal Lecturer in Science, Worcester College of Higher Education, Worcester

Alan Hunt
*Deputy Head, Marshlands High School, Newcastle-under-Lyme
(formerly Head of Science, Coundon Court Comprehensive School, Coventry and Head of Physics, St Thomas Aquinas Grammar School, Birmingham)*

Ken Swinswood
Head of Science, Ruskin High School, Crewe, Cheshire

E. J. Wenham
Consulting Editor

D. Bentley
Language Consultant

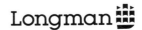
Longman

Acknowledgements

Longman Group UK Limited,
Longman House, Burnt Mill, Harlow,
Essex CM20 2JE, England
and Associated Companies throughout the world.

First published 1986

Set in 10/11 point Palatino

Printed in Great Britain
by Scotprint Limited, Musselburgh

I S B N 0 582 98584 6

We are grateful to the following for permission to reproduce photographs:

Addison-Wesley, *Physics: Concepts and Models*, Wenham, 27.3, 45.2, 51.1, 51.2, 51.3 and 90.2; Addison-Wesley Publishing Company, Reading, MA, *College Physics*, © 1980, Sears, Zemansky and Young, 51.7; BBC, 53.3; BICC/Trinity House, 62.2; Alan Brain, 46.2; Braun, 44.3; Paul Brierley, 64.2; British Aerospace, Hatfield, 23.6; British Antarctic Survey, 33.3 (photo G. J. Gilbert); British Rail, 25.3 and 31.5; W. Canning Materials, 83.3; J. Allan Cash, Section 4, 17.3, 20.1, Section 8 (photo K. Morgan), 35.1, Sections 12, 13, 14 and 64.3; CEGB, 1.2, Section 6, 83.1, 96.2, 96.3, 96.4 and 96.5; John Cleare/Mountain Camera, 38.1 and 44.4; Daily Telegraph Colour Library/Space Frontiers, Section 5, 55.3 and 56.7; Dreamland, 85.4 (photo Clive Holmes); Electricity Council, 84.7 and 86.2(b); EMI, 97.4; Vivien Fifield Picture Library, 11.2 and Section 23; Financial Times Photography, 68.5; Geoscience Features, 15.3, Sections 11, 16 and 71.1; Siebe Gorman, 12.6; Richard Hamnet, 14.1(b); Philip Harris, 18.1; HMSO, Crown ©, 104.3; Inmos, Section 18; International Technology Development Group/AATP, Section 9; ITN, Sections 1 and 22; Jones Cranes, Section 20; Clive Lambert, 14.1(a); Frank Lane Picture Agency, 13.1 (photo H. Eisenbeiss), 28.2 (photo R.P. Lawrence), 29.3 (photo Ray Bird), 38.1(b) (photo Arthur Christiansen) and 53.4 (photo R. P. Lawrence); Brian Lawrence, 20.3; Mere Green Studios, 113.9, Motor Industry Research Association, Nuneaton, 20.5; National Coal Board, 29.1 and 29.2; National Maritime Museum, 74.1; Philips Security Systems, 112.16; Photosource, Section 2, 16.3, 22.3 (all Keystone) and 54.2 (CLI); Pilkington Insulation, 39.4; Press Tige Pictures/Tony Tilford, Section 3; *PSSC Physics*, second edition, 1965, D. C. Heath and Company with Education Development Center Inc, Newton, MA, 19.4 and 22.4; David Redfern, Section 15; Ann Ronan Picture Library, 15.5; Royal Greenwich Observatory, 59.5; Science Photo Library, 39.5 (NASA), 53.2 (US Naval Observatory) and Section 17 (photo Nelson Medina); Seaphot, 9.1 (photo Dick Clarke); Science Museum, 2.1(a); Scottish Tourist Board, 20.2; Robert Startin, 7.5; Teltron, 99.2; Teltronix UK, 101.2; TI Creda, 85.5; Topham, 3.1(a) (photo Chapman) and 38.1(a); Transport and Road Research Laboratory, Crowthorne/Crown ©, 25.2 and Section 7; United Kingdom Atomic Energy Authority, 1.1, 76.3, 109.1, 109.3, 110.2 and 110.3; University of Cambridge Cavendish Laboratory, 106.3 (photo P.M.S. Blackett); USIS, 21.4; Vision International, 29.4 (photo Paolo Koch); Ted Wenham, 106.1; Longman Photographic Unit, 2.1(b) and (c), 3.1(b), 10.2, 11.1, 16.2, 32.1, Section 10, 63.4, 67.3, 77.4, Section 19, 85.8, 86.2(a), Section 21, Section 24, 112.3(b), 112.9, 112.18, 112.23(b), 112.24, 112.26(b), 113.2 and 113.8 (components by RS Components).

The cover photograph was taken by Paul Brierley and shows the masks used to produce the various layers in a microchip.

Preface

This book is about physics. It is divided into many short **units**. Most of these are only one or two pages long. Each unit explains a new idea. Units dealing with similar ideas are grouped into **sections**. At the end of each section you will find a **summary** of the main points.

Technical words are printed in **bold** the first time they are used. You will find an explanation nearby. There is also a short physics dictionary at the end of the book to help you.

This book is illustrated in colour and black and white. The illustrations are placed so that they are near the written explanation.

There are questions for you to try at the back of the book. These are arranged in section order.

This book will provide a good foundation for the work needed for the 16+ and new GCSE examinations. By the time you have worked through it you will have a grasp of physics and you will also see how and why physics plays an important part in our lives.

David Lucas
Mike Bowker
Alan Hunt
Ken Swinswood

Contents

Physicists and Physics Measurements

1 Who are the physicists?

The world we live in is full of examples of physics at work. For physics is about movement, forces, energy and power, structure, light, sound and so on. Physicists, the people who work in physics, have given us knowledge and theories which have led to many useful things in our lives. Some of these are: the silicon chip, power stations of all sorts, the smooth shapes of modern cars and aircraft, and many types of machinery (both simple and complicated).

Physicists work in industry, transport, hospitals, research and communications. You will also find them in government, universities, radar stations, the defence forces and engineering. Some of the jobs they do are shown here (Figs 1.1 and 1.2). You will find others elsewhere in the book.

Fig. 1.1 A radiographer at work with a patient.

Fig. 1.2 A power station control room.

2 Measurements and units

Physicists and engineers need to know the size, mass, temperature, strength, etc., of things. They find this out when they **measure**. Many different instruments can be used to measure. But each instrument is made to make one kind of measurement.

MEASURING MASS

If you buy some cheese, the grocer will put it on some scales to find out how much cheese you have to pay for. This is just what the physicist does to find the **mass** of an object. But the physicist uses a balance. Most modern balances, like the grocer's scales, have a pan on top. The object is put on the pan and the mass is read on a scale in grams (g) or kilograms (kg).

MEASURING TIME

Some clocks have a pendulum swinging from side to side (Fig. 2.1). This swinging pendulum controls the hands of the clock. Each swing takes the same time. The energy to drive the clock comes from a mass which is falling very slowly (p. 16).

Watches with springs have a balance wheel that turns back and forth. The swinging of the balance wheel controls the movement of the hands. The energy to drive the watch is stored in a coiled-up spring.

Modern electronic clocks and watches depend on the very regular vibrations of a tiny quartz crystal. These vibrations control the 'read-out'. The energy comes from a small battery.

MEASURING LENGTH

To find the length of a piece of wood or fabric you use a rule or tape. If you need to measure the length exactly you must take special care (Fig. 2.2). The end of a rule can be damaged easily. If the zero mark is at the end you could have difficulty deciding where it should be.

Place the rule as close to the object as possible. Choose a mark — the zero mark if it is clear or any other, e.g., 1 cm or 10 cm — and place it against the edge of the wood or fabric.

(a)　　　　　　　　　　　(c)

Fig. 2.1　Measuring time. (a) A grandfather clock. (b) A watch with springs. (c) A digital watch.

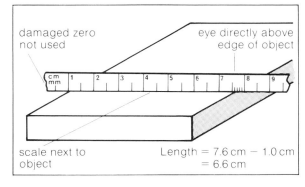

damaged zero not used

eye directly above edge of object

scale next to object

Length = 7.6 cm − 1.0 cm = 6.6 cm

Fig. 2.2　How to use a rule to measure the length of an object.

When the rule is in place, read off the length at the other end of the rule. If you use a metre or half-metre rule, try to read to one-half of a millimetre. Remember to keep your eye level with the mark you are reading.

MEASURING VOLUME

If you have a regular solid, such as a cuboid or a sphere, you can calculate its **volume**—the space it takes up—from measured lengths (Fig. 2.3). If the solid is not regular, a large bolt perhaps, you can use a measuring cylinder to find its volume (Fig. 2.4). Put some water in the cylinder and write down its volume. Lower the bolt carefully in the water and read the new volume. Find the difference between the two readings. This is the volume of the bolt.

SI UNITS

All scientific measurements are given in the International System of units (SI). Three of the basic units are the **kilogram**, the **second** and the **metre**. The names of smaller or bigger units are made by adding one of the following prefixes to the name of the base unit:

μ ..	micro	one-millionth
m ..	milli	one-thousandth
c ..	centi	one-hundredth
d ..	deci	one-tenth
k ..	kilo	one thousand times
M ..	mega	one million times

Table 2 shows some of the units for length, mass and volume. You can see that, for example:

one-thousandth of a metre (m) is a millimetre (mm);
a gram (g) is one-thousandth of a kilogram (kg);
a megawatt (MW) is one million watts (W).

VERY CAREFUL MEASUREMENTS

People who make and repair engines, sewing machines and other pieces of machinery have to make very careful measurements of length. A rule cannot be used because it is not accurate enough. Special tools called **vernier callipers** and **micrometer screw gauges** are used instead.

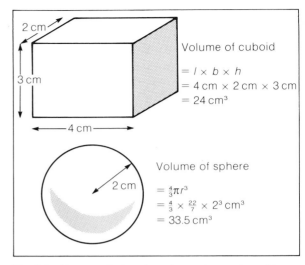

Volume of cuboid
$$= l \times b \times h$$
$$= 4\,cm \times 2\,cm \times 3\,cm$$
$$= 24\,cm^3$$

Volume of sphere
$$= \tfrac{4}{3}\pi r^3$$
$$= \tfrac{4}{3} \times \tfrac{22}{7} \times 2^3\,cm^3$$
$$= 33.5\,cm^3$$

Fig. 2.3 How to calculate the volume of a regular solid.

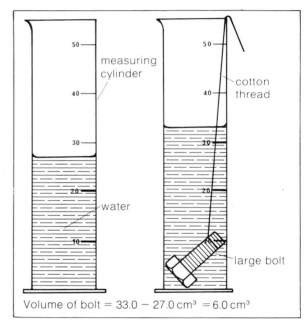

Volume of bolt = $33.0 - 27.0\,cm^3 = 6.0\,cm^3$

Fig. 2.4 How to use a measuring cylinder to find the volume of a large bolt.

Table 2 Some units for length, mass and volume

Length		Mass		Volume	
μm	micrometre	μg	microgram	mm³	cubic millimetre
mm	millimetre	mg	milligram	cm³	cubic centimetre
cm	centimetre	cg	centigram	dm³	cubic decimetre
m	metre	g	gram	m³	cubic metre
km	kilometre	kg	kilogram		

3 Forces

You can pull or push an object in many ways (Fig. 3.1). You could use your hands, a spring or a screw. You could also use a magnet as they do on doors of refrigerators. What other ways can you think of? Every push or pull is an example of a **force**. Forces are very important in physics and engineering. Forces allow us to move, walk and run. They can make bicycles, cars and trains go faster or slower. They can bend, stretch, compress or twist things.

(a)

(b)

Fig. 3.1 Examples of forces. (a) Horse pulling a sleigh. (b) A screw-jack raising a car.

MEASURING FORCES

The unit in which forces are measured is called a **newton (N)**. Forces are often measured with a spring balance. To do this, the balance has to be **calibrated**. This is done by marking numbers on it that measure in newtons.

Some spring balances can be used in any position, while others must be kept upright. Some measure pushes rather than pulls.

FORCES STRETCHING SPRINGS

If you increase the force on a spring by hanging an extra load or mass on the end the spring will get longer or extended. To find the extension of a spring, measure the length of the spring with a small load on it to open out the coils. Then measure the length of the spring with the extra force on it (Fig. 3.2). Subtract the first length from the second. You can then plot a graph of extension against the force. You should get a straight line that goes through the origin – the 0,0 point on the graph (Fig. 3.3, overleaf). You can see from the graph that the extension doubles if the force doubles and so on. This means that the

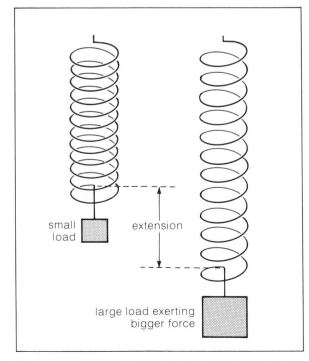

Fig. 3.2 When you add an extra load, the spring extends.

extension is proportional to the force. This is called **Hooke's law**. We say that the spring is **elastic**.

Example An open spring has a length of 12 cm. When a force of 100 N is applied the length becomes 20 cm. What will the length be if a force of 80 N is applied?

For a load of 100 N the extension is 20 cm − 12 cm = 8 cm. For 1 N the extension would be one-hundredth of this; that is, 0.08 cm. Therefore, the extension for 80 N will be 80 × 0.08 cm = 6.4 cm. The new length will be 12 cm + 6.4 cm = 18.4 cm.

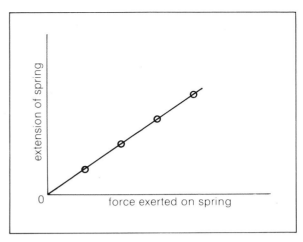

Fig. 3.3 The spring followed Hooke's law.

OVERLOADING A SPRING

If you put too much force on a spring the graph, which starts as a straight line, will become curved (Fig. 3.4). When you remove this large force, the spring will keep some of its stretch. It is permanently stretched, or **strained.** The point on the graph where the straight line ends is called the **elastic limit.**

STRETCHING A WIRE

If you take a length of about 30 cm of thin copper wire you will be able to stretch it. Hold the ends in your two hands and pull gently; then a little harder; a little harder still. It feels quite soft and then it breaks. Look at the broken ends very carefully.

Metal wires all stretch elastically at first. Then they reach the elastic limit and become permanently stretched. With larger forces a neck will form and then they will break.

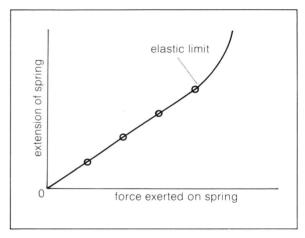

Fig. 3.4 Why has the graph become curved?

4 The pull of the earth

Look carefully at the two balances in Fig. 4.1. The spring balance is calibrated in newtons and we know it measures force. Hanging from it is a bag of sugar marked 2 kg. The balance tells us that the pull of the earth on the bag of sugar is 20 N. Scientists call this pulling force the **weight** of the sugar.

The balance or scales with the two pans compares two masses. There is a 2-kg bag of sugar on the left-hand pan. There are two standard 1-kg masses on the right-hand pan. Because the two pans balance we know that the bag of sugar has a **mass** of 2 kg.

The earth pulls a mass of 2 kg towards it with a force of 20 N.

You have to be very careful about the words *weight* and *mass*. The shopkeeper who sold the 2-kg bag of sugar said that its weight was 2 kg (p. 9). The scientist who bought it said that the mass of the bag of sugar was 2 kg and its weight was 20 N. Both are right! This is just the way we use these words. So be warned!

In this book, the word *weight* always means 'the pull of the earth on . . .'. Because it is a force, it is measured in newtons.

If an astronaut took the spring balance and the scales up to the moon the scales would still balance. The mass of the bag of sugar is still 2 kg. But the reading of the spring balance would be only a little over 3 N, not 20 N. This is because the moon doesn't pull as hard as the earth does.

On his way to the moon, the astronaut would find that the pull of the earth was getting smaller. At the surface of the earth the pull on each kilogram is 10 N. At a distance equal to the earth's radius from the surface (about 6400 km) it is only 2.5 N.

CENTRE OF GRAVITY

The earth pulls on every part of any object (Fig. 4.2). But there is one point in the object where the whole weight (pull of the earth) seems to act. This is the **centre of gravity** of the object. For a regular solid—a solid steel ball, say—the centre of gravity is at the centre. If a body is hanging freely, its centre of gravity is always directly below the **pivot**. This can help you find the centre of gravity if the solid is not a regular one.

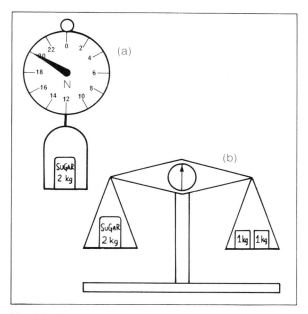

Fig. 4.1   You can (a) measure weight or (b) compare masses.

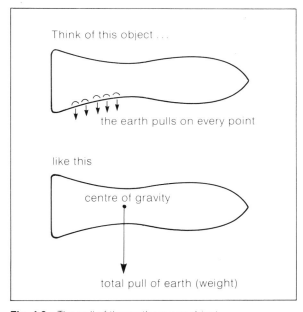

Fig. 4.2   The pull of the earth on any object.

5 Balancing forces

EQUILIBRIUM

If an object is not moving although several forces are acting on it, it is said to be in **equilibrium**; that is, the forces balance one another. There are three ways in which this can happen. To distinguish between them move an object a little.

1   If it returns to its original position it was in **stable equilibrium**.
2   If it stays in its new position it was and is in **neutral equilibrium**.
3   If it continues to move away from the original position it was in **unstable equilibrium** (Fig. 5.1).

STABILITY

A bus can lean over a long way before falling It is very stable. This is because the heavy engine is placed as low as possible. The centre of gravity (p. 13) of the whole bus is low. So long as the vertical line from the centre of gravity is still between the wheels when it is tilted, the bus will not topple over.

The filing cabinet with the drawers pulled out in Fig. 5.2(a) is likely to topple. Its centre of gravity is pulled to one side. The cabinet in Fig. 5.2(b) is stable; its centre of gravity is in the middle.

MOMENTS

Try to push a door open with one finger. You will find it easier if you push a long way from the hinges. The ability of a force to make something turn is called the **moment** or **torque** of the force.

To measure the moment or torque of the force, multiply together the force and the shortest distance from the pivot to the force:

$$\text{moment of a force} = \text{force} \times \frac{\text{shortest distance from pivot to force}}{}$$

The distance is measured at right angles to the force.

The moment of a force can be either clockwise or anticlockwise. Think which way the force would turn the object if it was the only force (Fig. 5.3).

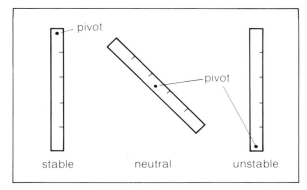

Fig. 5.1   What will happen if you give each of these three rules a little push?

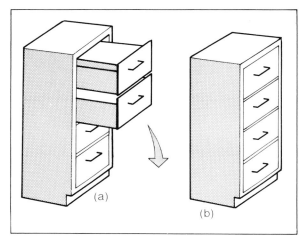

Fig. 5.2   Which of these filing cabinets is the more stable? Why are these cabinets usually screwed to the floor?

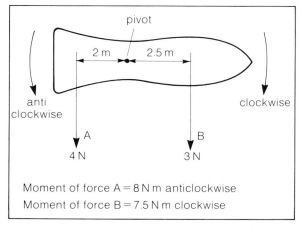

Moment of force A = 8 N m anticlockwise
Moment of force B = 7.5 N m clockwise

Fig. 5.3   Calculating and describing moments. Which way will this object turn−clockwise or anticlockwise?

THE PRINCIPLE OF MOMENTS

Two people want to play on a see-saw but one is heavier than the other. They will not balance if they sit at equal distances from the pivot. However, they may balance if the lighter person sits further from the pivot than the heavier one. Then the moments of their weights will be equal in size, but one will be clockwise while the other is anticlockwise.

The principle of moments applies to any system where turning forces are balanced. It states that if a system is in equilibrium the sum of the clockwise moments about any point equals the sum of the anticlockwise moments about that point. One very simple system has two masses hanging from a metre rule. The rule is pivoted at its centre (Fig. 5.4). You will always find that:

force$_1$ × distance$_1$ = force$_2$ × distance$_2$

If a third mass is added (Fig. 5.5), then to make it balance

force$_1$ × distance$_1$ = (force$_2$ × distance$_2$)
$$+ (force_3 × distance_3)$$

Example A metre rule pivoted at its mid-point has a mass that makes a force of 3 N hung from the 10-cm mark. A mass making a force of 6 N is hung from the 60-cm mark. What force must be exerted at the 80-cm mark to balance the system (Fig. 5.6)?

Find the moments about the pivot:

Moment due to the weight of 3 N
= (3 × 40) N cm = 120 N cm anticlockwise

Moment due to the weight of 6 N
= (6 × 10) N cm = 60 N cm clockwise

Moment due to the unknown force (F)
= (F × 30) N cm = 30F N cm clockwise

By the principle of moments, for balance:

anticlockwise = sum of clockwise
moment   moments
120 N cm = 60 N cm + 30F N cm
60 N cm = 30F N cm
F = 2 N

The unknown force is 2 N.

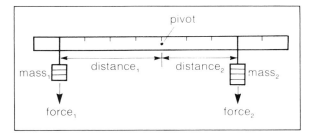

Fig. 5.4 A balanced system with two sets of masses.

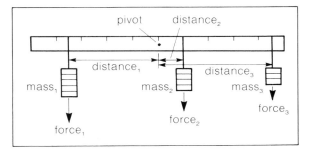

Fig. 5.5 A balanced system with three forces.

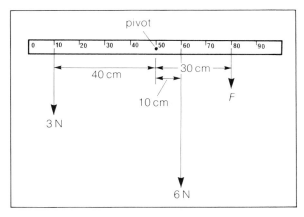

Fig. 5.6 What force must be exerted to balance the system?

6 Energy—a first look

FUEL FOR JOBS

Fuel is needed for most jobs. You use food to walk, petrol to drive a motor bike, coal to produce electricity and gas to cook food. All these fuels provide **energy**. You pay for energy when you get a gas or electricity bill.

The earth gets a lot of energy free—from the sun. That energy keeps us warm and is used by green plants in photosynthesis (p. 97) to produce starches and sugars from carbon dioxide and water. We depend on this process for our food. Animals eat plants. We eat plants and animals. The sun's energy also drives the winds, the waves and the weather as well.

There are a few jobs that don't need energy. For example, to put a 2-kg bag of sugar on a shelf needs food as fuel. But once the bag is there, it stays there without needing any more energy.

MEASURING ENERGY

If you lift a 2-kg bag of sugar out of a shopping bag on the floor and put it on a shelf 1.5 m high, you have to apply a force to overcome the pull of the earth on the bag. We already know that this force—the weight of the bag of sugar—is 20 N (p. 13). To calculate the energy stored in this way multiply the force by the distance moved in the direction of the force (Fig. 6.1):

energy = 20 N × 1.5 m = 30 newton metres

The unit newton metre (N m) is usually called a **joule (J)**.

You supplied 30 J of energy; you did 30 J of work.

work = force × distance moved in the
direction of the force

Work is measured in joules (newton metres).

Sitting up on the shelf, the bag of sugar has that extra amount of energy. This store of energy is called **potential energy**. To lift the bag you used much more than the 30 J of energy stored. To lift your arm your muscles had to work and your body warmed up a bit. That needed energy too. You probably used about 120 J of energy to get that bag of sugar

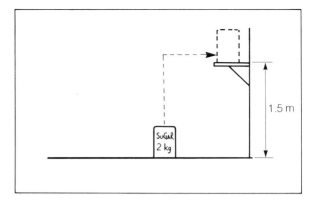

Fig. 6.1   What force do you have to overcome in lifting the bag of sugar?

up on the shelf. The energy came from the food you had eaten.

Now look back to Fig. 2.1 on p. 9. Winding up the driving mass in the pendulum clock stores up potential energy. As it falls very slowly down again, the potential energy is used to drive the hands of the clock. In many clocks of this sort, the energy stored will drive the clock for eight days.

Example   You try to push-start a car. This needs a force of 300 N and you manage to push the car for 20 m in a straight line. How much energy do you give to the car to get it started? Or, if you like, how much work do you do on the car?

$$\begin{aligned} \text{energy given} \atop \text{to the car} &= \text{work done} \\ &= \text{force} \times \text{distance moved} \\ &= 300 \text{ N} \times 20 \text{ m} \\ &= 6000 \text{ N m} \quad \text{or } 6000 \text{ J} \end{aligned}$$

7 Using measurements

DENSITY

You may have been asked the trick question: 'Which is heavier, a lump of lead or a bag of feathers?' Many people say that the lead is heavier. But a mass of feathers occupies more space than the same mass of lead. Its volume is larger. To avoid problems like this, a new idea, density is used (Fig. 7.1). **Density** is the mass (in g or kg) of unit volume (in cm^3 or m^3) of the substance:

$$\text{density} = \frac{\text{mass}}{\text{volume}}$$

Density is measured in kilograms per cubic metre (kg/m^3) or in grams per cubic centimetre (g/cm^3). Typical densities are shown in Table 7.

Table 7 Some densities

Material	Density (kg/m³)	Material	Density (kg/m³)
Helium	0.18*	Sea water	1 025
Air	1.3*	Glass	~2 600
Cork	240	Marble	2 600
Wood	650	Aluminium	2 710
Methylated spirit	790	Steel	7 860
Ice	920	Lead	11 340
Water	1 000	Gold	19 300

* At standard temperature and pressure.

If you have measured the mass and the volume of a body (p. 10) you can calculate the density of the material it is made from.

Example A block of concrete 2 m by 1 m by 10 cm has a mass of 480 kg. What is the density of concrete?

$$\text{volume} = \text{length} \times \text{breadth} \times \text{height}$$
$$= 2\,\text{m} \times 1\,\text{m} \times 0.1\,\text{m}$$
$$= 0.2\ \text{m}^3$$

$$\text{density} = \frac{\text{mass}}{\text{volume}}$$
$$= \frac{480\ \text{kg}}{0.2\ \text{m}^3}$$
$$= 2400\ \text{kg/m}^3$$

The density of concrete is 2400 kg/m^3.

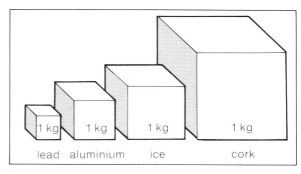

Fig. 7.1 The mass of each of these cubes is 1 kg.

SOLIDS IN LIQUIDS

If you place a piece of ice in some methylated spirit, it will sink. But if you place a similar sized piece of ice in water, it will float. Look at the table of densities (Table 7). Ice is denser than methylated spirit so it sinks. Ice is less dense than water so it floats.

Tie a piece of aluminium by a thread to a spring balance and lower it gently into some water. Watch the reading of the spring balance get smaller as more and more of the aluminium is covered with water. The more aluminium there is in the water, the more the water pushes up on it and the lighter the aluminium seems (Fig. 7.2). This apparent loss in weight is called the **upthrust**—the upward push. The upthrust on a solid immersed in any liquid or gas is equal to the weight of the liquid or gas pushed out of the way by the solid. This is called **Archimedes' principle**.

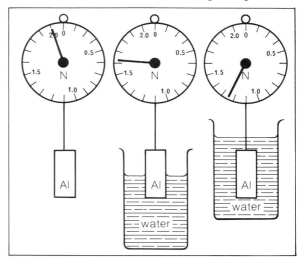

Fig. 7.2 What happens when a solid block of aluminium is gradually lowered into water?

FLOATING

Tie a piece of wood to a spring balance with a length of thread. Lower the wood into the water. Once again, the balance reading will get smaller. When the wood floats, the thread goes slack and the balance reads zero. The floating piece of wood seems to weigh nothing. The water must be pushing upwards on the wood with a push exactly equal to the pull of the earth on the wood. The upthrust is equal to the weight of the wood (Fig. 7.3(a)). Now do the same thing using methylated spirit instead of water. The wood will still float. But more of the wood will be in the methylated spirit (Fig. 7.3(b)). If you use sea water or brine instead of water, the wood again floats. But there is less of the wood in the sea water (Fig. 7.3(c)).

The denser the liquid (Table 7) the less wood below the surface. The weight of the liquid pushed out of the way is the same and the upthrust is the same. But because the density of the liquid is greater the volume pushed aside is smaller.

THE HYDROMETER

A **hydrometer** is an instrument specially designed to float in a liquid and measure its density (Fig. 7.4). Read the density where the surface of the liquid crosses the scale in the stem of the hydrometer. Special hydrometers are used to test whether a car battery is fully charged (Fig. 7.5) or whether milk contains too much water.

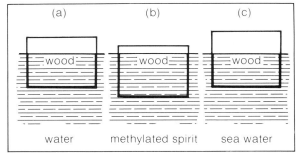

Fig. 7.3   A wood block floats most deeply in the least dense liquid.

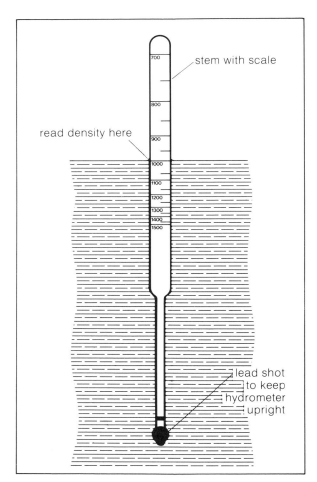

Fig. 7.4   Using a hydrometer to measure the density of a liquid.

Fig. 7.5 Using a hydrometer to check the density of the acid tells you whether the battery has been discharged.

BALLOONS

When a balloon contains a gas that is less dense than air it will rise. This gas could be hot air, hydrogen or helium. Hot air is normally used as hydrogen is dangerous because it can catch fire; helium is expensive.

The balloon rises because the upthrust of the air round it is greater than the total weight of the balloon, the gas inside it and the load that it is carrying. The movement up or down of a hot air balloon is controlled by altering the amount of hot air in the balloon or the temperature of the air. More or hotter gas is needed to make it go up. Less or cooler gas is needed to make it come down.

SUMMARY: PHYSICISTS AND PHYSICS MEASUREMENTS

- Balances are used to compare masses; the units are grams (g) or kilograms (kg).
- Lengths are measured with rules or, more accurately, with vernier callipers or micrometers; the units are millimetres (mm), centimetres (cm) or metres (m).
- Volumes of solids and liquids may be found by calculation or by using a measuring cylinder; the units are cm^3 or m^3.
- All scientific measurements are given in SI units.
- A force is a push or a pull.
- Forces may be measured with spring balances in units called newtons (N).
- The extension of a spring is proportional to the force up to the elastic limit (Hooke's law).
- The pull of the earth on a body is called the weight of the body. Weight is measured in newtons.
- The whole weight of a body appears to act at its centre of gravity.
- If a system is balanced under the action of several forces it is in equilibrium. Equilibrium may be stable, neutral or unstable.
- The moment of a force, or its torque, is its turning effect. It is equal to the force multiplied by the perpendicular distance from the pivot.
- A moment may be either clockwise or anticlockwise.
- When a system is balanced the sum of the clockwise moments about any point is equal to the sum of the anticlockwise moments about that point. This is the principle of moments.
- Energy is transformed from one form to another when a force moves along its own direction.
- Work is force multiplied by the distance moved in the direction of the force.
- Energy and work are measured in newton metres (N m) or joules (J).
- Density is mass divided by volume.
- A solid sinks in a liquid less dense than itself but floats in a liquid denser than itself.
- The upthrust on a solid body placed in a liquid is equal to the apparent loss in weight of the solid.
- The upthrust on a solid body in a liquid is equal to the weight of the liquid displaced (Archimedes' principle).
- The density of a liquid can be measured with a hydrometer, which floats in it.
- A rising balloon contains gas less dense than air.

Force and Pressure

8 Pressure

If you were forced to sit on a drawing pin would you rather have the point or the head upwards? It would be more comfortable with the head upwards. The area of contact between you and the drawing pin would be greater. The pressure would be less—and it would hurt less.

Pressure is force divided by area. If the force is measured in newtons (N) and the area in square metres (m²), the pressure will be in newtons per square metre (N/m²). This unit is called the **pascal (Pa)**.

At one time, dance-hall owners banned women wearing stiletto heels from going on to the dance floor (Fig. 8.1). The pressure set up by a woman putting all her weight on to one heel is greater than that caused by an elephant standing on one foot! You can often see marks on tarmac caused by stiletto heels.

Fig. 8.1 The girl with stiletto heels and the elephant!

Woman: Weight 480 N
       Heel 1 cm × 1 cm or
       0.01 m × 0.01 m

$$\text{Pressure} = \frac{\text{force}}{\text{area}}$$

$$= \frac{480\ \text{N}}{0.01\ \text{m} \times 0.01\ \text{m}}$$

$$= \frac{4\,800\,000\ \text{N}}{1\ \text{m}^2}$$

$$= 4\,800\,000\ \text{Pa}$$

Elephant: Weight 54 000 N
       Foot 30 cm × 30 cm or
       0.3 m × 0.3 m

$$\text{Pressure} = \frac{\text{force}}{\text{area}}$$

$$= \frac{54\,000\ \text{N}}{0.3\ \text{m} \times 0.3\ \text{m}}$$

$$= \frac{5\,400\,000\ \text{N}}{9\ \text{m}^2}$$

$$= 600\,000\ \text{Pa}$$

9 Pressure in liquids

PRESSURE AND DEPTH

The vessel shown in Fig. 9.1 can be used in very deep water. It is built to resist the great pressure exerted by the water when it is deep in the ocean. The deeper you go the greater the pressure becomes. Underwater vessels like this one are made of acrylic plastic which is very strong. The strength of the material and its ball shape help the vessel to withstand the great pressure.

Think about the tube of water shown in Fig. 9.2:

$$\text{volume of water} = \frac{\text{area of cross-section}}{} \times \text{height}$$

$$\text{mass of water (in kg)} = \text{volume} \times \text{density}$$

$$= (\text{area} \times \text{height}) \times \text{density}$$

A mass of 1 kg has a weight of 10 N. Therefore,

$$\text{weight of water (in N)} = \text{mass} \times 10$$

$$= (\text{area} \times \text{height}) \times \text{density} \times 10$$

The pressure at the bottom of the tube is

$$\text{pressure} = \frac{\text{weight}}{\text{area}}$$

$$= \frac{(\text{area} \times \text{height}) \times \text{density} \times 10}{\text{area}}$$

$$= \text{height} \times \text{density} \times 10 \quad (\text{in N/m}^2)$$

So the pressure increases with depth. It also increases with the density of the liquid.

PRESSURE AND DIRECTION

Use a red-hot pin to make some holes in a plastic syringe. When you fill the syringe with water and push the plunger in, water squirts out of the holes in all directions. The plunger exerts pressure on the water. This pressure acts in the liquid in all directions.

TRANSMISSION OF FLUID PRESSURE

In Fig. 9.3 the smaller syringe always wins. The plunger has a smaller area so more pressure is set up by pushing. The pressure is

Fig. 9.1 Why do you think this vessel is shaped like a ball?

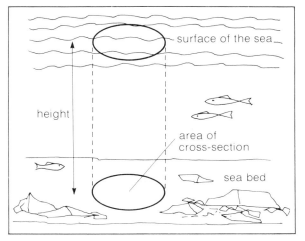

Fig. 9.2 Finding the pressure formula.

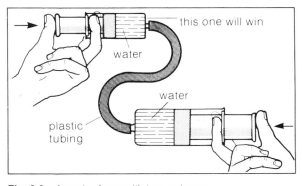

Fig. 9.3 A push-of-war with two syringes.

transmitted through the water and pushes the larger plunger out against the push. Liquids and gases transmit pressure because they can flow. They are also called **fluids**.

10 Hydraulic machines, fluid pressure and fluids flowing

Machines that are driven by the pressure of a fluid are called **hydraulic machines**. Any fluid will work in this way because all fluids transmit pressure (p. 21). A small force on a small area may give the same pressure as a large force on a large area. The fluid used in the machine is the one that suits it best. To avoid corrosion of metal parts, special oily mixtures are used, e.g., car brake fluid.

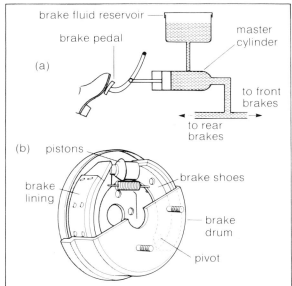

Fig. 10.1 Slowing down a car. (a) The hydraulic braking system. (b) A drum brake.

HYDRAULIC BRAKES

The foot brake on a car is a hydraulic machine. The hand brake uses a cable and works quite differently. When the driver presses the brake pedal a piston moves in the master cylinder (Fig. 10.1(a)). This increases the pressure on the brake fluid. The pressure is transmitted to the brakes on each of the four wheels. In drum brakes the increased pressure of the fluid makes the two pistons move outwards (Fig. 10.1(b)). Each piston forces the pivoted brake shoe to move out. The brake lining rubs on the brake drum and the car slows down.

There are many other types of hydraulic brakes. Modern cars and motor bikes often have disc brakes as well as or instead of drum brakes. In disc brakes the moving pistons squeeze brake pads on to a disc that turns with the wheel and so slows the car down (Fig. 10.2).

Fig. 10.2 A disc brake on a motor bike.

FLYING

When an aircraft moves through the air, air flows over its wings. The wings are shaped so that air flows more quickly over the top of the wing than over the bottom. The faster a fluid flows the lower the pressure; this is called the **Bernoulli effect**. The pressure below the wing is therefore higher than the pressure above the wing where the air is flowing fastest. As greater pressure means greater force, there is an upward force on the underside of the wing. This is called the **lift**. Lift accounts for the flight of birds as well as of aircraft. Try the experiment shown in Fig. 10.3 to see these effects.

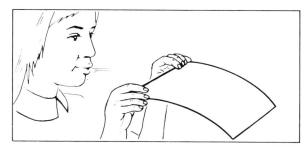

Fig. 10.3 As you blow out across the top of the paper it lifts, why?

11 Atmospheric pressure

Take a large plastic container with a good tap and put it on a sensitive balance. Record the mass of the container and the air inside it. Then use a foot pump to push more air into the container. Put it back on the balance and you will find that the mass has increased. The container looks much the same. The pull of the earth on the extra air tells us that the air has mass (p. 9).

The atmosphere is the layer of air round the earth. It is many kilometres deep. So there is a lot of air above us. Because it has weight it presses down on the earth's surface and on us. This pressure is called **atmospheric pressure**.

THE EFFECT OF ATMOSPHERIC PRESSURE

If air is slowly pumped out of a large tin, the tin is crushed by the pressure of the air outside it (Fig. 11.1). As the air is pumped out, the pressure of the air left in falls below the atmospheric pressure. Pumping the air out makes a partial **vacuum** inside the tin.

A classic experiment was carried out at Magdeburg in 1654 by Otto von Guericke, inventor of the vacuum pump. He had two hemispheres that fitted closely together round their rims. He pumped out the air from inside them. Two teams of horses could not pull the two large hemispheres apart (Fig. 11.2). Atmospheric pressure held them together despite the pull of the horses.

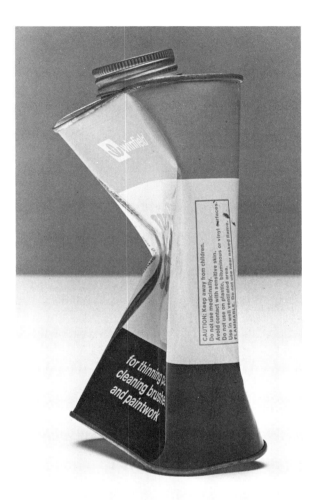

Fig. 11.1 A metal can crushed by the pressure of the atmosphere after air has been pumped out of it.

Fig. 11.2 von Guericke's experiment in 1654 to show the great force exerted by atmospheric pressure.

THE BAROMETER

A long glass tube, sealed at one end, is filled with mercury. It is then carefully turned upside down without letting the mercury escape. The open end is placed in a bowl of mercury. The mercury level in the tube falls until it is about 760 mm above the level in the bowl. The atmosphere can only push hard enough to support a column of mercury about 760 mm high. The space above the mercury is a vacuum. This can be shown by tilting the tube. The mercury then completely fills the tube (Fig. 11.3).

This instrument is called a **barometer**. It can be mounted and hung on the laboratory wall. A barometer may have extra parts, like a vernier scale (p. 10), to help measure the height of the mercury column more accurately. Atmospheric pressure, measured by the barometer, is important to the meteorologist (weather forecaster).

The average atmospheric pressure is 101 300 Pa. On weather maps, this is known as 1013 millibars. Very high atmospheric pressures go up to over 1040 millibars; very low ones down to 950 millibars (at sea level).

THE ANEROID BAROMETER AND THE ALTIMETER

Aneroid barometers have no mercury in them; *aneroid* means without liquid. They have a metal drum shaped like a concertina. Some air has been removed from inside this drum. As the atmospheric pressure changes the top of the drum moves up or down. Levers magnify this movement and move a pointer over a scale.

Air pressure falls as you go up from the earth's surface, or sea level. This is because there is less air above you to press down. A type of aneroid barometer used to measure height is called an **altimeter**. Pilots use altimeters to see how high they are flying.

STRAWS AND SYRINGES

When you suck milk from a glass with a straw you are really expanding your lungs. This action lowers the pressure in your mouth. Atmospheric pressure acting on the milk in the glass then pushes it up into your mouth (Fig. 11.4). The same thing happens when a hypodermic syringe is filled ready for an injection. With the needle in the liquid, the plunger is pulled back. This lowers the pressure in the syringe. Atmospheric pressure then forces the liquid into the syringe.

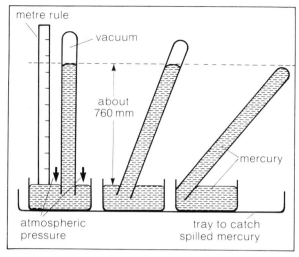

Fig. 11.3 Tilting a simple barometer tube shows that the space above the mercury is empty (a vacuum). How does it show this?

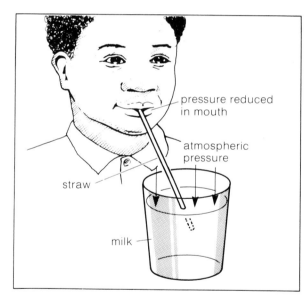

Fig. 11.4 When you suck milk up a straw you are really letting atmospheric pressure push the milk into your mouth.

12 Pressure in gases

You know that air exerts a pressure. How does it make this pressure? Scientists believe that all gases are made up of minute particles that move around quite freely at very high speeds. These particles collide with one another and bounce away again. They also hit the walls of a box containing them time and time again (Fig. 12.1). The pressure of a gas is due to the constant bombardment by these particles. The particles are called **molecules** (see also p. 66).

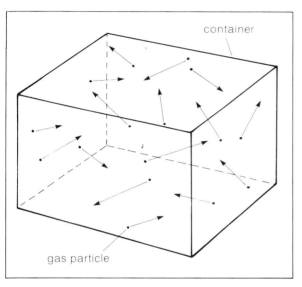

Fig. 12.1   A few gas molecules moving round in a box.

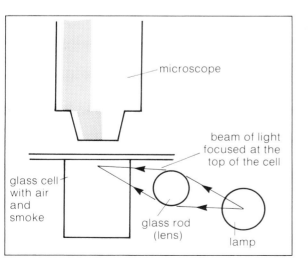

Fig. 12.2   Watching Brownian motion in a smoke cell.

BROWNIAN MOTION

Molecules are too small to be seen. You can, however, see them pushing smoke particles around if you use a microscope. A smoke cell is often used for this (Fig. 12.2). You see the smoke particles as tiny points of light that move zigzag in all directions. This movement is called **Brownian motion** and happens because the heavy smoke particles are hit at random by the fast-moving air molecules. Sometimes the smoke particles are knocked one way, sometimes another (Fig. 12.3). You may see a similar movement of tiny particles floating in a liquid.

MEASURING GAS PRESSURE

Connect a U-tube half filled with water to a gas tap. Turn on the tap. The water level goes down on one side and up on the other (Fig. 12.4). The difference in heights measures

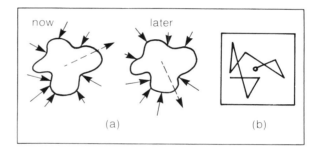

Fig. 12.3   (a) A smoke particle under bombardment by other molecules. (b) What the particle of smoke might do.

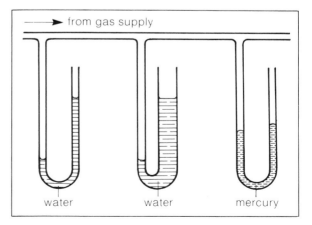

Fig. 12.4   Three manometers connected to a gas supply. The width of the tubes doesn't matter; but the density of the liquid does.

the gas pressure (above that of the atmosphere). This instrument is called a **manometer**. The diameter of the tubes does not matter but if a denser liquid such as mercury is used the difference in height will be smaller.

The tyre gauges used at garages use another principle. If you blow into a coiled paper tube it will uncoil (Fig. 12.5). A **Bourdon gauge** of the sort used to measure the extra pressure of the air in a tyre works on the same principle. It contains a curved tube made of metal. When the pressure inside the tube increases it uncoils a little. This movement is magnified by levers and moves a pointer over a scale.

Fig. 12.5 This paper tube works like a tyre gauge.

BOYLE'S LAW

A swimmer with an aqualung can stay under water for a long time (Fig. 12.6). The air needed for breathing is carried in the cylinder on the swimmer's back. This air is under pressure because a lot of it has been squashed into the small cylinder. The air is released through a regulator so that it returns to normal pressure before the swimmer breathes it. Gases are fairly easy to compress, or squash.

If you measure both the total pressure and the volume of a gas you can test **Boyle's law**. This states that: The product of the pressure and volume of a fixed mass of gas, i.e., some gas which is kept separate from any other, remains the same, i.e., constant, provided the temperature does not change. In other words:

$$\text{pressure}_1 \times \text{volume}_1 = \text{pressure}_2 \times \text{volume}_2$$

or

$$p_1 V_1 = p_2 V_2$$

This behaviour can also be shown by a graph (Fig. 12.7).

TYRE PRESSURES – A WARNING

Pressure gauges read the pressure above atmospheric pressure. So, if a pressure gauge records a pressure of 170 kPa, the total pressure inside the tyre is 170 kPa plus atmospheric pressure. That is a total pressure of about 270 kPa.

Fig. 12.6 A swimmer with a sub-aqua system on his back. The cylinders contain air at high pressure.

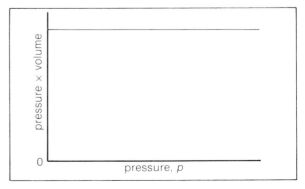

Fig. 12.7 A Boyle's law graph.

13 Surface tension

WALKING ON WATER

Figure 13.1 shows a pond skater standing on the surface of a pond. Its feet don't break through the water surface but simply bend it. The weight of the insect is supported by a force in the water surface called **surface tension**. When you overfill a glass tumbler so that the water's surface is a little above the edge of the tumbler, as in Fig. 13.2, surface tension is the force that keeps the water there.

REDUCING SURFACE TENSION

Make a little boat from a small piece of the expanded polystyrene used for packing. It will float easily on water. Place a little piece of soap or a crystal of camphor at the rear and the boat will move forward. The soap or camphor dissolves slowly in the water and reduces the surface tension at the back of the boat. The difference in surface tension between the front and back of the boat pulls it forward (Fig. 13.3).

DROPS AND BUBBLES

A drop has only one surface. A bubble has two: there is air inside and outside a bubble. But bubbles of air in a glass of water are really air drops like raindrops in air. It is surface tension that pulls the drop or bubble into its round shape. Surface tension also makes the pressure of the air inside the bubble greater than that outside it. The smaller the bubble the greater the extra pressure.

WETTING SURFACES

If clean water is put on to a greasy surface, surface tension pulls the water into lots of little drops. The water will not wet the greasy surface. When you add detergent to the water, it spreads out over the surface. The detergent lowers the surface tension of the water and it will wet the greasy surface. This is why detergent helps to wash greasy pots or clothes.

Fig. 13.1   A pond skater standing on water.

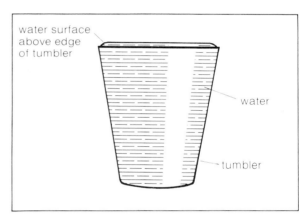

Fig. 13.2   What force holds the water above the edge of this tumbler?

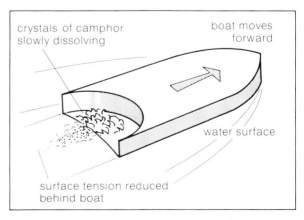

Fig. 13.3   A model boat moving across the surface of water as the soap or camphor lowers the surface tension behind the boat.

CAPILLARITY

A **capillary tube** has a very narrow hole down the middle. You can easily make one. Heat an ordinary glass tube in a bunsen burner flame to make it soft, then pull it out. If you put one end of a capillary tube in water, the water rises up the tube. The narrower the capillary tube the higher the water rises (Fig. 13.4). The water rises because surface tension pulls it up the narrow tube. This force is called **capillarity**. The same force causes water to move across a paper towel when it is placed on spilt water.

If mercury is used instead of water, the level in the capillary tube drops below the level of the mercury in the container.

The **meniscus** is the curve of the liquid at the top of the tube. Mercury curves in the opposite way to that of water (Fig. 13.5).

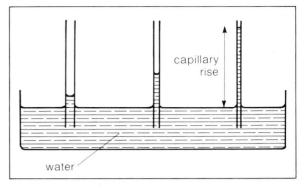

Fig. 13.4 The narrower the capillary tube, the higher the water rises.

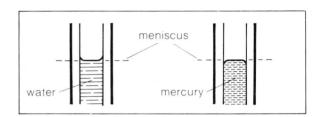

Fig. 13.5 The shape of a water meniscus and a mercury meniscus.

SUMMARY: FORCE AND PRESSURE

- Pressure is force divided by area. It is measured in pascals (Pa) or newtons per square metre (N/m^2):1 Pa = 1 N/m^2.
- The deeper down in a liquid the greater the pressure.
- Denser liquids give greater pressures at the same depth.
- Pressure in a liquid acts in all directions.
- Both liquids and gases are called fluids.
- Fluids transmit pressures applied to them.
- A small force on a small area can give the same pressure as a large force on a large area.
- A valve is a device that only lets a liquid or a gas go one way through it.
- Any machine worked by fluid pressure is a hydraulic machine.
- The atmosphere presses on us and everything around us.
- Atmospheric pressure is measured by mercury or aneroid barometers.
- Atmospheric pressure forces liquid into your mouth when you use a straw.
- Gas pressure is due to bombardment by gas molecules.
- Brownian motion is due to the uneven bombardment of particles by gas molecules.
- Gas pressure can be measured by a manometer or a Bourdon (curved-tube) gauge.
- Boyle's law states that for a fixed mass of gas at constant temperature:

  pressure$_1$ × volume$_1$ = pressure$_2$ × volume$_2$

- The force in the surface of a liquid is called surface tension.
- Surface tension of a liquid is reduced by impurities, such as soap or camphor in water.
- Adding detergent lowers surface tension and helps water wet a greasy surface.
- Smaller bubbles have a greater pressure inside them than larger bubbles.
- Water rises up a capillary tube. The narrower the tube the higher the water rises.
- Mercury goes down in a capillary tube.
- A water meniscus curves the opposite way to a mercury meniscus.

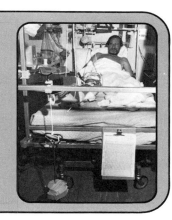

SECTION 3

Machines Alter Forces

14 Pulleys

A machine helps you do a job more easily or more conveniently. It allows a force applied at one point to move a load at another (Fig. 14.1). Many machines are very complicated. However, they usually contain simple parts that are arranged to do a complex job. All the parts obey similar rules.

PULLEY SYSTEMS

Several pulley wheels may be used at the top and the bottom of the system. In real pulley blocks the pulley wheels are usually side by side. We shall draw them one above the other. This makes it easier to see what is going on.

Fig. 14.1 (a) Lifting a car engine using a simple pulley system.   (b) More complicated pulley systems in use.

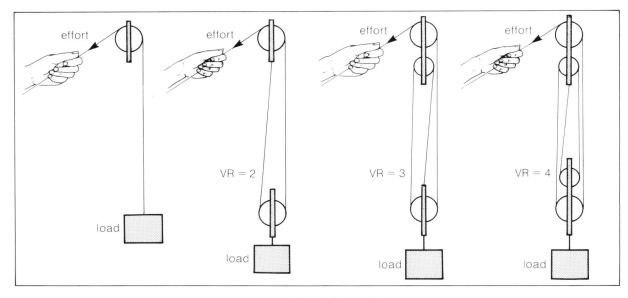

Fig. 14.2 Which of these pulley systems only alters the direction of the pull?

In the pulley systems shown in Fig. 14.2 you pull on the cord to lift the load. The force, or pull, you exert on this cord is called the **effort**. You can measure the effort, in newtons (p. 11), with a spring balance.

In the laboratory the load is usually a set of masses. The force on the load—its weight—is also recorded in newtons. Note that a single fixed pulley just alters the direction of a force.

MECHANICAL ADVANTAGE AND VELOCITY RATIO

In most experiments with machines you measure the load (in N) and the effort (in N) you need to move it. By comparing these two measurements you can calculate the **mechanical advantage**:

$$\text{mechanical advantage} = \frac{\text{load}}{\text{effort}}$$

Another quantity that you can find at the same time is the **velocity ratio (VR)**:

$$\text{velocity ratio} = \frac{\text{distance moved by effort}}{\text{distance moved by load}}$$

You can calculate this from your measurements of distance. In the pulley system shown in Fig. 14.3 imagine that the load is raised a distance of 10 cm. As both of the two cords will be shortened by 10 cm, the effort must be

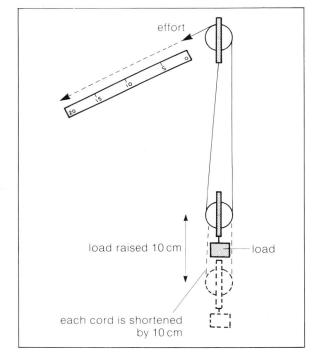

Fig. 14.3 How to find the velocity ratio of a pulley system.

moved through 20 cm to take up the slack. Therefore, the velocity ratio is 20/10 = 2. The velocity ratio equals the number of cords in a pulley system that support the load (see Fig. 14.2).

15 More useful machines

LEVERS

How would you get the top off a tin of custard powder? How would you open a packing case that had been firmly nailed down? How would you get the tyre off the rim of a car or a bicycle wheel? In each case you would probably use some sort of lever.

A lever, e.g., a length of steel, sometimes with a bend in it, can be used to give a larger force. Place one end of the steel bar over a pivot near the place where the force is needed (Fig. 15.1). Press on the other end to exert the force. The principle of moments (p. 15) tells you that the products of each force and the distance from it to the pivot are the same. Therefore the force near the pivot must be the larger one. So a small force—where you press on the bar—produces a larger one to do the job.

Levers can be used to do a job more easily rather than to increase a force. A pair of tweezers is an example of this. Sometimes levers are used to make a movement bigger as in the aneroid barometer (p. 24). A bicycle is another good example of this way to use a lever. Only a small force is needed to move a bicycle along a road. If you push down harder on the pedal to turn the large chain wheel round once, the rear wheel will turn round several times. Try to find out how many more times.

BICYCLE CRANK AND CHAIN-WHEEL

If the pedal of a bicycle is pushed so that the crank turns right round, the chain-wheel also turns right round (Fig. 15.2). Because the pedal is further from the centre of the wheel than the bicycle chain is, the force on the chain is increased by the principle of moments.

The velocity ratio of the system can be calculated as follows:

$$\text{velocity ratio} = \frac{\text{distance moved by the effort}}{\text{distance moved by the load}}$$

For one turn this ratio equals

$$\frac{\text{circumference of circle in which pedal moves}}{\text{circumference of chain-wheel}}$$

As the circumference of a circle is the product of a constant (2π) and the radius:

$$\text{velocity ratio} = \frac{\text{radius of circle in which pedal moves}}{\text{radius of chain-wheel}}$$

$$= \frac{\text{length of crank}}{\text{radius of chain-wheel}}$$

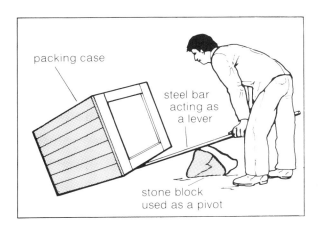

Fig. 15.1 You can use a steel bar to lift a packing case.

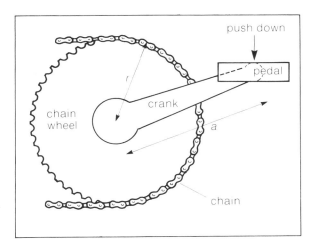

Fig. 15.2 Each time you push down on the pedal of your bicycle you operate a lever.

GEARS

A bicycle uses toothed wheels that are linked by a chain. Many other machines have toothed wheels that mesh or fit nicely into one another. These are called **gear wheels**. Sometimes, as in a derailleur drive of a bicycle, there are several sets of gear wheels placed in a group and a lever lets you choose which set to use. In a motor bike or car engine this is called a **gear box**.

If a large gear wheel drives a smaller one, the small one turns faster. If a small gear wheel drives a larger one, the larger one turns more slowly, but the force is increased (Fig. 15.3).

Fig. 15.3   A geared windless used to haul up a boat. The pull is increased by using gears.

THE INCLINED PLANE

Even something as simple as a plank fixed to the back of a lorry can act as a type of machine. It is easier to roll drums of material up a slope and on to a lorry than to lift them directly (Fig. 15.4). A slope like this is called an **inclined plane**. In this example the effort is the push you give up the slope. The load is the weight of the drum. To get the drums on to the lorry, the effort must move the length of the plank. The load only moves usefully through the height of the back of the lorry. So the velocity ratio is:

$$\frac{\text{length of the slope}}{\text{vertical height risen}}$$

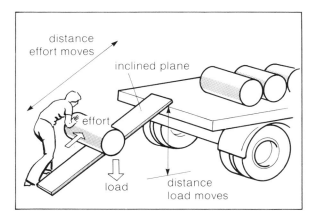

Fig. 15.4   Rolling drums up an inclined plane on to a lorry makes the job easier!

THE SCREW

If a car tyre gets a puncture the motorist has to change the wheel. A **jack** helps to lift one corner of the car (see Fig. 3.1(b) on p. 11). Most jacks include a screw. Some have both a screw and levers. Other have a screw and some gears. In all cases the screw acts as a type of machine.

A screw is also used in some types of press (Fig. 15.5). One metal plate is forced down on to a fixed base by turning the handle. Whatever is put between the plates is well squashed. The effort is applied to the handles of the press. The load is put on to the object being squashed. A wood or metal worker's vice works in the same way.

Fig. 15.5   A screw-operated press.

16 Improving machines

It is always important to know how well a machine is doing the job you are using it for. You can measure the **efficiency** of a machine as the ratio of the machine's energy output to energy input. As the efficiency is usually given as a percentage, you must multiply the answer by 100. The efficiency of a machine is always less than 100 per cent because some of the energy is wasted, e.g., as heat. The energy is put into the machine by your effort and the output is the energy gained by the load. So

$$\text{efficiency} = \frac{\text{energy given to load}}{\text{energy put in by effort}}$$
$$= \frac{\text{work done on load}}{\text{work done by effort}}$$

Example   A machine produces a force of 20 N when an effort of 5 N is applied. The effort has to move 10 m to move the load 2 m. What is the efficiency of the machine?

$$\text{efficiency} = \frac{\text{work done on load}}{\text{work done by effort}}$$
$$= \frac{20 \text{ N} \times 2 \text{ m}}{5 \text{ N} \times 10 \text{ m}}$$
$$= \frac{40}{50}$$
$$= 0.8$$

Therefore the machine's efficiency is 80%.

If you make measurements on a simple machine you can work out how the efficiency varies with the load. A graph of efficiency against load is shown in Fig. 16.1. As the load rises so does the efficiency. The efficiency is always less than 100 per cent although it gets nearer to that value as the load rises. There are two reasons for this.

Whenever two surfaces rub on one another, a force called **friction** acts against the movement between them. An old bicycle with a rusty chain and bearings may be difficult to use because of friction. However, if the parts are oiled the bicycle moves much more easily. All moving surfaces in a machine must be **lubricated** with the correct grade of oil (Fig. 16.2).

Friction wastes energy. Most of the wasted energy warms the machine up so the efficiency is never 100 per cent.

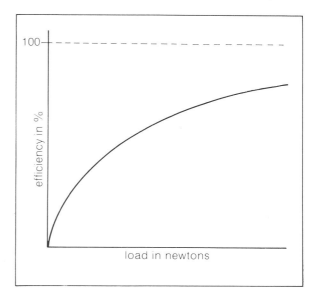

Fig. 16.1   How the efficiency of a machine can increase with the load.

Fig. 16.2   A bicycle that is kept oiled works much more efficiently than one that isn't.

In Fig. 16.3 you can see people travelling on an escalator. They have been brought up from a lower level on the moving treads. Energy was needed just to move these heavy treads. Therefore this energy was wasted and the efficiency was reduced. The same amount of energy is wasted this way whether the escalator is crowded or not. When there are fewer people a bigger fraction of the total energy is wasted. For small loads the efficiency is reduced more than it is for larger loads.

Fig. 16.3   People on an escalator.

SUMMARY: MACHINES ALTER FORCES

- A machine is a device that helps you do a job more easily or more conveniently.
- The force that is applied to a machine is called the effort.
- The force that the machine gives is called the load.
- Mechanical advantage is load divided by effort.
- Velocity ratio is distance moved by effort divided by distance moved by load.
- In a pulley system the velocity ratio is equal to the number of cords helping to support the load.
- Efficiency is defined as the ratio of energy output from a machine to energy input into the machine.
- The efficiency of a machine increases as the load increases.
- The efficiency is always less than 100 per cent because of friction and the effect of the moving parts of the machine itself.

SECTION 4

Moving Along

17 Moving along a line

When you look at a bus or railway timetable there is a lot more information there than the time of the most suitable bus or train for your journey. Have a look at the timetable for the Square-Wheel Bus Co. shown in Table 17. It sets out times for two journeys between Alantown and Homer.

Table 17   Timetable for the Square-Wheel Bus Co.

Bus stop	Distance (km)	Departures (d) and arrivals (a)	
Alantown (Bus Station)	0	d 8.10	10.10
Bradwell (Market Street)	2	d 8.20	10.20
Corfield (Tree Inn)	5	d 8.26	10.26
Desloe (Centre Square)	8	a 8.32	10.32
		d 8.40	10.40
Evenodd (Crossroads)	11	d 8.46	10.46
Fiveroads (Roundabout)	21	d 8.58	10.58
Glentfield (Superstore)	24	d 9.06	11.06
Homer (Bus Station)	26	a 9.15	11.15

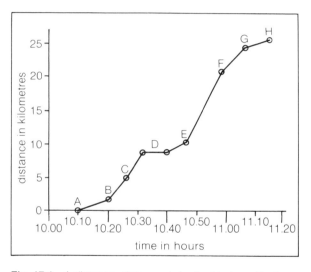

Fig. 17.1   A distance—time graph for the trip from Alantown to Homer.

DISTANCE—TIME GRAPHS

The information in the timetable can be shown on a graph. The distance from Alantown can be plotted against the time to give the **distance—time graph** shown in Fig. 17.1.

1   Why is the graph horizontal between 10.32 and 10.40? The bus was waiting in Desloe's centre square; that is, it was not moving! Therefore a horizontal part of a distance—time graph means that the speed is zero.

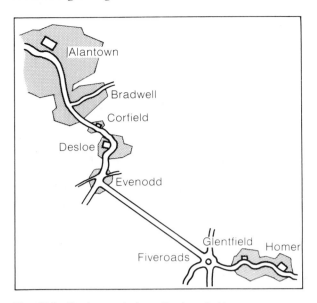

Fig. 17.2 The bus route from Alantown to Homer.

2 Why does the steepness of the slope of the
line change? Compare the part of the
journey between 10.10 and 10.20 with that
between 10.46 and 10.58. The first part is
from Alantown to Bradwell. As this is a
built-up area (Fig. 17.2), there will be a lot
of traffic and the bus can only travel slowly.
The second part is from Evenodd to
Fiveroads. This is along a main road in
open country and so the bus can travel
faster. The faster the bus travels the greater
the slope of the graph.

SPEED

Speed is found by measuring the distance
travelled in a certain time:

$$v = \frac{s}{t}$$

where v is speed, s is distance and t is time
(Fig. 17.3). Speed is measured in metres per
second (m/s) or kilometres per hour (km/h). If
you look back at the timetable in Table 17 you
will see that the bus travelled 10 km in
12 minutes between Evenodd and Fiveroads.
So the speed was 10 km/0.2 h (since 12 minutes
is 12/60 or 0.2 hours), which is 50 km/h.

Fig. 17.3 If the cats' eyes on this motorway are 15 m apart,
the driver feels a double bump every 2 s when the car
drives over them. Why does the driver feel a *double* bump?
How fast is the car going?

MEASURING SPEED

In a car you read the speed on the
speedometer. On a train you could watch for
the yellow posts that are at the sides of the
track every quarter of a mile. If you measure
the time it takes to pass from one to the next
you can work out the speed of the train.

18 Speed−time and velocity−time graphs

VELOCITY

Velocity is speed in a given direction. For example, a man walking at a speed of 6 km/h decides to walk due south. His velocity is 6 km/h from north to south. For many purposes this difference between speed and velocity is not important and so the two words are often mixed up.

Fig. 18.1 A laboratory ticker-timer. It makes dots on a paper tape every fiftieth of a second.

MEASURING SPEED IN THE LABORATORY

A moving object, such as a trolley, pulls a length of paper tape through a **ticker-timer** (Fig. 18.1). This timer marks the paper tape with a dot every fiftieth of a second (Fig. 18.2).

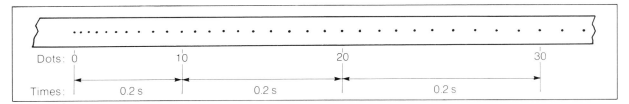

Fig. 18.2 A piece of paper tape after it has been pulled through a ticker-timer making dots every fiftieth of a second. Each millimetre on the drawing represents 1 cm of tape.

The distance between one dot and the next is the distance travelled by the trolley in a fiftieth of a second (0.02 s). Since these distances are quite short, the tape is usually cut up into ten-dot lengths (starting to count dots at 0). Each ten-dot length is the distance travelled by the trolley in a time of $(10 \times 1/50)$ second or 0.2 s. The lengths of tape may be stuck on to a piece of paper side-by-side and in the right order to make a **tape-chart** (Fig. 18.3). Since the length of each ten-dot tape is the distance travelled in 0.2 s, the speed of the trolley is

$$\frac{\text{length of ten-dot tape}}{0.2} \text{ m/s}$$

which is the same as $(5 \times$ length of ten-dot tape) m/s.

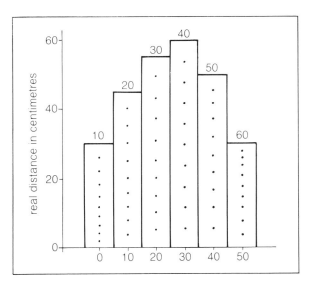

Fig. 18.3 The paper tape cut into ten-dot lengths. These have been stuck side-by-side to make a tape-chart. Each millimetre represents 1 cm.

VELOCITY–TIME GRAPHS

Figure 18.4 is a **velocity–time graph** plotted from the measurements in Fig. 18.2. If the velocity keeps changing the graph is curved. But if the velocity does not change the graph is a horizontal line (Fig. 18.5).

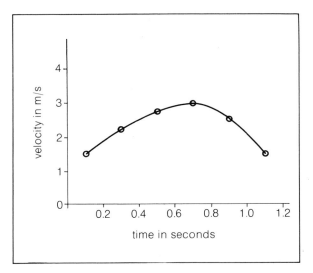

Fig. 18.4 A velocity–time graph drawn for the tape-chart in Fig. 18.3. Why have the points been plotted at the middle of each time interval?

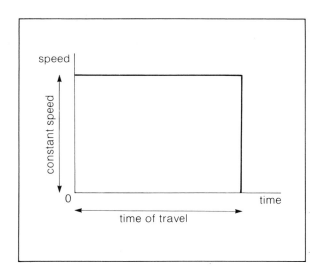

Fig. 18.5 The graph for an object moving at constant speed.

Example A car's velocity along a straight road increased steadily from 0 to 20 m/s in 10 s. The velocity then remained the same for the next 15 s. When the driver applied the brakes, the car came steadily to rest in 25 s. Draw a velocity–time graph for this journey.

In order to draw the graph the time axis must cover the total time involved. This is 10 s + 15 s + 25 s = 50 s. The maximum velocity was 20 m/s. So you can draw axes as in Fig. 18.6. Then add the information given in the question. The four values of time and velocity that can be plotted are as follows:

Time (s)	Velocity (m/s)
0	0
10	20
25	20
50	0

As all the changes were steady and as the velocity did not change between 10 and 25 s the points can be joined by straight lines. This gives the velocity–time graph (Fig. 18.6).

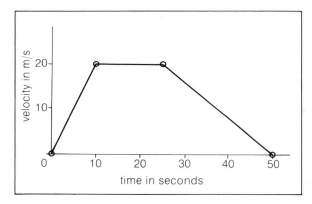

Fig. 18.6 The points joined up to give the velocity–time graph.

AVERAGE SPEED

For a complete journey the average or mean speed is the total distance divided by the total time. For example, the average speed of the bus from Alantown to Homer was 26 km/65 minutes, or 24 km/h.

19 Speeding up

Suppose you made a note of the speed of a bus as it started off and every second after that. Perhaps the speed was 5 km/h after 5 s and 7 km/h after 6 s. The speed had gone up by 2 km/h in one second. This is an **acceleration**. You have measured it in a strange sounding unit—the kilometre per hour in a second. A more usual unit would be the metre per second in a second; for short, the metre per second squared.

$$\text{acceleration} = \frac{\text{change in speed}}{\text{time taken for the change}}$$

A car manufacturer might tell you that a car can build up its speed (accelerate) to 90 km/h in 12 s; 90 km/h is 25 m/s, so the acceleration is

$$\frac{25 \text{ m/s} - 0 \text{ m/s}}{12 \text{ s}}$$

which is 2.1 metres per second squared, or 2.1 m/s^2.

MEASURING ACCELERATION

Acceleration as well as speed can be found from a tape-chart. In Fig. 19.1 the real distances and speeds for each 0.2 s are:

Each 0.2 s	1st	2nd	3rd	4th	5th	6th
Distance (cm)	30	45	55	60	50	30
Real speed (cm/s)	150	225	275	300	250	150
Real speed (m/s)	1.5	2.25	2.75	3.0	2.5	1.5

Strictly speaking, these are average speeds over each 0.2 s. Between the first and the second ten-dot lengths the speed of the trolley increases by (2.25 − 1.5) m/s which is 0.75 m/s. The time taken for this change in speed is 0.2 s. Therefore the acceleration of the trolley is:

$$\frac{0.75 \text{ m/s}}{0.2 \text{ s}} = 3.75 \text{ m/s}^2$$

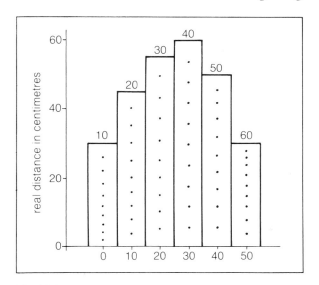

Fig. 19.1

You can work out the acceleration for the other parts of the tape-chart. The results should be:

Time (s)	0.2	0.4	0.6	0.8	1.0
Acceleration (m/s^2)	3.75	2.5	1.25	− 0.25	− 0.05

The minus sign shows that the trolley is slowing down. It has a negative acceleration. This is often called **retardation**.

CONSTANT ACCELERATION

People, cars and lorries often move with an acceleration that keeps changing—like the trolley in Fig. 19.1. However, there are some very important cases where there is **constant** or **uniform acceleration**. If something moves with constant acceleration the change in velocity in equal periods of time must be the same. For example, consider these figures:

Time (s)	0	2	4	6	8
Velocity (m/s)	0	10	20	30	40
Change in velocity (m/s)		10	10	10	10
Acceleration (m/s²)		5	5	5	5

The graph of velocity against time for this case is shown in Fig. 19.2. It is a straight line. Constant acceleration always gives a straight line on a velocity—time graph. The slope of the graph, which is called the **gradient**, gives the acceleration (Fig. 19.3).

ACCELERATION DUE TO GRAVITY

Things that fall freely have a constant acceleration called the **acceleration due to gravity**. This is so important that it is given a special symbol, g. The value of g depends on where you are. On the surface of the earth it is nearly 10 m/s². On the surface of the moon it is 1.6 m/s², about one-sixth of the value on earth.

MEASURING g

A heavy falling object can pull a paper tape through a ticker-timer. The tape-chart should give a constant value for the acceleration. However, it is likely that the value will be too small. This is because friction between the tape and the timer slows the tape down.

A **stroboscopic** photograph can be taken of a falling object (Fig. 19.4). The light of the **strobe** flashes a known number of times each second. The photograph shows where the falling object is each time the light flashes. Knowing the scale of the photograph you can work out the speeds and the acceleration. Why don't you try it?

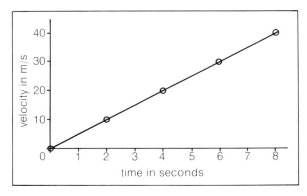

Fig. 19.2 A velocity—time graph for a body moving with constant acceleration.

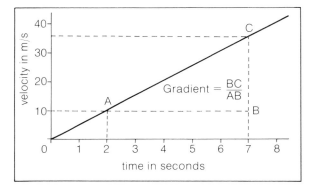

Fig. 19.3 Finding the slope (or gradient) of a velocity—time graph.

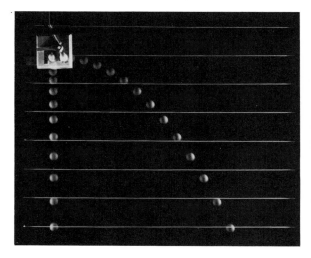

Fig. 19.4 A strobe picture of two golf balls falling freely. One was dropped vertically down; the other was shot out sideways. Light flashes were recorded every thirtieth of a second. The white strings are 15 cm apart. What can you say about the way the two balls fell?

20 What has force to do with moving?

A supertanker is not an easy ship to steer. It only responds slowly to any change that is needed (Fig. 20.1). A tiny dinghy is much more responsive. It will change course quickly. There is the same sort of difference between a bus and a moped. In the same way, a football filled with water would be much more difficult to control than an ordinary one. The more massive the object, the harder it is to change its motion. Heavier objects have more **inertia**.

THE FIRST LAW OF MOTION

Sir Isaac Newton set out three very important laws to describe motion. The **first law** states that: A body continues at rest or in uniform motion along a straight line unless a force acts on it.

It is easy to see that an object on a surface has to be pushed or pulled to start it moving. But the other part of the first law does not seem to fit with everyday life. When a car is travelling at constant speed on a level road its engine is working steadily. But Newton said no force was needed to keep something moving at constant speed. Was Newton wrong?

Suppose you pushed a sledge first over rough ground and then along some smooth ice. What differences would you notice? On the ice the object would go much further and take much longer to slow down and stop (Fig. 20.2). Resistance to motion is greater over the rough ground than over smooth ice.

A car engine has to keep working to overcome the resistance of the road and air. Without resistance, the engine could be switched off and the car would travel on and on at constant speed. Newton was right. Perhaps the best example of motion without resistance is that of a spacecraft or satellite in orbit round the earth.

RESISTANCE TO MOTION

Friction is one cause of the resistance to motion. At greater speeds air resistance is high. Resistance to motion can be a nuisance. A car has to use extra fuel and energy is wasted. Resistance is also a help. Without it the car could not move, nor could we walk. In

Fig. 20.1 A supertanker may take 3 km to stop.

Fig. 20.2 A game of curling.

Fig. 20.3 One way to slow down.

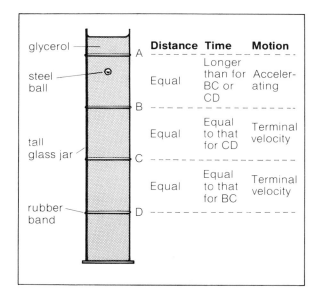

Fig. 20.4 A ball bearing falling through glycerol soon reaches its terminal speed.

Fig. 20.3 the parachute behind the aircraft increases resistance. This helps the aircraft to slow down after it has landed.

Raindrops fall from a great height. If they fell freely they would reach a very high speed and could be dangerous. But air resistance slows them down. A model shows you what happens.

Let some small steel balls taken out of ball bearings fall through glycerol (antifreeze) (Fig. 20.4). This is a thick or **viscous** liquid that does not flow easily. You can time the balls as they fall through the liquid. They accelerate for the first part of their journey. Then they settle down to a steady speed. They travel equal distances in equal times. This is the result of liquid friction. The maximum velocity that they reach is called their **terminal velocity**. Because of air resistance raindrops also reach a terminal velocity.

REDUCING RESISTANCE TO MOTION

Designers often try to reduce resistance to motion to allow something to move faster or to save fuel. The shape of an object affects its air resistance. Tests in a wind tunnel (Fig. 20.5) show what happens using models.

In the school laboratory, friction can spoil experiments on motion. A tilted track or runway is used to overcome this (Fig. 20.6). The runway or **friction-compensating slope** is tilted until the object, perhaps a trolley, runs at constant speed on its own. It has to be given a push to get it moving. Then the effect of any extra force (p. 43) can be investigated.

Fig. 20.5 Testing a car body for air resistance in a wind tunnel.

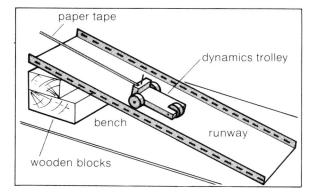

Fig. 20.6 Tilting a trolley runway to offset the effect of friction.

21 Forced to accelerate

A trolley on a suitable downward slope will move at constant speed (p. 42). What happens if a force is applied to the trolley? You can apply a force with an elastic thread kept at the same amount of stretch—**extension**—all the time. The force applied is constant (Fig. 21.1). The trolley accelerates as you apply the force and you can make a tape-chart to work out the acceleration (p. 39). Repeat the experiment with two similar elastic threads side-by-side (Fig. 21.2). This doubles the force. Three similar elastic threads will treble the force.

You can work out the accelerations from the tape-charts (Fig. 21.2(b)). These are the results from a similar experiment:

> One trolley, one elastic thread, force F:
> acceleration 1.2 m/s^2
> One trolley, two elastic threads, force $2F$:
> acceleration 2.4 m/s^2
> One trolley, three elastic threads, force $3F$:
> acceleration 3.6 m/s^2

If you double the force you get twice the acceleration and so on. Acceleration is proportional to force.

What will happen if you double or treble the mass of the trolley? It is easy to put one trolley on top of another and do the experiment again without changing the force (Fig. 21.3(a)). See the tape-chart in Fig. 21.3(b). The results will look like this:

> One trolley, one elastic thread, force F:
> acceleration 1.2 m/s^2
> Two trolleys, one elastic thread, force F:
> acceleration 0.6 m/s^2
> Three trolleys, one elastic thread, force F:
> acceleration 0.4 m/s^2

If you double the mass you get half the acceleration and so on. Acceleration is inversely proportional to mass.

The acceleration of a fixed mass is proportional to force.

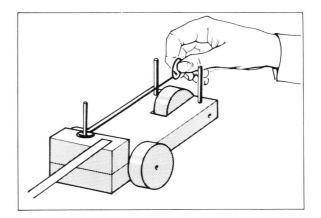

Fig. 21.1 Use one elastic thread to accelerate a trolley.

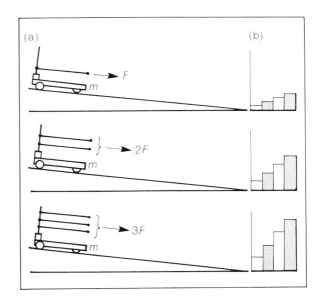

Fig. 21.2

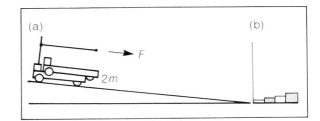

Fig. 21.3

NEWTON'S SECOND LAW OF MOTION

Newton put all these results together in his second law. You can write the **second law** as:

force = mass × acceleration

If we measure mass in kilograms and acceleration in metres per second squared, the force is measured in newtons (N). Remember, that is the unit you used to calibrate the spring balance (p. 11).

THE UNIT OF FORCE

Forces are measured in newtons (see p. 11). You can now see more clearly what a newton is. In the equation

force = mass × acceleration

if the mass is 1 kg and the acceleration is 1 m/s^2, then the force is 1 N. So 1 N is the force that will give a mass of 1 kg an acceleration of 1 m/s^2.

WEIGHT

An object falling freely near the surface of the earth has an acceleration due to gravity (g) of about 10 m/s^2 (p. 40). If the object has a mass of 1 kg, the force acting is given by:

force = mass × acceleration
    $= 1 \text{ kg} \times 10 \text{ m/s}^2 = 10 \text{ N}$

This is the force we call the weight. A mass of 1 kg has, near the surface of the earth, a weight of 10 N (p. 13). In general:

weight = mass × acceleration due to gravity

Example A spanner weighs 20 N on the surface of the earth. What would its mass and weight be on the surface of the moon? (Acceleration due to gravity on the moon is 1.6 m/s^2.)

You need to find the mass of the spanner on the surface of the earth using

force = mass × acceleration
20 N = m × 10 m/s^2
    $m = 2 \text{ kg}$

Taking the spanner to the moon does not change its mass. So on the surface of the moon:

force = mass × acceleration
    $F = 2 \text{ kg} \times 1.6 \text{ m/s}^2 = 3.2 \text{ N}$

On the surface of the moon the object would have a mass of 2 kg, as on the earth, and a weight of 3.2 N. No wonder astronauts on the moon find it easy to jump about—their weight is so much less although their masses stay the same (Fig. 21.4).

Fig. 21.4 This astronaut's mass is the same as on the earth, but his weight is less.

22 Going round and round

You can make a model car driven by a battery go round in a circle if you tie a piece of string to it. Tie the other end to a fixed object. When the car starts, it has to move in a circle (Fig. 22.1).

Anything moving in a circle has to be forced to do so. The string pulled the car towards the centre of the circle. The force on the car is called **centripetal force**. The outward pull of the string on the fixed object at the centre of the circle is called **centrifugal force**.

When you untie the string, the toy car will move in a straight line (Newton's first law; p. 41) (Fig. 22.2). There is nothing pulling it to the centre of the circle any more. The straight line the car travels in is a **tangent** to the circle.

There are two main points about moving in a circle:

1 There has to be an inward force towards the centre of the circle.
2 If this force disappears the object moves along a tangent to the circle.

OTHER EXAMPLES OF MOVING IN A CIRCLE

A motor-cyclist riding on the wall of death moves in a circle because the push from the walls on the tyres of the motor bike is towards the centre of the circle (Fig. 22.3).

Put a coin on the turntable of a record-player. If the friction between the coin and the turntable is big enough, the coin will move round with the turntable. Stop the turntable and cover it with a disc of very smooth paper. The frictional force is now not so big. The coin does not move in a circle. How does it move?

You can swing a bucket of water in a vertical circle. It can go above your head without spilling a drop! Your pull on the bucket handle keeps it moving in a circle.

GRAVITY

Any two pieces of matter attract one another with a force. You are attracted or pulled towards the earth by a force called **gravity**. Because the mass of the earth is so huge, this force, which is your weight, is large.

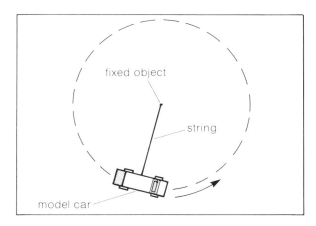

Fig. 22.1 The string pulls the model car inwards and it moves in a circle.

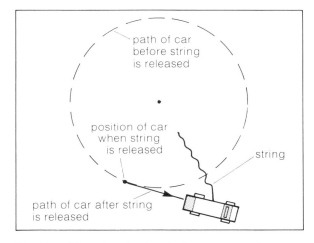

Fig. 22.2 When the string breaks the car moves along a tangent to the circle.

Fig. 22.3 Is it really the wall of death?

Look at Fig. 22.4. This shows what happened to two falling balls. The picture is a multiflash photograph. The ball on the left fell straight down. The ball on the right moved to the right at the same time because it was shot off the table. The pull of the earth accelerated both of them towards the floor. See how they stayed level with one another as they fell. But the right-hand ball went on moving to the right at the same speed. It followed a curved path. This path is called a **parabola**.

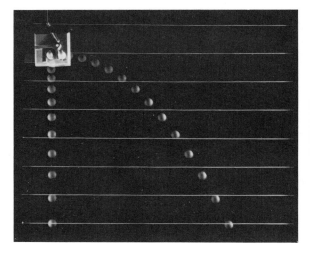

Fig. 22.4 Multiflash photograph of two golf balls released at the same time. One drops straight down. The other also moves from left to right.

SATELLITES

Many satellites travel round the earth. The moon is a natural satellite. There are also hundreds of artificial ones, all moving in circles or near-circles. Satellites have no rope pulling them into the circular path. It is gravity that supplies the inward pull towards the earth. Gravity pulls the earth, Mars and the other planets towards the sun; they move round the sun like satellites move round the earth.

People say that the things inside a satellite are **weightless**. They don't mean that at all! A man inside a satellite is still pulled towards the centre of the earth. And so is everything around him. That is what keeps the satellite and the man in orbit. They don't have to resist the earth's pull in the way that a chair does when you sit on it. So they *feel* weightless. It would be better if we said that things in a satellite are in **free fall**.

SUMMARY: MOVING ALONG

- Information about a journey can be displayed on a distance−time or velocity−time graph.
- Speed is distance divided by time: $v = s/t$.
- On a distance−time graph the slope of the graph measures the speed.
- Velocity is speed in a given direction.
- Speed can be calculated from a tape-chart.
- Average speed is total distance travelled divided by the time taken.
- Acceleration is change in speed divided by time taken for the change.
- Acceleration is measured in metres per second squared (m/s^2).
- Acceleration can also be calculated from a tape-chart.
- If a speed−time graph is a straight line, the acceleration is uniform; the slope of the graph measures acceleration.
- The acceleration of an object that is falling freely is called the acceleration due to gravity, g. The value of g depends on where you are.

- Newton's first law of motion states that an object stays at rest or continues in uniform motion along a straight line unless acted upon by a force.
- Friction affects experiments on motion.
- When an object is falling through a fluid it reaches a maximum or terminal velocity.
- Newton's second law of motion leads to the following equation:
  force = mass × acceleration.
- The newton is the force that will give a mass of 1 kg an acceleration of 1 m/s^2.
- Weight is mass multiplied by acceleration due to gravity.
- Objects move in a circle if there is a constant pull, or centripetal force, to the centre.
- If that pull is removed the object moves off along a tangent to the circle.
- Gravity is the name given to the pull exerted by one mass on another.
- Gravity is the inward force that keeps satellites moving in orbit round the earth and the planets round the sun.
- A ball struck by, say, a tennis racquet moves along a curved path called a parabola.

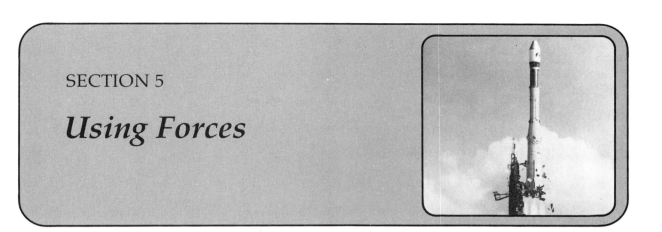

SECTION 5

Using Forces

23 Action, reaction and engines

FORCES GO IN PAIRS

Have you ever tried to hit or slap someone who suddenly moved out of the way? Did your hand then hit a wall or a table? If so, you will know that your hand hurt. You exerted a force on the wall or table. There was an equal force on your hand.

NEWTON'S THIRD LAW

Newton's third law is about forces like this. The **third law** states that: Action and reaction are equal and opposite and act on different bodies. This means that if a force—the action—is exerted by one object, A, on another object, B, an equal and opposite force—the reaction—is exerted by object B on object A.

When a rifle is fired, the force on the bullet makes it accelerate down the barrel of the rifle. But an equal backward force makes the rifle kick backwards or recoil (Fig. 23.1).

If you step from a small boat on to a landing stage, you push backwards on the boat in order to use the reaction of the boat on your foot to move you forwards. This makes the boat move away from the landing stage; so be careful, or you might finish up in the water (Fig. 23.2)!

When an object falls, the earth's pull—gravity—makes the object accelerate downwards. An equal and opposite force makes the earth move towards the object.

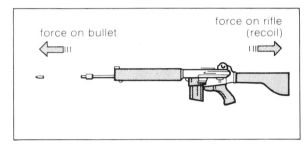

Fig. 23.1 The recoil of a rifle can hurt your shoulder!

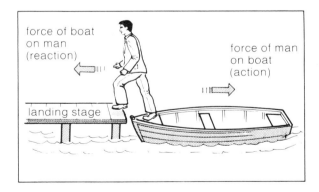

Fig. 23.2 Be careful not to miss the jetty!

However, the mass of the earth is so great compared to that of the falling object that this movement is quite impossible to detect (Fig. 23.3).

PULLING A TOBOGGAN

Suppose you are pulling a friend along on a toboggan. You push backwards on the ground which pushes forwards on you—action/ reaction. The ground pushes you forward so you and the toboggan will move forward. Figure 23.4 shows four pairs of action and reaction forces for you and the toboggan.

ROCKETS

All rockets from the smallest firework to the biggest space rocket work in the same way. They contain their own fuel. When they are lit the fuel burns. The hot gas that is produced escapes from the back of the rocket. So by Newton's third law there must be an equal but opposite force on the rocket. It is this force that drives the rocket forward. When the fuel is used up the empty rocket motor may be pulled back to earth by gravity. A rocket motor is able to work in a vacuum, unlike a jet engine which depends on air.

JET ENGINES

The jet engine is similar to a rocket in that it forces out hot gas at the rear. By Newton's third law there must be an equal and opposite force on the engine and so on the aircraft. The big difference is that the air needed to burn the fuel is taken in from the atmosphere. The jet engine works continuously so long as it has enough fuel.

The principle of the jet engine is shown in Fig. 23.5. Air is drawn in and compressed by a compressor, a complicated fan. Fuel is then added and the mixture is burnt. The hot gas produced drives a turbine (see later). The turbine then drives the compressor—they are linked by a shaft. Hot gas then comes out of the jet engine at high speed to force the aircraft forward. Most modern jet engines (Fig. 23.6) work on this principle.

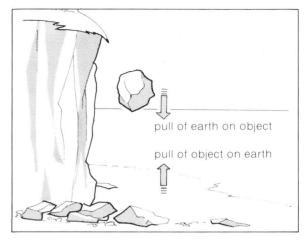

Fig. 23.3 The rock falls towards the earth; the earth rises to meet the rock (but not much!).

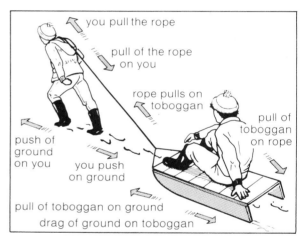

Fig. 23.4 Four pairs of horizontal forces are involved when you drag a toboggan. There are also two pairs of vertical forces. What are they?

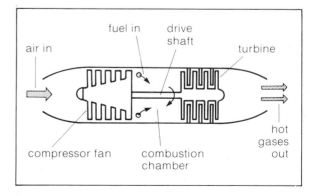

Fig. 23.5 Inside a jet engine.

Fig. 23.6 A modern jet engine.

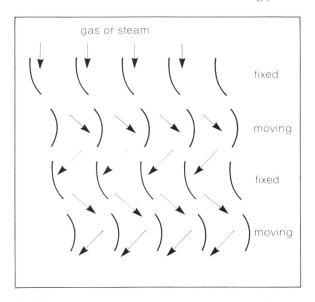

Fig. 23.7 A turbine has many sets of fixed and moving blades. It is the flow of fluid through them that makes the moving blades turn.

TURBINES

A turbine is a machine driven by a fluid. In many turbines the fluid is a hot gas, often steam. Fixed blades direct the hot gas on to movable blades (Fig. 23.7). This turns the **rotor**.

Turbines help to make electricity. Water is heated by energy from coal, oil or a nuclear reactor to produce steam. This makes the turbine rotate. The turbine drives a generator (p. 182) to produce electricity. Generators in hydroelectric power stations are driven by turbines rotated by water.

THE TWO-STROKE ENGINE

Small motor-bike engines have no valves, (Fig. 23.8) unlike a car engine. When the piston rises the petrol/air mixture above the piston is compressed. At the same time more mixture enters below the piston. The sparking plug fires when the piston is near the top of the cylinder. This ignites the mixture above the piston. The expansion of the exploding gases drives the piston down. This allows the burnt gases to escape through the exhaust port. Fresh mixture is driven from below the piston to above it. The shape of the piston helps to keep the exhaust gases and the fresh mixture separate.

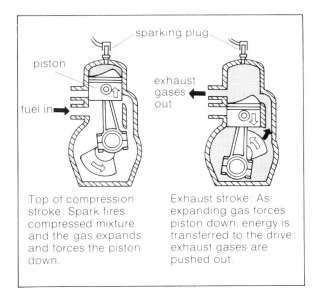

Fig. 23.8 How a two-stroke engine works.

24 Building structures

Imagine you build a very simple bridge across a stream by putting a wooden plank over it (Fig. 24.1). Then you walk across the plank. Your weight W_1 and the weight of the plank itself W_2 are supported by forces F_1 and F_2 at the ends of the plank bridge. And, if the plank doesn't collapse,

$$W_1 + W_2 = F_1 + F_2$$

The plank itself is in equilibrium. But, of course, it will bend under your weight. Like a spring (p. 11), the wooden plank is elastic. The top side of the wood is compressed a little; the lower side is stretched a little. As you walk off the bridge, the plank returns to its original shape and size because it has elasticity.

All bridges, floors and even aircraft wings bend like that. Even railway bridges made of heavy steel beams bend a little as the trains pass over them. But no one will want them to bend very much. In many cases, the designer of the bridge will use a girder to make the bridge less likely to bend (Fig. 24.2).

Sometimes beams are pushed out from a wall and only fixed at that end. This arrangement is called a **cantilever**. The wing of an aircraft is a very good example (Fig. 24.3). The wing bends a little under its own weight and it flexes a little more and a little less all the time the aircraft is in the air. The wing can do this because it is elastic—just like the spring and the wooden plank. As different forces are applied it bends and as they are removed it returns to its original shape.

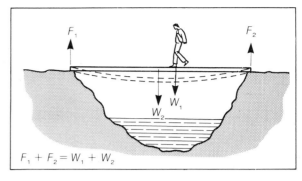

Fig. 24.1   The plank bridge. The dotted line shows what really happens, but still $F_1 + F_2 = W_1 + W_2$.

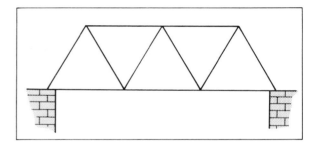

Fig. 24.2   A steel-girder bridge.

Fig. 24.3   The wings of aircraft are cantilevers fixed to the fuselage.

SUMMARY: USING FORCES

- Forces always occur in pairs.
- Newton's third law states that action and reaction are equal and opposite and act on different bodies.
- A rocket carries all its own fuel. As this is burnt the hot gases are forced out of the back of the rocket and the rocket itself is pushed forward.
- A jet engine needs to take in air from the atmosphere to burn its fuel. Again, hot gases forced out set up a forward push on the plane.

- In a turbine a fluid, usually hot gas, is directed by fixed blades to turn movable blades.
- The stages of a two-stroke engine are intake—compression—firing and power—exhaust—transfer.
- Bridges, floors and girders are elastic and bend a little when forces are applied.

Energy and Power

25 Forms of energy and energy changes

Fuels provide the energy you need to get useful jobs done (p. 57). What about the energy from a two-stroke engine (p. 49)? When the fuel burns in air and gives off hot gas, the store of **chemical energy** in the mixture of fuel and air is changed into **thermal energy** or heat. When the hot gases expand and push the piston down, some of the thermal energy of the hot gas is changed into the energy of motion or **kinetic energy** of the piston. The kinetic energy of the piston is then used to turn the drive shaft, the gears and the wheels.

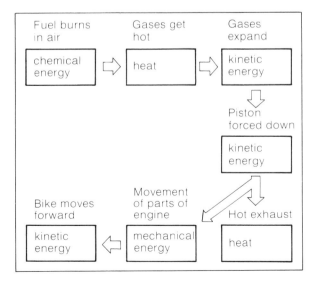

Fig. 25.1 The chain of energy changes in a motor-bike engine.

The bike moves forward and has kinetic energy. This chain of energy changes is shown in Fig. 25.1.

POTENTIAL ENERGY

An object has potential energy by reason of its position. The mass used to drive the clock in Fig. 2.1 on p. 9 is given **gravitational potential energy** every time it is wound up against the pull of the earth. This potential energy is used to drive the clock.

You can work out gravitational potential energy by multiplying the weight of the body lifted by the vertical height it moves through.

$$\text{potential energy} = \text{weight} \times \text{vertical height}$$

$$= \left(\text{mass} \times \text{acceleration due to gravity}\right) \times \text{vertical height}$$

If the mass is in kilograms (kg), the acceleration in metres per second squared (m/s^2) and the height in metres (m), then the potential energy is in joules (J) (p. 16).

The energy stored in a wound-up spring is another form of potential energy; but this is harder to calculate.

KINETIC ENERGY

This is the energy a body has because it is moving. The faster a body moves the more kinetic energy it has—since more work has to be done to accelerate it. It is the kinetic energy

51

Fig. 25.2 The kinetic energy of the car crushes the car and does a lot of damage.

Fig. 25.3 An Inter-City 125 engine at speed.

of a car that causes the damage when a car is in a crash (Fig. 25.2). You can work out kinetic energy from the formula:

$$\text{kinetic energy} = \tfrac{1}{2}\,\text{mass} \times \text{speed}^2$$

If you double the speed, you have four times the kinetic energy! That is why crashes at high speed do so much damage.

CHEMICAL ENERGY

Energy is given out (or taken in) in every chemical reaction. Probably the most important type of reaction in this connection is burning. Burning may be violent, e.g., in an explosion, under firm control, e.g., in a gas fire, or very slow, e.g., food being used up in our bodies. In each case chemical energy is being made available to do a job of work.

THERMAL ENERGY OR HEAT

Hot gases from burning coal, natural gas or oil not only keep our homes warm, they drive turbines to make electricity (p. 182; see Fig. 29.1 on p. 57) and oil powers diesel locomotives which haul trains (Fig. 25.3).

WAVE ENERGY

Light from the sun brings energy to the earth. Light waves carry energy; so do sound waves. Your eyes respond to light energy and you see. Your ears respond to sound energy and you hear. All types of waves carry energy from one place to another. This is why waves are so

important. One day engineers hope to get large supplies of energy from the waves of the sea. But many problems have to be overcome before this will be possible on a large scale.

ELECTRICAL ENERGY

People depend very greatly on electrical energy. Many of the things you use everyday are worked by electricity (p. 161). They do many different jobs. For example, electric fires provide warmth; electric refrigerators keep food cool and fresh; electric motors drive all sorts of machines. TV and radio sets need an electricity supply. The electrical energy is usually supplied along cables from the power station; this is mains electricity. Other appliances contain batteries which supply the electrical energy.

A thunderstorm (see the photograph on p. 140) is a violent display of electrical energy. Unfortunately this energy cannot be controlled and may do a lot of damage.

NUCLEAR ENERGY

Changes in the nuclei of atoms (p. 196) can result in a great deal of energy being made available. Scientists have found two ways of using this energy. One way can lead to the nuclear bomb, which can cause great devastation.

The second way is much less violent. In a nuclear power station the nuclear energy is carefully controlled. This is a valuable source of energy. It is likely to become more important in years to come.

26 More energy changes

When something happens energy changes from one form to another. As the change takes place a job of work is done. It is often useful to trace all the energy changes that take place, as we did for the motor bike.

Example Jill hammers a nail into a piece of wood.

The original energy for this job came from the chemical energy in the food that Jill ate. This energy was released in her body and converted to kinetic energy by her muscles. Her arm raised the hammer and the hammer gained potential energy. When the hammer came down towards the nail, the potential energy was changed to kinetic energy. When the hammer hit the nail, altering its position and the position of the wood fibres, a little of the kinetic energy must have changed back into potential energy. Most of it was changed into heat (Fig. 26.1). A nail will get quite hot if you keep hammering it.

Example Electric current from a coal-fired power station lights an electric lamp.

The original energy in this case is in the coal taken to the power station (see Fig. 29.1 on p. 57). This is chemical energy. When the coal is burnt, the chemical energy is used to boil water to make hot energetic steam. This drives the turbine. The turbine uses its kinetic energy to drive a generator. So the kinetic energy becomes electrical energy. This is transmitted through cables until it reaches your home and lights the lamp. The electrical energy changes into light energy and heat.

In all these energy changes some useful job is done and some energy is wasted. But the energy is not used up. Every time energy changes something happens. Energy is a bit like money. You give the shopkeeper some money for a bag of sweets. The shopkeeper pays the wholesaler and gets goods to sell to you. The wholesaler pays the manufacturer and gets goods to sell to the shopkeeper. The manufacturer pays for materials to make things. And so the chain goes on.

In long chains of energy changes like those just described, some energy is wasted at each link in the chain, often by warming something up. Look again at Fig. 29.1 on p. 57. Try to draw the chain of energy changes for the power station starting with the coal in the wagons of the train. End with the lamp in your room at home. Don't forget the wasted energy, especially from the cooling towers, which produce all the steam, and from the power station chimney!

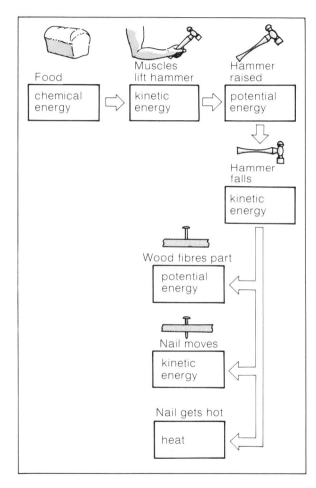

Fig. 26.1 How the energy changes when a nail is driven into some wood.

27 The conservation of energy

There is some similarity between money and energy (p. 53). When money changes hands, something is bought or sold. When energy changes form some useful work is done. Neither the money nor the energy is used up. But both can be wasted!

The idea that energy cannot be used up but only changed from one form to another is the **law of conservation of energy**—the most basic law in physics. It says that energy can neither be created nor destroyed.

TESTING THE LAW

The unit of energy is the joule or newton metre. It is named after James Joule, the man who carried out so many different experiments on energy. His work convinced scientists that the law was correct. In his most famous experiment, two falling masses drove a paddle wheel which churned up some water in a metal can (Fig. 27.1). He measured:

1   The work done, or the energy transformed, by the masses as they fell.
2   The rise in temperature of the water.

He found that the two amounts of energy were always the same. All our experience since then agrees with these results.

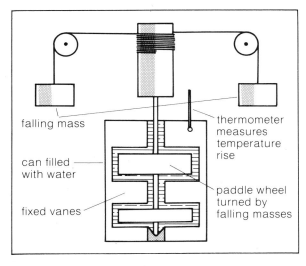

Fig. 27.1   Joule's paddle wheel experiment showed that the energy supplied by the falling masses was equal to the energy used to warm the water.

EFFICIENCY

When you read that an engine is only 30 per cent efficient, it means that the engine wastes 70 per cent of the energy put into it. But this energy is not lost. It just cannot be made use of. For example, a lot of the input energy—the energy put into the engine—is changed into heat energy, which cannot be used. The hot exhaust gases from a car share their energy with the air. A lot of the input energy finishes up as low-temperature heat, which is wasted. When you measure the efficiency you compare the useful output energy to the total energy input. When you compare the total output, including all the wasted energy, to the total input they are always the same.

The power station shown in Fig. 29.1 on p. 57 is about 40 per cent efficient—that is quite a high figure. About 28 per cent of the energy originally supplied in the coal is used to heat water in the cooling towers and to produce the waste steam; the rest is wasted in the exhaust gases and elsewhere in the station. There is very little that engineers can do to get a better efficiency than this!

OSCILLATORS AND ENERGY

An oscillator is something that repeats a to-and-fro motion time after time, like a pendulum (Fig. 27.2). The strobe photograph in Fig. 27.3 shows a similar pendulum swinging from side to side. Each time the

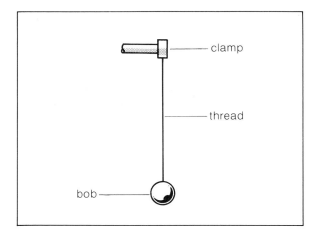

Fig. 27.2   A simple pendulum.

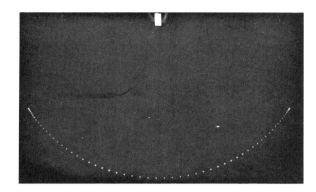

Fig. 27.3 A strobe picture of a pendulum swinging. The strobe rate was 100 per second.

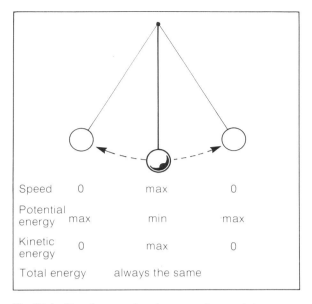

Speed	0	max	0
Potential energy	max	min	max
Kinetic energy	0	max	0
Total energy		always the same	

Fig. 27.4 How the energies change as the pendulum swings.

strobe light flashes the film records the position of the pendulum. Like the dots on a ticker-tape, the positions are at equal time intervals.

Look carefully at Fig. 27.3. The distance between the positions of the pendulum at the lowest point of the swing is larger than at other parts of the swing. When the pendulum gets near to the end of its swing, this distance becomes very small. The speed of the pendulum is high when the distance between the positions is large. The speed is low when the distance between the positions is small.

So the pendulum moves quickest at the bottom of its swing and slowest at the ends of its swing. Careful investigation will show that the pendulum actually stops moving at the end of each swing and starts to swing back at once.

The kinetic energy of the pendulum is continually changing. It is zero at each end of each swing and at a maximum in the middle of the swing when the pendulum is in its lowest position.

To provide the changes in kinetic energy, the potential energy of the bob of the pendulum also changes. At the ends of the swing the bob is in its highest position, so it has maximum potential energy. At the middle of its swing it is in its lowest position, so it has its smallest amount of potential energy. If potential and kinetic energy are added together the amount is always the same. Total energy is conserved. Energy can only change from one form to the other and back again (Fig. 27.4). Some energy is wasted as kinetic energy used to move air around and so the pendulum eventually stops.

The same sort of thing occurs in other oscillating systems. A mass bobbing up and down on a spring has kinetic energy, gravitational potential energy and potential energy which is stored in the spring. But the amount of energy always remains the same. When a balance wheel of a watch oscillates, energy changes between the potential energy of the spring and the kinetic energy of the movement.

28 Power

A powerful person will get a job of work done more quickly than a weaker one because energy is changed from one form to another more quickly. **Power** is defined as energy transformed or work done divided by time taken.

Power is measured in **watts (W)**. One watt is 1 joule per second (1 W = 1 J/s):
1 kilowatt (kW) = 1000 W;
1 megawatt (MW) = 1 000 000 W.

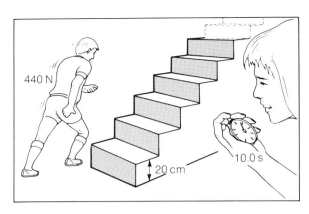

Fig. 28.1   Measuring your own power.

MEASURING YOUR OWN POWER

If you know your weight (in newtons) you can measure your own power by finding how long it takes for you to run up a flight of stairs. Remember, you need to measure the height of the stairs.

Example   Stephen has a weight of 440 N and can run up a flight of stairs in 10.0 s. There are 25 stairs each of height 20 cm (Fig. 28.1). Calculate Stephen's power.

$$\text{total distance climbed} = 25 \times 0.2 \text{ m} = 5.0 \text{ m}$$

$$\text{work done} = \text{force} \times \text{distance}$$
$$= 440 \text{ N} \times 5.0 \text{ m}$$

$$\text{power} = \frac{\text{work done}}{\text{time taken}}$$

$$= \frac{440 \text{ N} \times 5.0 \text{ m}}{10.0 \text{ s}} = 220 \text{ W}$$

If you measure your power doing a different job you will probably get a different answer. However, in every case the answer will be quite small. A human being is not very powerful. A horse can exert a steady power of about 750 W (once known as one horsepower) (Fig. 28.2). A one-bar (1 kW) heater has a power of 1000 W. At the price paid for electricity (p. 165) a person is worth about a penny an hour!

Fig. 28.2   Two horsepower.

the time it takes, you can find the power of the engine:

$$\text{work done} = \text{force} \times \text{distance}$$

$$\text{power developed} = \frac{\text{force} \times \text{distance}}{\text{time taken}}$$

Now

$$\frac{\text{distance}}{\text{time}} = \text{speed}$$

Therefore

$$\text{power} = \text{force} \times \text{speed}$$

If a car accelerates or starts to go uphill but keeps the same speed, the force it exerts has to increase and so does the power. The car engine will have to work harder and use petrol more quickly. Powers of bike and car engines are often given in the old-fashioned brake horsepower (bhp) unit. A 100-bhp engine produces about 75 kW.

THE POWER OF A CAR

Even on level ground a car engine must keep working. This is because it has to overcome the resistance to motion (friction). If you know this resistance, the distance the car goes and

29 Energy today and tomorrow

Where do we get the energy we need to run our homes, our industry, our transport, our farms from? Nearly all of it comes from burning coal, oil or gas (Fig. 29.1). Some also comes from hydroelectric schemes and nuclear fuels. Coal, oil and gas are **fossil fuels**. They are found in the earth – brought to the surface and burned to do the useful jobs we must have done (Fig. 29.2).

It is quite easy to understand why people talk about an energy problem. Think of one coal mine or one oil field. When all the coal has been dug and all the oil pumped out there is no more left to dig or to pump.

To get more we have to open another mine where there is more coal or find another oil field. Sooner or later, these too will run out. And so on. The same is true of the uranium mines from which nuclear fuels come.

What happens when all the coal has been found and dug up and when all the oil has been found and pumped out? It must happen! How long have we got before it does? We don't know! We don't know how much fossil fuel is left for us to discover. We don't know how fast we shall use it all up. But we do know that the more we use today, the less is left for tomorrow.

Fig. 29.1 Good neighbours. Coal from the mine is burnt in the furnaces of the power station.

Fig. 29.2 Cutting coal in a Nottinghamshire pit.

Fig. 29.3 Harvesting grain from wheat plants, which use photosynthesis to store energy from the sun.

Fig. 29.4 Solar panels that use energy from the sun to warm water for use in the home.

This is why governments are giving money for research on renewable energy sources. The best place to start looking for these is in the sun itself. Energy from the sun falls on the earth all the time—and it is free! In Britain the rate is about 200 W/m² in daylight hours. Plants already make use of this energy in photosynthesis (p. 97) (Fig. 29.3). The air and the sea are stirred up by it to give us winds and waves. We might use windmills and wave machines. We might fit solar panels (which warm water) to our houses to help us keep warm (Fig. 29.4).

But none of these is yet able to keep our industry, our farm tractors and our transport running.

One thing we can do is to waste as little of our precious energy as we can: switching off the lights when we don't need them, insulating our houses and factories and cutting out draughts, and making trains and cars more efficient so that they use less fuel for each kilometre.

SUMMARY: ENERGY AND POWER

- Energy comes in different forms: mechanical—potential and kinetic, chemical, thermal, electrical and nuclear. All types of waves also carry energy.
- Potential energy is the energy an object has due to position. For a raised object, the potential energy is mass $\times g \times$ height raised.
- Kinetic energy is motion energy. It is given by $\frac{1}{2}$ mass $\times$ speed² ($\frac{1}{2} mv^2$).
- Energy often changes from one form to another. This change can be used to do a job of work.
- Energy cannot be created or destroyed. This is the law of conservation of energy.
- Energy is measured in joules: $1\,J = 1\,N\,m$.

- In a pendulum there are continual changes between kinetic and potential energy. However, the total energy remains constant, if no energy is wasted.
- Power is work done, or energy transformed, divided by the time taken. It is measured in J/s or watts (W).
- For a car on a level road, power is force exerted multiplied by speed.
- Coal, oil and natural gas are fossil fuels; when they have been used up, there will be no more.
- Energy from the sun is used by plants in photosynthesis as they produce crops and in solar panels to warm water.
- Energy from the sun causes winds to turn wind turbines.

SECTION 7

Expanding Solids, Liquids and Gases

30 Expanding solids

If you heat a solid it **expands**, i.e., it gets bigger. When it cools it **contracts**, i.e., it gets smaller. For solids, the expansion is usually very small. Special pieces of apparatus (Fig. 30.1) are made to show this expansion. After heating, bar A will not fit into the gauge. After heating, ball B will not go through the ring. When rod C is heated the pointer is pushed over the scale.

Solids expand in all directions. When bar A in Fig. 30.1 is cold it fits into the hole in the gauge. When the bar is hot it's too fat to fit. Ball B is bigger in all directions when it is hot.

FORCE OF EXPANSION AND CONTRACTION

Expanding or contracting solids can push really hard. If you stop a solid from contracting or expanding a very large force may be set up. Another special piece of apparatus shows this (Fig. 30.2). The steel bar is held firmly by the nut at one end and the cast iron pin at the other. When the bar is heated it expands. The nut is turned so that the hot rod is firmly held. Then the rod cools. Very soon the pin snaps in two.

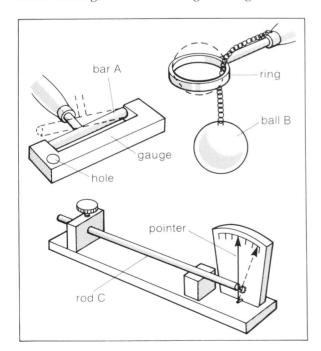

Fig. 30.1 Some experiments on expansion and contraction. Do the dotted lines show the apparatus when it is hot or cold?

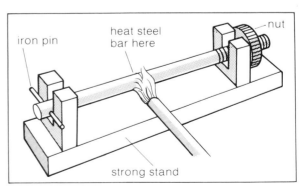

Fig. 30.2 When metals expand or contract they can develop very large forces.

59

Table 30 The expansion of rods (1-m long) made of different materials when heated from 0 to 30 °C

Material of rod	Expansion (mm)
Aluminium	0.8
Copper	0.5
Steel	0.4
Window glass	0.3
Oak	0.2
Pyrex glass	0.1
Invar	0.03

DIFFERENT EXPANSIONS

If you heat different solids so that they get equally hot, they expand by different amounts (Table 30). The expansion of a solid by heat is usually too small to see. The 0.8-mm expansion for 1 m of aluminium is about the thickness of 10 pages of this book. However, if the object is large, the expansion is more noticeable. The middle span of the Humber Estuary Bridge is 1410 m long. It is about 50 cm longer in summer than in winter. A jumbo jet is 10 cm shorter in the cold upper air than when it stands in tropical sunshine at an airport.

BIMETALLIC STRIP

A **bimetallic strip** (or compound bar) is made of two strips of different metals fixed together. The strip is straight when at room temperature. However, it bends when heated because one metal expands more than the other. When the strip is hot, the metal that expands more is always on the outside of the curve (Fig. 30.3).

Some **fire alarms** have a bimetallic strip. When the strip is hot it bends. The electrical contacts then touch so that current flows and rings the bell (Fig. 30.4).

The contacts of a **room-heating thermostat** fitted with a bimetallic strip move apart when the strip is hot. This switches off the heater or the pump that sends hot water through the central-heating radiators. When the bimetallic strip cools the contacts close. This switches the heating on again. The thermostat keeps the room at a steady temperature. To raise the temperature screw the top contact downwards (Fig. 30.5). The contacts then stay closed for longer periods.

Thermostats in aquaria and in some electric irons work similarly. When an automatic kettle boils the steam makes the thermostat switch the kettle off.

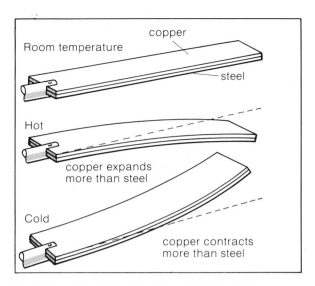

Fig. 30.3 A bimetallic strip will bend if it is heated or cooled.

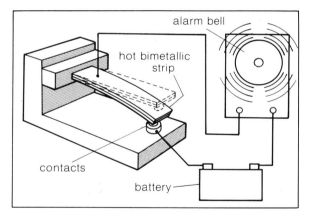

Fig. 30.4 A fire alarm. The dotted lines show the position of the bimetallic strip when it is cold.

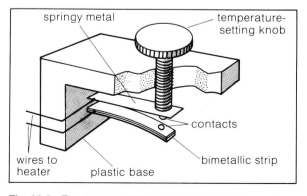

Fig. 30.5 The thermostat has opened the contacts and so switched the heater off.

31 Expansion—friend and foe

EXPANSION AND CONTRACTION ARE HELPFUL

Some of the ways in which expansion and contraction can be used are shown below.

Metal lids   If you cannot unscrew a metal lid, pour hot water carefully on to it. The lid will expand and should be easier to unscrew. Take care not to get the hot water on the glass of a glass jar (p. 62).

Rivets   Rivets are used to fix steel plates firmly together. One type of rivet is put into a hole when it is hot. When the rivet contracts it pulls the plates together (Fig. 31.1).

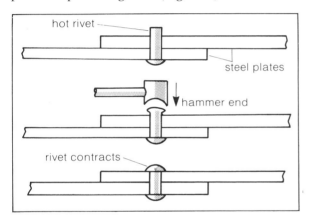

Fig. 31.1   Hot riveting.

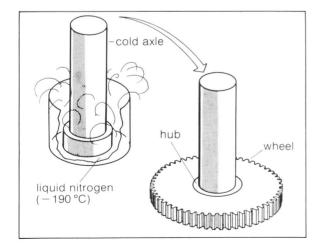

Fig. 31.2   The cold axle fits into the hub. When it warms up, it grips the hub very firmly.

Axles for wheels   An axle can be cooled and fitted into a wheel. When the axle warms and expands it grips the hub (centre part) of the wheel (Fig. 31.2). Sometimes the wheel is heated and put on the axle. The wheel grips the axle when it contracts again. This also shows that the hole in a piece of metal gets bigger when the metal is heated.

Gas oven thermostats   Gas oven thermostats have a rod of Invar (Fig. 31.3). **Invar** is a type of nickel—steel alloy that hardly expands when heated. Its length is almost INVARiable, or constant. When you first light the gas the gap at the left-hand end of the Invar bar is large. So plenty of gas flows through. As the big flames heat the oven, the brass tube expands and the Invar rod pulls the valve head along. The gap gets smaller and less gas gets through. The flames then decrease and the oven reaches a steady temperature. Turning the control knob screws the valve head along the Invar rod so you can widen the gap. This lets more gas flow and the oven gets hotter. If the valve shuts, enough gas goes through the by-pass to keep small flames lit.

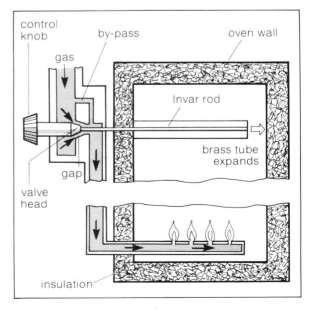

Fig. 31.3   The gap in the thermostat controls the gas flow.

EXPANSION AND CONTRACTION CAUSE TROUBLE

Some of the ways in which expansion and contraction can cause trouble follow.

Bridges The metal of a bridge expands in hot weather and contracts in cold weather. To make sure the bridge is safe it rests on rollers at one end. When the metal expands it rolls on the rollers (Fig. 31.4). There is also a sliding joint in the road surface at the moving end to allow for movement.

Concrete road surfaces Some roads are made of concrete blocks a few metres long. The joints between the blocks are made of a soft material. When the blocks expand the soft material is squashed. But the blocks are not damaged and the road surface remains smooth. The photograph on p. 59 shows another way of joining road sections together to allow for expansion.

Steam pipes Cold pipes expand when steam or hot water goes through them. They often creak as they move in their brackets. A long pipe needs an expansion loop to allow for the movement.

Telephone wires Telephone wires expand and sag in the summer. They are straighter and tighter in the winter. When the wires are put up this must be allowed for in case they sag too far in warm weather or snap in cold weather.

Sudden change in temperature can crack glass If you pour very hot water into a thick tumbler or milk bottle the glass might crack. The inside expands while the outside is still cold. This strains the glass. **Pyrex** and similar materials expand only about one-third as much as ordinary (soda) glass. Sudden heating or cooling is less likely to break them.

Railway tracks A solid track of rail might buckle because of expansion in hot weather. This could derail a train. Rails used to be about 20 m long. But gaps between the ends of the rails got smaller as the rails expanded. Rails are now welded into lengths of about a kilometre. Strong sleepers hold most of the length still. The last few metres of each rail expand. A sliding joint lets the rail move without buckling (Fig. 31.5).

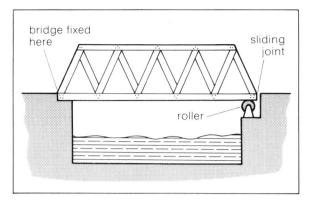

Fig. 31.4 A steel-girder bridge is fixed at one end. The other end rests on a roller.

Fig. 31.5 A joint in a modern railway track.

32 Expansion of liquids

WATCHING WATER EXPAND AND CONTRACT

Pour boiling water into a heated milk bottle. Fill the bottle to the top and leave it until it is cool. You will find that the water level drops about 3 cm. This suggests that water contracts as it cools.

Many modern cars have an expansion tank (Fig. 32.1) attached to the radiator. When the water in the radiator gets hot it expands and flows into this tank. This stops water (and antifreeze) from being lost from the car. When the water cools, it goes back into the radiator.

If you heat the apparatus shown in Fig. 32.2 the water level in the tube falls at first. This is because the flask warms up and expands. Soon the water too heats up. Now it rises in the tube. This shows that the water expands as you heat it. No water escapes as you heat the apparatus. The mass of water stays the same. The volume of the water increases, so the density of the water becomes less:

$$\text{density} = \frac{\text{mass}}{\text{volume}} \qquad \text{(see p.17)}$$

The hot water is less dense than the cold water.

OTHER LIQUIDS EXPAND DIFFERENTLY

All liquids expand when heated. Look at Fig. 32.3. This experiment shows that some expand more than others. Many **thermometers** contain a liquid that expands as it is heated (p. 69). The apparatus in Fig. 32.2 can act as a thermometer if you mark a temperature scale on the card. It is not a good thermometer because it is too big. The expansion of the flask could cause a problem. Also, water expands in an unusual way (p. 64).

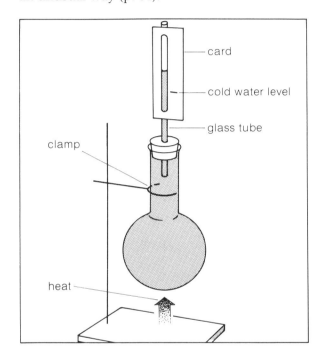

Fig. 32.2 If you heat the water in the flask, the level rises in the tube.

Fig. 32.1 When does the water flow from the radiator to the expansion tank?

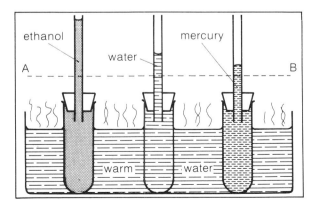

Fig. 32.3 Three different liquids being warmed. All the liquid levels were at the same level (AB) before warming.

33 The odd behaviour of water

A mixture of ice and water will be at 0 °C. Water can still be liquid although it is ice-cold. If you warm ice-cold water from 0 to 4 °C it contracts. This is odd behaviour. Other liquids expand when you warm them. But if you warm water above 4 °C, it expands like other liquids.

If you cool water it contracts until it reaches 4 °C, then it expands as it cools from 4 to 0 °C. Water shows this **anomalous expansion** only between 0 and 4 °C (Fig. 33.1). When you warm water from 0 to 4 °C the mass of water does not change but the volume gets smaller. Since density is mass divided by volume, the density of water must also change as you warm it. As the water contracts, its density increases. Water has its maximum density at 4 °C.

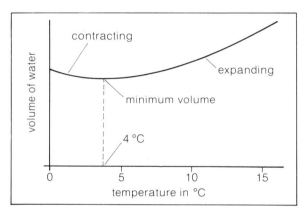

Fig. 33.1 Ice-cold water contracts as its temperature rises from 0 to 4 °C; then it expands.

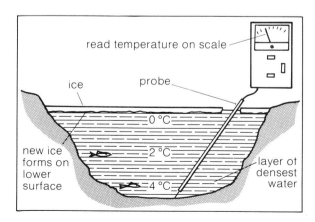

Fig. 33.2 Temperatures in a frozen pond. The temperature probe reads the temperature electrically.

PONDS FREEZING

In very cold weather a layer of dense water at 4 °C forms at the bottom of the pond. This layer lets fish swim and feed even if the top is frozen over (Fig. 33.2).

WHY DO PIPES BURST?

Most liquids contract as they freeze. But water at 0 °C expands by almost one-tenth of its volume as it freezes to ice. This is why pipes burst in very cold weather. Of course, we don't know it has happened until the thaw comes!

If milk freezes the expansion pushes the top off the bottle. If you put a watery liquid, e.g., soup, in a freezer you must allow space for it to expand as it freezes. If you freeze a lettuce, ice forming bursts the cells and the lettuce is soggy and limp when the ice in the cells melts.

THE DENSITY OF ICE

One dm^3 (1000 cm^3 or 1 litre) of water weighs 1 kg (1000 g). If water freezes the ice still weighs 1 kg. Its volume is 1.09 dm^3, or 1090 cm^3.

$$\text{density of ice} = \frac{1 \text{ kg}}{1.09 \text{ dm}^3} = \frac{1000 \text{ g}}{1090 \text{ cm}^3}$$
$$= 0.92 \text{ g/cm}^3$$

This is less dense than water, so ice floats on water (Fig. 33.3).

Fig. 33.3 An iceberg floating: only one-tenth of it is above the water line.

34 Gases expand when heated

If you put an open bottle, mouth down, into hot water, air will bubble out (Fig. 34.1). As the air in the bottle warms up, it takes up more space (expands). Because it takes up more space, the air becomes less dense.

All gases expand when heated. That's one reason why meringues, souffles, bread and cakes rise. It's also the reason why hot air balloons rise in the atmosphere.

To find out how large this expansion is, you can warm some air in a gas syringe. You can measure the expansion as the plunger moves past the calibrations, or volume marks, on the syringe barrel (Fig. 34.2). When 60 cm^3 of air or any other gas is warmed from 20 to 80 °C it expands to about 72 cm^3. No air escapes; no air gets in. The mass of the air stays the same, remains constant. The pressure of the air outside the syringe stays the same. The pressure inside the syringe stays the same. Only the temperature and the volume of the air increase.

Figure 34.3 shows the graph for this experiment. The line BC is a straight one. When you extend the line back to the temperature axis at A, the temperature is −273 °C. This is the lowest possible temperature; it is called **absolute zero** (p. 68).

The graph shows two scales of temperature; the ordinary **Celsius scale** in **°C** and the **Kelvin scale** in **K**. The Kelvin scale starts at absolute zero and uses the same sized divisions as the Celsius scale. To convert degrees Celsius to kelvin you add 273. For example:

$$20 \,°C = (20 + 273) \,K = 293 \,K$$
$$0 \,°C = 273 \,K$$
$$-273 \,°C = 0 \,K$$

Fig. 34.1 Air bubbling out of a bottle put into hot water. Why are the bubbles at the top bigger than the ones at the bottom?

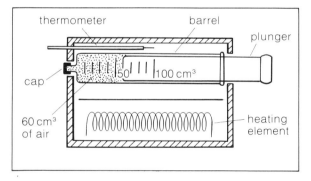

Fig. 34.2 Heating air in a gas syringe.

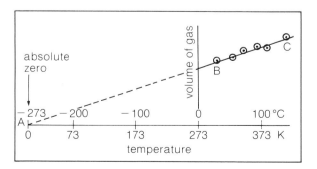

Fig. 34.3 How a gas expands when heated (constant mass and pressure).

COMPRESSION HEATING

The end of a bike pump gets hot in use (Fig. 34.4). This is because air gets hot as it is **compressed**, or squashed up. All gases get hot as they are compressed. Diesel engines compress air and fuel so much that the mixture explodes. These engines have **compression ignition**. Similarly, gases cool when they expand suddenly. Air rushing from a tyre valve is colder than it was in the tyre. (See also the section on refrigerators, on p. 83).

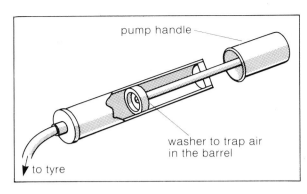

Fig. 34.4 A bicycle pump.

KINETIC THEORY OF GASES

Scientists think that gases are made of lots of tiny particles called **molecules**. Gas pressure is the result of collisions between the gas molecules and the walls of their container (p. 25). The molecules rush about like the bearing balls in the kinetic theory model (Fig. 34.5). When the motor in the model speeds up, the balls move faster and push the piston up. The force on the piston increases. Similarly, if a gas is given energy by being heated its molecules move faster and the gas exerts a bigger force on the container (see Fig. 34.3). If you stop a heated gas from expanding, its molecules hit the walls faster and more often. This means the gas pressure increases. The model shows this if you hold the piston down and make the ball bearings move faster. There are more collisions and harder collisions between the balls and the piston.

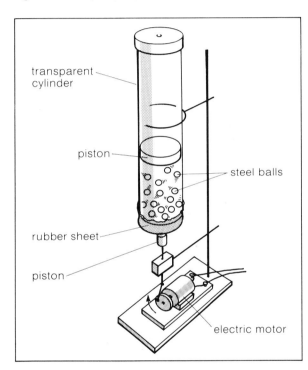

Fig. 34.5 A model of a gas. As the motor turns, the piston goes up and down and the bearing balls whizz about.

SUMMARY: EXPANDING SOLIDS, LIQUIDS AND GASES

- Solids expand when heated.
- If solids are prevented from expanding or contracting they can produce large forces.
- Different solids expand by different amounts when heated through the same temperature change.
- A bimetallic strip bends when heated.
- Expansion is used in thermostats, fire alarms, riveting and fitting wheels to axles.
- Engineers allow for expansion in bridges, road surfaces, steam pipes and railway tracks.
- Different liquids expand differently when heated through the same temperature change.
- Water contracts when heated from 0 to 4 °C.
- Water is densest at 4 °C.
- Water expands when it freezes.
- All gases expand equally when heated through the same temperature change.
- Absolute zero is − 273 °C, or 0 K (kelvin).

Measuring Temperature

35 Heat or temperature?

Look at Fig. 35.1: the horseshoe is red-hot. You would use a special thermometer to measure how hot the horseshoe was. The reading on a thermometer is the **temperature**. It is a measure of how hot something is.

The horseshoe was made red-hot by the energy put into it in a furnace. It was in the blacksmith's fire for quite a short time. The more energy put in, the faster the particles that make up the metal move. Unlike the particles in a gas, those in a solid move by vibrating about some fixed position. The amount of energy needed to heat up a body depends on:

1 What sort of particles make up the body, i.e., what the body is made of;
2 How many particles there are; and
3 How quickly the particles are moving to begin with, i.e., the temperature of the body before you start to heat it.

A red-hot spark from a firework is hotter than a pan of boiling water. If the spark fell on your hand you would hardly notice it. But if the boiling water fell on you, you would have to be rushed to hospital! Even though its temperature is lower, the boiling water has much more energy than the red-hot spark.

Fig. 35.1   The red-hot horseshoe.

36 Temperature scales

Temperatures are measured in **degrees Celsius** (°C). Anders Celsius, a Swedish astronomer, thought of this scale. He fixed two points on a scale and made 100 equal divisions between them. That is why it was called a hundred-division, or centigrade scale. One of the fixed points is the **ice point** (Fig. 36.1). This is the temperature of pure melting ice. The other is the **steam point** (Fig. 36.2). This is the temperature of steam boiling from water at standard atmospheric pressure (p. 23).

When a thermometer is made these fixed points are marked on the stem. Then the length of stem between them is divided into 100 divisions. This is called **calibrating** or **graduating** the thermometer.

OTHER TEMPERATURE SCALES

As you have seen, the **Kelvin scale** uses Celsius-sized divisions called **kelvin (K)**. The freezing point of water is 273 K. There are 100 kelvin between the freezing and boiling point of water. The boiling point of water is 373 K. The lowest temperature on the Kelvin scale, zero kelvin (0 K), is called **absolute zero** (p. 65).

The **Fahrenheit scale** is not often used now. This has 180 °F between the freezing (32 °F) and boiling point (212 °F) of water.

ABSOLUTE ZERO

A temperature of less than one-millionth of a kelvin has been reached in an experiment. It is impossible to cool something to absolute zero, (0 K). If a gas existed at 0 K it would shrink to zero (no) volume (see Fig. 34.3 on p. 65). But all known gases liquefy before reaching this temperature.

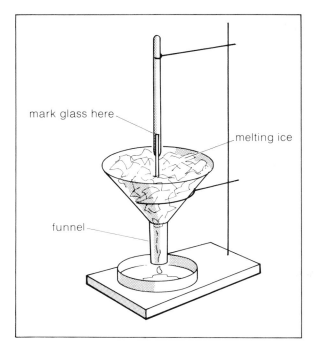

mark glass here

melting ice

funnel

Fig. 36.1 Marking the ice point (0 °C) on a thermometer.

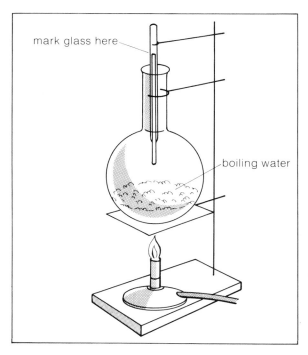

mark glass here

boiling water

Fig. 36.2 Marking the steam point (100 °C) on a thermometer.

37 Thermometers

LIQUID-IN-GLASS THERMOMETERS

Mercury and alcohol (spirit) are used as liquids in thermometers (Table 37). Liquids expand when heated. This expansion pushes a thread of the liquid out of the bulb and up the glass tube (Fig. 37.1). Look at the stem of a broken mercury thermometer. The hole, or **bore**, is about the same thickness as a hair. Such very fine tubes are called **capillary tubes**. A small expansion of the liquid in the bulb pushes the thread a long way up a narrow tube.

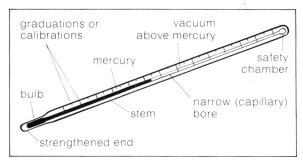

Fig. 37.1 A mercury thermometer: the round glass stem acts as a lens so that you can read the temperature easily.

Table 37 A comparison of the properties of mercury and alcohol, for use in thermometers

Mercury	Alcohol
Expensive—use small bulb	Cheap—large bulb may be used
Conducts heat well—shows temperature quickly	Expansion six times that of mercury
Easy to see—silvery colour	Colourless—dye must be added
Freezes at (− 39 °C)—can't always be used in very cold places	Freezing point low (− 115 °C)—can be used in very cold places
Boiling point high (357 °C)	Boiling point 78 °C—can't use in, for example, boiling water
Poisonous vapour—dangerous if thermometer breaks	Non-poisonous

MAXIMUM-RECORDING THERMOMETERS

These thermometers show the highest temperature reached in a day. One type uses mercury and has a light steel **index** in the bore (Fig. 37.2). When the mercury expands it pushes the index along. Note, the index doesn't break through the surface tension (p. 27). When the mercury contracts it leaves the index behind. You reset the index by using a magnet or by tilting the thermometer.

MINIMUM-RECORDING THERMOMETERS

This type of thermometer contains alcohol. It also has an index, like that in Fig. 37.2, inside the alcohol thread. When the thread expands the index stays where it is to mark the lowest temperature reached. Again, you reset the index by using a magnet or by tilting the thermometer.

MAXIMUM-AND-MINIMUM THERMOMETERS

One type of thermometer can record both the highest and lowest temperatures reached (Fig. 37.3, overleaf). The alcohol in the round bulb on the left expands or contracts as the

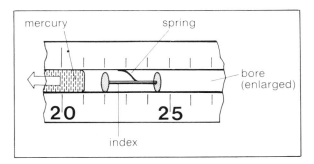

Fig. 37.2 The index in a maximum thermometer. What was the maximum temperature?

temperature changes. This moves the mercury thread and the two indices. The temperatures are read as shown.

CLINICAL THERMOMETERS

These are a type of maximum thermometer (Fig. 37.4, overleaf). The mercury expands and forces its way past the **constriction**, which is a narrow neck in the bore. When the thermometer cools and the mercury contracts again, the mercury that has gone past the constriction stays where it is. You jerk the

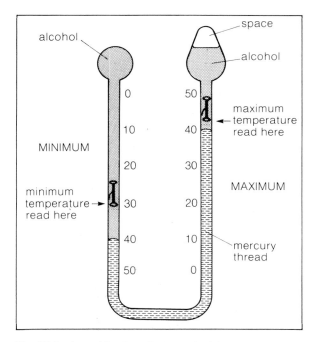

Fig. 37.3 A combined maximum-and-minimum thermometer works by the expansion and contraction of the alcohol in the left-hand bulb.

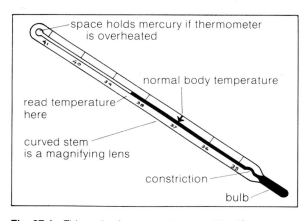

Fig. 37.4 This patient's temperature was 38.4 °C.

mercury back again by shaking the thermometer. Normal body temperature is about 37 °C.

BIMETALLIC THERMOMETERS

Bimetallic strips bend when heated (p. 60). A coiled bimetallic strip can act as a thermometer (Fig. 37.5). It is strong and cheap, but not very accurate. In better types the moving end of the strip turns a pointer through gears.

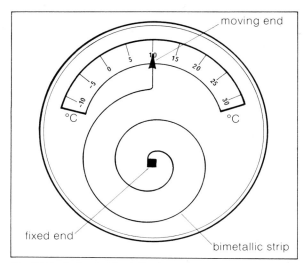

Fig. 37.5 A simple bimetallic thermometer.

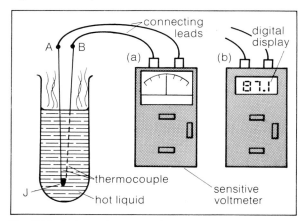

Fig. 37.6 Using a thermocouple.

THERMOCOUPLES–ELECTRICAL THERMOMETERS

A thermocouple has two wires of different metals. They are twisted together at one end. Heating the twisted end makes a voltage appear across the other end. In Fig. 37.6 the more the temperature of J is raised above the temperature of A and B, the bigger the voltage. A thermocouple is often put into a thin stainless steel case. The thermocouple and case together are called a **temperature probe.**

Thermocouples of metals such as platinum and rhodium can be used to measure temperatures up to 1500 °C. To produce a bigger voltage, thermocouples are connected in series. A group of them connected in this way is called a **thermopile.**

38 Zero kelvin and upwards!

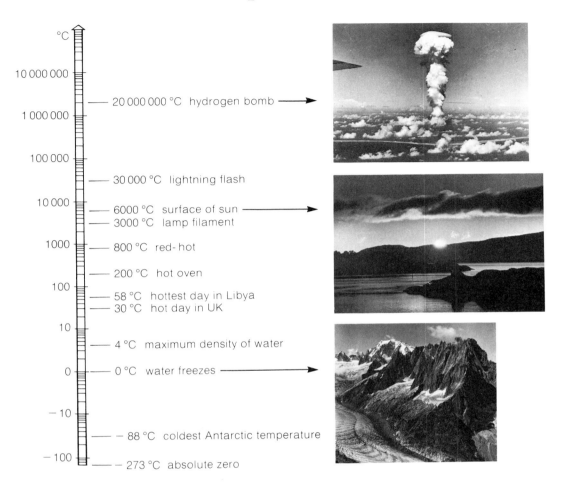

°C

10 000 000

1 000 000 ── 20 000 000 °C hydrogen bomb ──→

100 000

10 000 ── 30 000 °C lightning flash

── 6000 °C surface of sun ──→
── 3000 °C lamp filament

1000 ── 800 °C red-hot

── 200 °C hot oven

100 ── 58 °C hottest day in Libya
── 30 °C hot day in UK

10

── 4 °C maximum density of water

0 ── 0 °C water freezes ──→

− 10

── − 88 °C coldest Antarctic temperature

− 100 ── − 273 °C absolute zero

SUMMARY: MEASURING TEMPERATURE

- Temperature tells us how hot something is.
- To heat a body you must give it energy. This energy is often called heat.
- The amount of energy needed to raise the temperature of a body depends on its mass, the material it is made of, and its temperature to start with.
- Scientists measure temperature in degrees Celsius (°C) or in kelvin (K).
- The ice point (0 °C) and the steam point (100 °C) are used to calibrate the scales on thermometers.
- Absolute zero, − 273 °C, is 0 K (zero kelvin).

- Absolute zero is the lowest temperature possible.
- Mercury and alcohol are used in liquid-in-glass thermometers.
- The index of a maximum thermometer is pushed along by the mercury surface and left at the highest temperature.
- The mercury thread of a clinical thermometer breaks as the bulb cools.
- The strip of a bimetallic thermometer curves when it is heated.
- A thermocouple is made of two different metal wires, twisted together.
- The voltage of a thermocouple increases with temperature.

SECTION 9

Moving and Stopping Energy (Heat)

39 Conduction in solids

In Fig. 39.1 rods of copper, steel and glass are shown being heated. The flame heats the rods equally giving energy to them. The energy moves fastest along the copper rod. It moves slowest along the glass rod. We say that copper is a better thermal conductor than steel, which is much better than glass. When heat moves through a substance and the substance itself does not move, **thermal conduction** is taking place.

GOOD AND BAD CONDUCTORS

Most metals are good thermal conductors. The metal drawing pins (Fig. 39.2) conduct energy away from paper. The wood does not conduct energy away so well. The paper scorches over the wood but not over the drawing pins. This shows that a metal drawing pin is a better thermal conductor than a piece of wood.

On a cold day the metal frame of your bike feels colder than the saddle although they are both at the same temperature. This is because the metal conducts energy away from your hand quickly. The leather or plastic saddle is not such a good conductor. A piece of expanded polystyrene is a very poor thermal conductor. It conducts so little energy from your hand that it feels warm to touch. A very poor thermal conductor is a **thermal** or **heat insulator**.

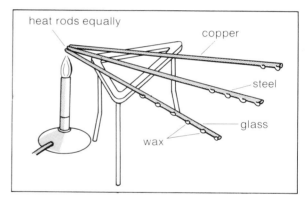

Fig. 39.1   As energy travels along the rods from hot to cold parts, the blobs of wax melt. Which of these three rods is the best insulator?

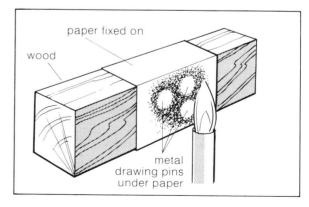

Fig. 39.2   The flame scorches the paper except where the metal drawing pins are stuck in.

72

CONDUCTION IN LIQUIDS AND GASES

Fill a test-tube almost to the top with water. Hold it carefully at the bottom and warm up the top couple of centimetres of water (Fig. 39.3). The water will soon come to the boil. But your fingers holding the bottom of the tube will still be quite comfortable. Water is a poor thermal conductor.

Air is another poor conductor of heat. It is often used to keep heat or energy in. Birds fluff up their feathers in cold weather. This traps air in the feathers and cuts down the energy loss from their bodies. The same idea works in eiderdowns and duvets and loft insulation (Fig. 39.4). The idea is also used in industry in freezers and refrigerators and in lorries carrying refrigerated foods. In double glazing the layer of air trapped between the two sheets of glass is good at cutting down the energy loss through a window. All these things use little pockets of air to help reduce energy wastage.

Fig. 39.3 Water boiling at the top of the tube, but keeping cool at the bottom.

Fig. 39.4 Cutting down energy losses from a house by laying an insulating blanket in the roof space.

SOME POOR CONDUCTORS IN USE

An oven cloth keeps your hands cool when you take a hot dish out of the oven. If you have a polished table, you will probably stand the hot dish on a table-mat. The mat is a poor conductor and protects the table. Kettles, saucepans and electric irons usually have plastic or wooden handles. And you soon learn to use a wooden spoon to stir boiling jam, which is very hot.

The space shuttle is covered with special insulating tiles (Fig. 39.5). They keep the shuttle body from getting too hot. As it returns from its orbits round the earth, the shuttle meets the air and this causes friction, which tends to heat up the shuttle.

SOME GOOD CONDUCTORS IN USE

Aluminium and copper-bottomed pans conduct energy very easily to the food being cooked in them. The copper bit of a soldering iron conducts energy from the electric heater inside it to the solder. Copper and aluminium are both good thermal conductors.

Fig. 39.5 The insulating tiles on a space shuttle.

40 Convection

CONVECTION IN WATER

Fill a test-tube almost to the top with cold water. Hold it carefully near to the top and warm up the water at the bottom. You will very soon put it down to stop your fingers from being burnt. You know that water is a bad thermal conductor (p. 73) so some other process of heat or energy transfer is working here. This process is called **convection**.

Next try warming a beaker containing water and some sawdust (Fig. 40.1). Don't use a gauze. You will see water carrying the sawdust flowing upwards from the warm spot X. The water and the sawdust then return to the bottom of the beaker at other places. A flow of liquid rising from a warm place is one kind of **convection current**. Instead of sawdust, you could use a dye, such as potassium manganate(VII) (potassium permanganate), to show the movement or circulation of the water. Put a crystal at X by dropping it down a glass tube. Gently remove the tube. The crystal slowly dissolves and colours the water in the upward convection current purple. Soon all the water will be coloured as the downward convection currents spread the dye.

CONVECTION IN AIR

In Fig. 40.2 a candle is setting up a convection current. A hot flame makes a warm, rising current. This is why you see smoke and sparks rising from a fire. Convection currents carry them upwards.

A cold substance, such as a lump of ice, makes a cold convection current. This flows downwards. In winter there is a downward convection current underneath a cold window. Open a refrigerator door just a little, put your hand below it and you will feel a cold convection current.

WHY CONVECTION TAKES PLACE

Heated air expands and becomes less dense than colder air (p. 65). The cold, dense air then sinks, pushing the warmer air upwards. Cold water sinks and hot water rises for similar reasons. Convection takes place only in liquids and gases, not in solids. In solids the particles cannot move around.

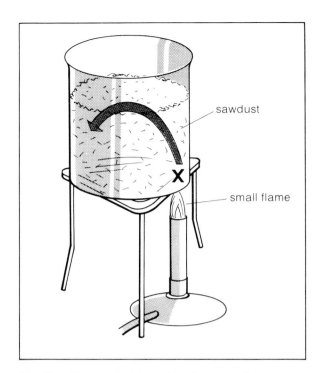

Fig. 40.1 The sawdust shows how the convection current moves.

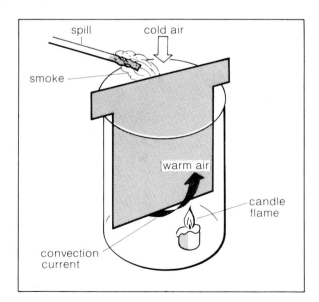

Fig. 40.2 The burning candle produces a convection current. Cool, smoky air moves down one side of the card. Air warmed up by the candle rises on the other side.

HOW WE MAKE USE OF CONVECTION CURRENTS

Convection moves energy through liquids and gases. When you warm a pan of water, the convection currents move through the water so that it warms up all through.

Radiators and **convector heaters** warm the air round them. The warm air then rises and travels up to the ceiling. This warms up the ceiling as the air current moves across it. The ceiling is often the warmest part of a room (Fig. 40.3). Cooler air falls and moves across the floor to the radiator or convector. If a radiator is placed directly under a window this stops cold downward convection currents.

A gas or solid fuel fire makes a hot convection current up the chimney. Although this wastes energy, fresh, cool air comes into the room through the windows, ventilators and cracks round the doors. So the air in the room is changed; the room is ventilated.

Strong convection currents flow in factory chimneys. They carry the waste gases and a lot of energy high into the air and away from the factory.

A HOT-WATER SYSTEM FOR A HOUSE

In an **indirect hot-water system**, water heated in a boiler flows upwards by convection and round a closed loop of pipes (Fig. 40.4). In the hot-water cylinder, the warm water passes through a coiled pipe. It loses heat to the cool water in the cylinder and this water is warmed. This part of the system is a **heat exchanger** or **calorifier**. The water flowing out of the coiled pipe returns to the boiler and so on. When you draw hot water off through a hot tap, it comes from the top of the store of hot water in the cylinder. Cold water flows from the cold tank in the roof to keep the cylinder full. Any central-heating radiators are on a different closed loop of pipes.

In a **direct system**, hot water from the boiler flows straight into the cylinder. There is no calorifier.

STOPPING CONVECTION

To keep energy or heat in, you must prevent convection as well as conduction. Animals' fur, birds' feathers and mineral wool insulation in lofts do this. They keep the air in little pockets so that convection doesn't occur.

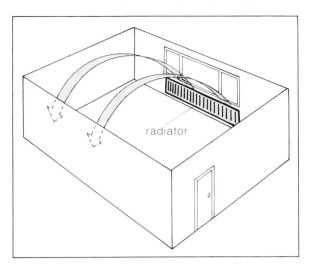

Fig. 40.3 A radiator spreads warm air through a room by convection. Only a little energy is radiated.

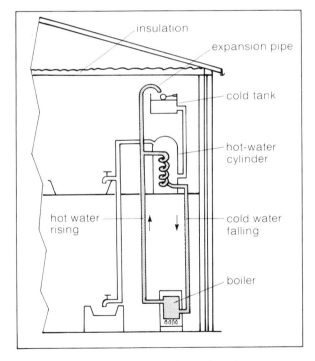

Fig. 40.4 A simplified diagram of an indirect hot-water system. Water from the boiler doesn't reach the hot taps.

41 Radiation of energy

Energy reaches us from the sun. Because there is a vacuum between us and the sun, conduction and convection cannot take place. The energy travels as electromagnetic waves (p. 95) by the **process of radiation**. The waves travel at the speed of light. It takes about eight minutes for them to reach us. If the sun changed colour you wouldn't know until eight minutes after it happened.

HOW DO WE KNOW IT'S THERE?

You can feel the radiation on your skin or detect it with a thermometer. The radiation warms the thermometer and the reading goes up. This works even better if you blacken the thermometer bulb. You can also use a thermocouple, or electrical thermometer (p. 70), to detect radiation.

WHAT GIVES OUT RADIATION?

Anything hot radiates. The hotter it is the more energy it radiates. It is easy to feel the radiation from a red-hot fire or cooker grill.

Take an empty tin can and paint one-half dull black. Fill it with boiling water (Fig. 41.1). The two sides of the tin are at the same temperature. Hold the backs of your hands at equal distances from the two sides. You can feel that the black side radiates more energy than the shiny side. In the same way, a thermometer would show a higher temperature at B than at A. Dull, black surfaces are good radiators. Shiny, light-coloured surfaces are poor radiators.

USES OF GOOD AND POOR RADIATORS

A shiny metal teapot is a poor radiator. This helps to keep the tea warm. You may cover the pot with a tea-cosy to reduce energy loss by conduction and convection. If you want something to emit (give out) radiation, make it dull and black. One example is the cooling coil at the back of a refrigerator. This helps it to lose energy by emitting radiation. It loses even more energy by conduction and convection.

HOW DOES A VACUUM FLASK WORK?

The silvering on the inner surface of a vacuum

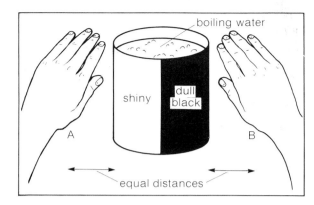

Fig. 41.1 Hold the backs of your two hands at A and B. Which surface radiates more heat?

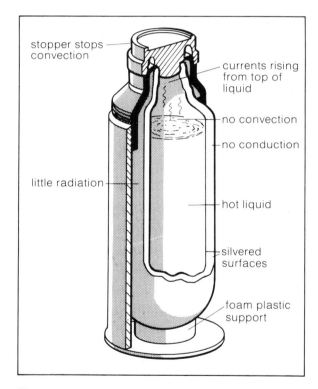

Fig. 41.2 How a vacuum flask keeps heat in.

flask is hot if the flask contains hot soup (Fig. 41.2). But as shiny surfaces are poor radiators, little energy escapes by radiation. Since energy cannot be conducted or convected across the vacuum, very little energy escapes. The soup stays hot.

If there is something cold in the flask, energy is kept out in a similar way. The cold liquid will stay cold.

WHAT ABSORBS RADIATION?

The red-hot element of an electric fire radiates a lot of energy. If you wrap the back of your hand in shiny foil you can hold it near the hole in a screen right in front of the element for a long time (Fig. 41.3). Now paint the foil dull black. Put your hand back in the same position. Don't hold it there for more than a second or two!

This experiment shows that a dull, black surface absorbs more radiation than a shiny, light-coloured one. Shiny surfaces reflect radiation (Fig. 41.4). Dull, black surfaces are good at both absorbing and emitting radiation.

USES OF GOOD AND POOR ABSORBERS OF RADIATION

1 If you wear light-coloured clothes you absorb less radiated heat than if you wear dark ones.
2 Houses in hot countries are often painted white to keep them cooler.
3 A light-coloured car stays fairly cool in the sun. A dark-coloured car absorbs radiation and gets quite hot.
4 The shiny reflector of an electric fire does not absorb radiation. It stays cool even if the fire has been on for hours.
5 Solar-heating panels are dull black. They absorb radiation very well.

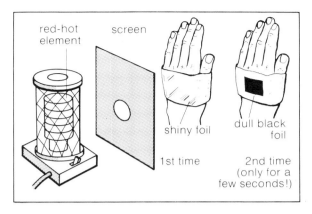

Fig. 41.3 Blackened foil absorbs more radiation than shiny foil. *Be careful*, this experiment can burn your hand very quickly!

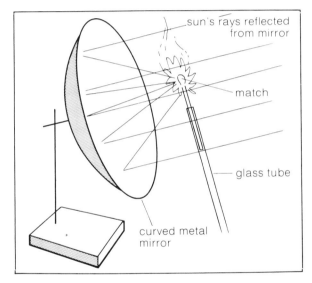

Fig. 41.4 Concentrating radiation from the sun to light a match. (The solar cooker on p. 72 also works like this.)

SUMMARY: MOVING AND STOPPING ENERGY (HEAT)

- Metals are good thermal conductors.
- Liquids and gases are not good conductors.
- Good insulators are poor conductors.
- Convection is the process of heat or energy transfer in a liquid or gas.
- Hot convection currents flow upwards.
- Cold convection currents flow downwards.
- Density changes cause convection currents.

- Water from the boiler of an indirect water-heating system flows in a closed loop.
- Radiation transmits energy as electromagnetic waves.
- Dull, black surfaces are good emitters and absorbers of radiation.
- Light, shiny surfaces are poor emitters and absorbers of radiation.
- A vacuum flask keeps hot things hot and cold things cold because there is no conduction or convection and little radiation from its walls.

SECTION 10

Energy and Changes of State

42 Measuring energy in a heating experiment

When a gas is cold its particles move slowly. When it is hot the particles move more quickly. They are more energetic (p. 66). Remember, energy is measured in joules (J) and temperature is measured in kelvin (K) or degrees Celsius (°C).

USING JOULES

When you strike a match and let about half of it burn, it gives out about 1000 joules (1000 J), or 1 kilojoule (1 kJ).

A joule is only a small amount of energy. A gas burner or an electric kettle may supply 2000 J of energy every second. As the gas burns, some of the energy of the hot flame warms up the kettle. The element of an electric kettle changes energy from the electrical form and this warms up the water. The warm water has more energy than the cold. It is easier to measure electric currents than it is to measure the flow of gas. That is why we prefer to use electrical heating and a **joule meter** to measure the quantity of energy given to something.

SPECIFIC HEAT CAPACITY

The block of aluminium in Fig. 42.1 has a mass of 1 kg and contains a thermometer and a small heating coil. A joule meter measures the energy given to the aluminium when the electric current in the heater is switched on.

First measure the temperature of the block.

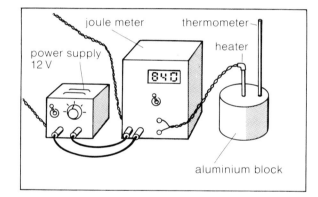

Fig. 42.1 Measuring the energy needed to warm 1 kg of aluminium through 1 °C.

Then switch on and wait for the temperature to rise by 1 °C—from, say, 18 to 19 °C. Then switch off and read the joule meter. It will probably tell you that about 800 J of energy were needed to raise the block's temperature by 1 °C.

The energy needed to raise 1 kg of a substance through 1 °C is called the **specific heat capacity** (c) of the substance. The specific heat capacity of aluminium therefore must be about 800 joules per kilogram per °C, J/kg °C.

This is rather a rough figure. To improve your measurement you could wait for a temperature rise of 10 °C and then divide the joule meter reading by ten. By lagging the block with a good thermal insulator you can reduce heat loss.

Table 42 Specific heat capacities

Material	Energy needed to raise the temperature of 1 kg through 1 °C (J)
Lead	130
Copper	380
Aluminium	840
Glycerine	2400
Water	4200

Table 42 shows some specific heat capacities. Notice how big the number for water is. No wonder we use it in our central-heating systems (see below).

HOW MUCH ENERGY IS NEEDED?

Try the experiment in Fig. 42.1 using some water in a light polystyrene cup instead of the aluminium block. You will find it takes 4200 J to raise the temperature of 1 kg of water by 1 °C. Using 2 kg you need twice as much energy for the 1°C rise, i.e., 8400 J. Raising the 2 kg by 10 °C would take 10 times as much energy as raising it by 1 °C, i.e., 84 000 J. These findings can be written:

$$\begin{array}{c}\text{energy}\\\text{supplied}\\\text{(in J)}\end{array} = \begin{array}{c}\text{mass}\\\text{(in kg)}\end{array} \times \begin{array}{c}\text{specific}\\\text{heat}\\\text{capacity}\\\text{(in J/kg °C)}\end{array} \times \begin{array}{c}\text{temperature}\\\text{change}\\\text{(in °C)}\end{array}$$

The same formula gives energy loss when substances cool.

Example How much energy is given out when 0.2 kg of water cool from 80 to 20 °C? (The specific heat capacity (c) of water is 4200 J/kg °C.)

The fall in temperature is (80 °C − 20 °C) = 60 °C. Therefore

$$\begin{aligned}\text{energy loss} &= \text{mass} \times c \times \text{temperature fall}\\ &= 0.2 \text{ kg} \times 4200 \text{ J/kg °C} \times 60 \text{ °C}\\ &= 50\,400 \text{ J}\end{aligned}$$

So 50 400 J (50.4 kJ) are lost when 0.2 kg of water cools from 80 to 20 °C.

FINDING SPECIFIC HEAT CAPACITIES

Example 13 500 J will raise the temperature of 1.5 kg of iron from 18 to 38 °C. What is the specific heat capacity of iron?

The rise in temperature is (38 °C − 18 °C) = 20 °C. Therefore using the formula given above:

$$\begin{array}{c}\text{energy}\\\text{supplied}\end{array} = \text{mass} \times c \times \begin{array}{c}\text{temperature}\\\text{rise}\end{array}$$

$$13\,500 \text{ J} = 1.5 \text{ kg} \times c \times 20 \text{ °C}$$

$$13\,500 \text{ J} = 30 \text{ kg °C} \times c$$

$$c = \frac{13\,500 \text{ J}}{30 \text{ kg °C}} = 450 \text{ J/kg °C}$$

Therefore the specific heat capacity of iron is 450 J/kg °C.

EFFECTS OF THE HIGH SPECIFIC HEAT CAPACITY OF WATER

Water needs a lot of energy to warm it up. So, once it is warm it holds a good store of energy. This is because its specific heat capacity, 4200 J/kg °C, is very high. A small mass of water in, say, a hot-water bottle, holds quite a lot of energy (Fig. 42.2). That is why water is the best liquid to use in central-heating systems and to use as a cooling liquid in such machines as petrol engines.

Islands like Great Britain, which are surrounded by water, keep cooler in summer and don't get so cold in winter as countries like Austria which are in the middle of a continent. The sea is a great reservoir of thermal energy and this helps to keep Britain neither too hot nor too cold.

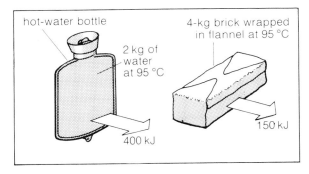

Fig. 42.2 In cooling to luke warm, the hot-water bottle will give around 420 kJ, the brick around 150 KJ. And the brick has twice the mass of the water!

43 Melting and boiling

Ice forms round the cold box of a refrigerator. Some people melt this ice and use the pure melted water in their steam iron. Ice is the **solid state** of water. Energy is needed to melt it to the **liquid state**. In the steam iron, water boils to the **gaseous state**, steam or water vapour. Cooling takes energy away and condenses steam back to water. Further cooling freezes the water. These changes are called **changes of state** (Fig. 43.1).

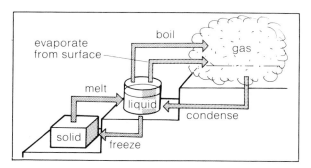

Fig. 43.1 The change-of-state staircase. To go up, add energy (warm). To come down, take energy away (cool).

On cool window panes in winter you often see **condensation**, drops of liquid water. If the glass is very cold these might freeze into ice. You can use the word **freeze** for any change of state from liquid to solid. Water freezes at 0 °C; mercury freezes at − 39 °C. A goldsmith melts gold and pours it into a mould to make a ring. The gold freezes at 1063 °C. These are also the **melting points**, the temperatures at which these substances melt. Some solids, such as bread and wood, do not melt when heated. They may burn or go through some other chemical change.

FREEZING SOLUTIONS

Rock pools that are left when the tide goes out contain sea water. This is a solution of salt in water. When rainwater pools freeze, salt-water pools often remain liquid. This is because salt water, brine, has a lower freezing point than pure water. Sea water freezes at about − 3 °C.

Any dissolved substance **depresses**, or lowers, the freezing point of a liquid. Antifreeze is added to water in car radiators. This can lower the freezing point of the

Fig. 43.2 Safety first. The ice−salt mixture is at − 2 °C, which is higher than the freezing point (− 4 °C), so the ice melts.

mixture to − 15 °C. (The temperature in Britain seldom falls to − 15 °C.) Therefore, the water with antifreeze in doesn't freeze. If it did, it would expand and damage the car engine (p. 63).

Salt is often put on icy paths and roads to help to melt the ice (Fig. 43.2).

BOILING SOLUTIONS

A sample of water containing antifreeze from a car radiator might boil at 104 °C. Antifreeze lowers the freezing point and raises the boiling point of water. Any solution in water has a boiling point above that of pure water. You can show this for yourself. Find the boiling point of some pure water. Then add salt to the water and find the new boiling point. Add more salt and so on (Fig. 43.3).

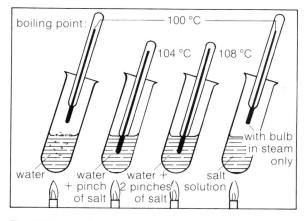

Fig. 43.3 To raise the boiling point add a little more salt.

COOLING

Try watching a liquid as it turns into a solid.
Naphthalene is a good substance to use. Put a
little naphthalene in a large test-tube and melt
it by dipping the tube into boiling water.
When it has melted, take the tube out of the
water. Put a thermometer in the naphthalene
and measure the temperature every minute as
it cools.

The graph in Fig. 43.4 shows some results.
From A to B the naphthalene cools in the
ordinary way. But at 80 °C the temperature
stops falling (curve BC is straight). It must still
be losing energy to the air but the temperature
doesn't change. It is getting energy from
somewhere else at the same rate. This energy
was locked up (stored) in the naphthalene
when it was melted. As the liquid turns back
to solid this hidden or **latent** energy is given
up. Once it has all frozen to the solid form, it
starts to cool down again (curve CD).

LATENT HEAT OF VAPORISATION

Boiling turns water at 100 °C to steam at
100 °C. The energy put in while the water is
boiling does not increase the temperature. This
energy is hidden in the steam. The energy
needed to vaporise a liquid is called its **latent
heat of vaporisation**. This latent heat is given
out again when the vapour condenses back to
a liquid.

Example In an experiment a 2000-W kettle
vaporises 0.25 kg of water in 300 s. How much
heat is needed to vaporise 1 kg of water?
(2000 W means 2000 J/s.)

In 300 s the kettle uses

300 s × 2000 J/s = 600 000 J

Since this energy vaporises 0.25 kg of water,
then 1 kg needs

$$\frac{600\,000 \text{ J}}{0.25 \text{ kg}} = 2\,400\,000 \text{ J} \quad \text{or } 2400 \text{ kJ or } 2.4 \text{ MJ}$$

So 2400 kJ are needed to vaporise 1 kg of
water.

The **specific latent heat of vaporisation** of
water is the amount of energy (in joules or
kilojoules) needed to vaporise 1 kg of water at
100 °C. A careful experiment, with no energy
lost to the bench or the air, would give a value
of 2260 kJ/kg of water.

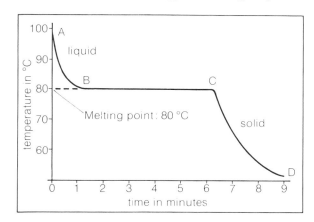

Fig. 43.4 The cooling curve of naphthalene. What happens
to the temperature as naphthalene freezes?

For any mass of water at 100 °C:

energy needed to vaporise water (in kJ)	=	specific latent heat of vaporisation (in kJ/kg)	×	mass of water (in kg)

It takes about seven times as much energy to
vaporise a mass of water as it does to heat that
water from room temperature to 100 °C.

LATENT HEAT OF FUSION (MELTING)

Energy is needed to turn ice at 0 °C into water
at 0 °C. This energy is called the **latent heat of
fusion**. The **specific latent heat of fusion** of ice
is the amount of energy (in joules or kilojoules)
needed to melt 1 kg of ice at 0 °C. It takes
340 000 J (340 kJ) to do this.

For any mass of ice at 0 °C:

energy needed to melt ice (in kJ)	=	specific latent heat of fusion (in kJ/kg)	×	mass of ice (in kg)

44 Evaporation

After a rain fall the streets soon dry up. If you leave the top off a felt-tipped pen it soon won't write. In both cases a liquid has turned to vapour. The liquid has changed its state. It has **evaporated**.

Take a cupful of water and pour half into a saucer. You will find that the water in the saucer evaporates more quickly than the water in the cup. This is because evaporation goes on at the surface. The bigger the surface area, the quicker the evaporation.

ALL LIQUIDS EVAPORATE

Some liquids, alcohol and petrol for example, evaporate more quickly than others. This is why you can smell them easily. Even a liquid like mercury evaporates but much more slowly; it gives off a dense harmful vapour.

You may have seen air bubbled through ether, which evaporates easily (Fig. 44.1). To do this the ether needs energy. It takes this energy from itself and its surroundings and gets colder. It may get cold enough to freeze water. If the flask stands on a wet bench, it could freeze to the bench.

When a liquid evaporates it gets its latent heat of vaporisation from the surroundings, cooling them. This is how cologne or

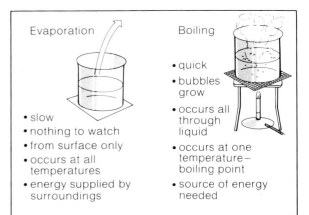

Evaporation
- slow
- nothing to watch
- from surface only
- occurs at all temperatures
- energy supplied by surroundings

Boiling
- quick
- bubbles grow
- occurs all through liquid
- occurs at one temperature – boiling point
- source of energy needed

Fig. 44.2 The differences between boiling a liquid and allowing it to evaporate.

aftershave cools your skin. Figure 44.2 shows how boiling is a special case of evaporation.

HOW WE USE EVAPORATION

Sweating cools your body. A hot, humid or muggy day feels unpleasant. This is because there is a lot of water vapour already in the air and your sweat, or perspiration, does not evaporate easily.

To dry hair with a hairdryer you blow hot air through it (Fig. 44.3). The warmth speeds evaporation. The movement of air carries the water vapour away. It also separates the strands, increasing the surface area. For the same reasons washing dries best on a warm, dry, windy day.

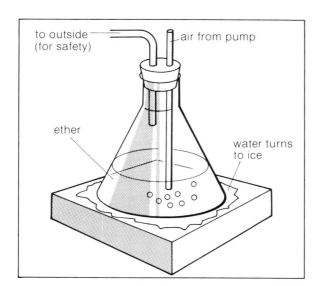

Fig. 44.1 The ether evaporates quickly, cooling the flask and freezing the water on the bench.

Fig. 44.3 This hairdryer dries hair in three ways. What are they?

EVAPORATION CAN BE DANGEROUS

You might want to prevent evaporation. Evaporation from wet socks can make your feet very cold.

Climbers and mountain walkers carry **exposure bags** (Fig. 44.4). If they get wet they crawl, feet first, into the bag if they need to rest. This prevents evaporation and keeps them warmer. Without it they might die from exposure.

Fig. 44.4 Mountain walkers sheltering in exposure bags to prevent evaporation.

A COMPRESSION REFRIGERATOR

The gas that is pumped through the tubes of a refrigerator or freezer (Fig. 44.5) is squashed (compressed) by the pump. As the gas flows through cooling tubes on the outside of the back of the refrigerator it turns to liquid and gives up its latent heat of vaporisation. As it does so it cools and the outside air warms up. The liquid then flows through a valve and expands into the tube surrounding the icebox. That is where it evaporates into a gas again. It takes its latent heat of vaporisation from the icebox. So the icebox gets cold. The gas then goes back to the **compressor** or pump and so round the circuit once again. The refrigerator pumps heat from the icebox through the cooling tube into the outside air. Some people think that heat pump would be a better name!

The substance used in refrigerators is called a **Freon** or an **Arcton**. The temperature inside the cabinet is controlled by a thermostat. This switches the pump motor on when the inside temperature gets too high and switches it off when it gets too low.

Why are the cooling tubes coloured black? Why are they made of metal?

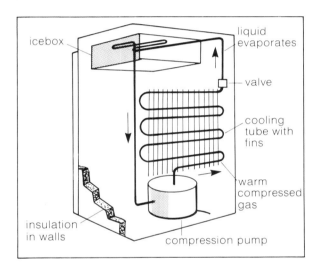

Fig. 44.5 Remember the refrigerator cycle — compress, cool, condense, evaporate.

ICING UP

The walls of a refrigerator contain a good thermal insulator. This is to keep out as much energy as possible. When you open the door of a refrigerator, cold, dense air falls out and warm, damp air flows in at the top. The moisture condenses to water and eventually to ice on the icebox. But ice is a poor thermal conductor. So now the refrigerator doesn't work so well as it should since the energy has to be removed through this layer of ice. The motor has to run for longer periods and the running costs go up! This is why refrigerators are defrosted. The motor is switched off so the ice melts. When the water from the ice has been removed the motor is started up again.

45 More kinetic theory

The pressure of a gas can be explained by the bombardment of a surface by fast-moving gas molecules. Brownian motion is evidence for this idea (p. 25). The theory of moving particles, the **kinetic theory**, should help us explain other observations.

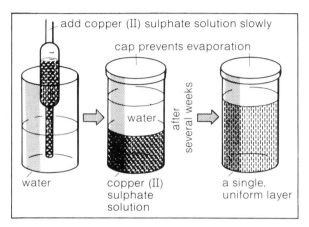

Fig. 45.1 Diffusion—the liquids mix because their particles move around all the time.

DIFFUSION

Two gases put in the same container always mix. Air in a room does not separate into layers of carbon dioxide, oxygen, nitrogen and so on. It stays mixed even though carbon dioxide is a denser gas than the others. Layers of liquids usually mix without even being stirred (Fig. 45.1). Their particles are moving all the time and this makes them move into all the space available—this is the process of **diffusion**.

Bromine is a red-brown liquid at room temperature. It is a dangerous liquid and must be handled with great care in special apparatus (Fig. 45.2). Liquid bromine evaporates easily. If you release some into a vacuum the brown vapour spreads right through the space almost at once. The molecules of bromine must be moving very quickly. If the bromine is released into a similar space full of air the brown colour spreads right through but much more slowly. The bromine molecules still travel very quickly. However, they now keep hitting air molecules which get in the way. Therefore, they do not spread out so quickly.

SOLIDS, LIQUIDS AND GASES

The kinetic theory says that solids, liquids and gases are made of particles that move all the time (Fig. 45.3).

Solids have fixed shapes. Each particle in the solid vibrates about a fixed place. The warmer the solid, the bigger the vibration.

Liquids flow and take the shape of the vessel they are in. They have a definite surface. The particles are free to move around in the liquid, but it is hard for them to leave it. They stay in a definite volume.

Gases have no shape, no surface and no fixed volume. They spread out to fill any vessel they are in. The particles are free to move around. They don't all move with the same speed but the average speed is very high. The molecules that make up air travel at over 1200 mph even at ordinary temperatures.

HEATING AND KINETIC THEORY

If you put one end of a steel poker into a hot fire, that end is heated. The poker takes energy

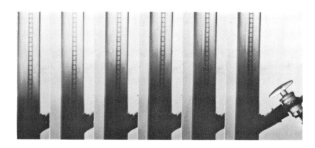

Fig. 45.2 Bromine vapour diffusing into air. The photographs were taken at intervals of 100 s.

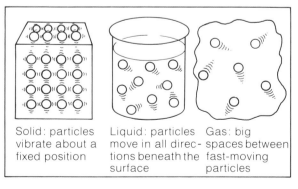

Solid: particles vibrate about a fixed position

Liquid: particles move in all directions beneath the surface

Gas: big spaces between fast-moving particles

Fig. 45.3 How we think molecules move in solids, liquids and gases.

from the burning fuel. The particles at the hot end vibrate more. This larger vibration is passed on from particle to particle up to the cool end of the poker. You already know that steel is a good thermal conductor and now you can see why. Because the particles are vibrating more, they move very slightly further apart as the poker gets hot. So the poker gets a little longer and fatter, or expands.

As a liquid is heated its particles bump about more vigorously and the liquid expands.

When a gas is heated in a container its temperature rises, its particles move faster and they hit the walls more often and harder. So the pressure of the gas increases. If the walls move back (as in Fig. 34.2 on p. 65) the gas takes up more space, i.e., its volume increases.

CHANGES OF STATE

As a solid is heated its particles vibrate more and more vigorously. Eventually they may have enough energy to break away from their fixed places and move freely. The solid has then melted. Most of the particles stay within the liquid. But some of the more energetic ones may escape from the surface. Some of these may bump into particles of air above the liquid, and then bounce back into the liquid. Others may move away. If they do we say the liquid is evaporating.

As a liquid evaporates it loses its fastest particles (Fig. 45.4). Slower ones are left. This means the liquid is cooler. Evaporation cools the liquid, as you have seen.

The hotter the liquid gets, the faster its particles move. There are then more quick ones to escape, so the liquid evaporates faster. When the average speed of the particles is fast enough for them to escape, the liquid boils.

The particles in the gaseous state are very much farther apart than they are in the liquid state. This is why gases have low densities. One cubic centimetre of boiling water produces about 1600 cm^3 of steam.

BOILING AND FREEZING IMPURE LIQUIDS

Salt solution (brine) contains particles of salt. These get in the way of any water molecules which are trying to escape. You have to heat the solution to a temperature above 100 °C before it boils (p. 80).

When salt water freezes, water molecules try to form into ice crystals. But salt particles get in the way. So salt, and other dissolved substances, lower the freezing point of water (p. 80).

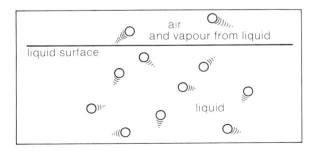

Fig. 45.4 Molecules escaping from an evaporating liquid. One molecule is about to get away. Which one?

46 Boiling and freezing under pressure

It is not enough to say water boils at 100 °C. If the water is impure it boils at a higher temperature (p. 80). Pressure also alters the boiling point.

It is correct to say pure water boils at 100 °C under normal atmospheric pressure (760 mm of mercury or 100 kPa).

BOILING UNDER REDUCED PRESSURE

The experiment shown in Fig. 46.1 allows you to boil water at around 30 °C! The water bubbles and vaporises just like water boiling in a pan. But it is only warm, not hot, and it **is** boiling. You can boil cold water if you reduce the pressure far enough. On mountains the effect is very obvious. At the top of Snowdon, water boils at 97 °C. At the top of Everest, where air pressure is only one-third that at sea level, water boils at 72 °C. You can't make good tea with water at 72 °C!

SUGAR AND MILK

Boiling at low temperatures under reduced pressure is very useful. It's cheaper to boil off water this way. You don't have to heat the liquid so much and you don't use so much fuel. In a sugar mill, the cane or beet sugar is mixed with water. This makes a sugar solution. The solution is boiled at 60 °C under low pressure until granulated sugar crystals separate. This is cheaper than boiling it at 100 °C and the low temperature stops the sugar from darkening.

Evaporated milk is made by boiling milk under reduced pressure. Some of the water vaporises, leaving a thicker liquid. To make sweet condensed milk, sugar is added before evaporating.

BOILING UNDER INCREASED PRESSURE

When a pressure cooker is working the pressure inside it is twice normal atmospheric pressure. At this pressure, water boils at 120 °C. Food cooks more quickly at 120 °C than at 100 °C and a pressure cooker saves time and fuel.

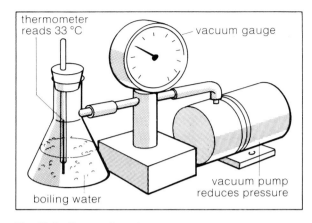

Fig. 46.1 If you reduce the pressure to about one-twentieth of normal, water boils at about 33 °C.

Fig. 46.2 An autoclave.

An **autoclave** is a special type of pressure cooker (Fig. 46.2). It is used to sterilise surgical instruments and culture plates by heating them to a high temperature.

SUPER-HEATED STEAM

When you heat a gas, you make its particles move faster. The gas then has more energy. Steam is often heated to very high temperatures for this reason. It is called **super-heated steam**. In electricity-generating stations, the steam used to run the turbines may be as hot as 600 °C—hot enough to make the steam pipes glow dull red.

MELTING AND PRESSURE

Increasing the pressure lowers the melting point of a solid. Try passing a loop of copper wire carrying a large mass over a block of ice. Leave it for a few minutes. You will see that the wire has moved into the ice (Fig. 46.3). The pressure caused by the weight of the mass lowered the freezing point. The ice melted—the wire moved—the water behind the wire froze again. This process continues and eventually the wire goes right through the block. But the block remains in one piece. This is called **regelation**.

Take two ice-cubes and press them together hard. They stick together. First, the surfaces melt under the pressure. When you release the pressure the water refreezes and the blocks freeze to each other. Squeezing snow makes a snowball in the same way.

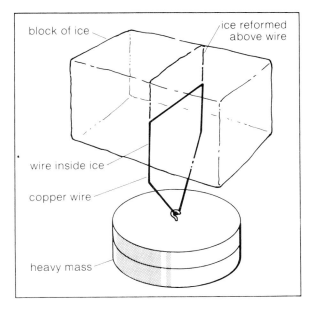

Fig. 46.3 Ice melts under pressure, but freezes again when the pressure is removed.

SUMMARY: ENERGY AND CHANGES OF STATE

- Energy is measured in joules: 1000 joules = 1 kilojoule (kJ).
- The specific heat capacity of a substance is the energy needed to raise 1 kg of the substance by 1 °C.
- Water has a very high specific heat capacity (4200 J/kg °C).
- Energy supplied (J) equals mass (kg) multiplied by specific heat capacity (J/kg °C) multiplied by temperature rise (°C).
- Solutions have freezing points lower and boiling points higher than those of water.
- Latent heat is the hidden energy that has melted a solid to a liquid or vaporised a liquid to a gas.
- The specific latent heat of vaporisation of a liquid is the amount of energy needed to vaporise 1 kg of the liquid.
- Specific latent heats are measured in J/kg or kJ/kg.
- The specific latent heat of fusion of a solid is the amount of energy needed to melt 1 kg of the solid.
- The horizontal part of the cooling curve of a liquid marks the freezing point of the liquid. This is the same temperature as the melting point of its solid.
- Evaporation of a liquid causes cooling.
- The gas in a compression refrigerator is compressed, cooled and condensed, then evaporated, taking energy from the icebox.
- A refrigerator needs regular defrosting.
- Kinetic theory explains gas pressure, diffusion, evaporation, melting and boiling in terms of the motion of particles.
- The particles of a solid can only vibrate about a fixed position.
- The particles of a liquid can move within the liquid.
- The particles of a gas can move freely and rapidly.
- Increasing the pressure raises boiling points and lowers melting points.

SECTION 11

Waves

47 What are waves?

Everybody knows that we use light waves to
see, sound waves to hear, radio waves to send
messages through space and so on. But what is
a wave? To find out, you can look at some
waves you can really see. Ripples, small waves
on the surface of some water, are best. They
are easy to make, easy to see and easy to
control.

WAVES TRAVELLING

Touch the surface of still water with your
finger. You will see circles spreading out from
the spot you touched (Fig. 47.1). These are
ripples, tiny waves on the surface. As these
circular waves move outwards, the water
surface moves up, down, up, down, forming a
smooth curve. Each part of the water surface
hands the motion of the wave on to the next.
This handing-on is called **wave propagation**.

If you keep on moving your finger up and
down, you send out one circular wave after
another. Your finger provides the energy to
disturb the water surface. It is the **wave source**.
The waves that travel away from the source
carrying energy are called **progressive waves**.
The water surface is the **medium** in which they
travel.

A small out-of-balance electric motor
screwed to a long bar can make a single dipper
send out a continuous progressive wave in a
ripple tank. The long bar bounces up and
down on the two rubber bands shown in
Fig. 47.2. The dipper is a **point source** of waves.

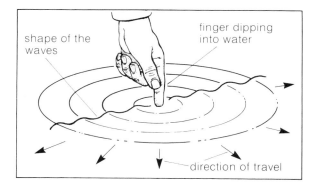

Fig. 47.1 Circular ripples (waves) on water.

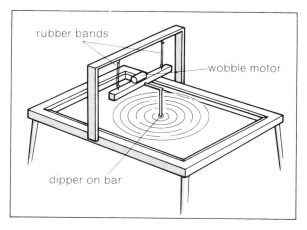

Fig. 47.2 A ripple tank with a wobbling dipper giving
circular waves.

If you take the dipper off the bar and let the bar just touch the water surface all along its length, you will see **plane** (straight) waves travel across the water (Fig. 47.3).

WAVES CARRY ENERGY

You have seen that something is needed to drive the wave motion. If your finger or the vibrating bar stops moving, the wave dies out. The **oscillator** (p. 54) gives energy to the wave.

UP-AND-DOWN AND SIDE-TO-SIDE WAVES

Each water drop in the water surface moves up and down as the wave passes. Energy is handed on from drop to drop. It is easier to watch what is happening if you use a long spring—a slinky-toy perhaps. Hold one end of the spring firmly on a smooth floor and ask your friend to stretch the spring out a bit across the floor. If you then waggle one end from side to side (Fig. 47.4) you will see a progressive wave travelling along.

Each of the coils of the spring moves in the same way as the one you are driving. So the particles of the medium (here the coils in the spring) move from side to side while the wave travels along. Waves in which the particles move across the direction in which the wave is travelling are called **transverse waves**.

Watch a small piece of cork floating on the water in a ripple tank. Send plane waves across the tank. The cork will move up and down; that is, across the direction in which the waves move. We see that water waves are transverse waves.

IN-LINE WAVES

There is another way to send waves along a spring. Pull and push one end of the slinky-toy and continue doing this. A wave is sent along the spring. It is a s-t-r-e-t-c-h—squash wave. The parts move backwards and forwards, in line with the direction the wave is moving. These are **longitudinal waves** (Fig. 47.5).

THE MEDIUM DOES NOT MOVE ALONG WITH THE WAVE

When you did the experiments with the slinky-toy, the wave moved a long way but the coils of the spring did not. Nor did the

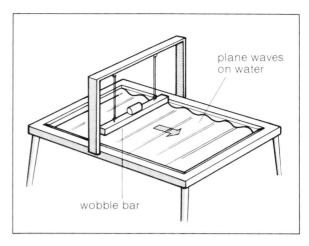

Fig. 47.3 A ripple tank with a wobbling bar giving plane waves.

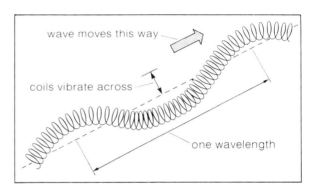

Fig. 47.4 A side-to-side (transverse) wave travelling along a slinky spring.

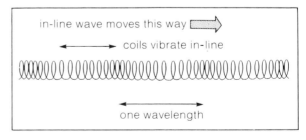

Fig. 47.5 A to-and-fro (longitudinal) wave travelling along a slinky spring.

molecules of water move very much as the wave passed. They simply vibrated about an average position in the middle. They passed their motion and energy on to their next neighbour; the wave moved on but the molecules stayed where they were.

48 Measuring waves

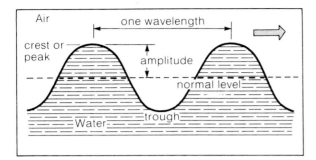

Fig. 48.1 Wave measurements.

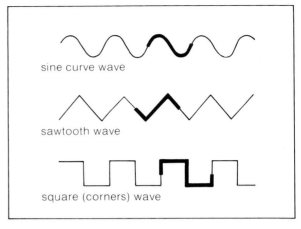

Fig. 48.2 Three wave-forms. Notice how each wave-form repeats exactly, wavelength after wavelength.

You can make many sizes and shapes of wave with a slinky-toy. You can move your hand from side to side by different amounts. You can move your hand slowly or quickly. You can move it smoothly or in jerks. So we must have some way of describing what a wave really looks like.

The top of a wave is called the **crest** or **peak** (Fig. 48.1); the bottom is the **trough**. The height of the crest above or the depth of the trough below the middle position is the **amplitude** of the wave.

A boat, riding on the waves offshore, goes up and down from trough to crest and back again; this is twice the amplitude of the waves. The number of crests that pass a fixed point in 1 s is the **frequency** of the wave. It is also the frequency of the oscillator that produces the wave. Frequency is measured in **hertz (Hz)**; 1 Hz is one complete vibration per second.

The distance from one crest to the next one is called the **wavelength**. It is usually measured in metres. The **wave-form** is the shape of one wavelength (Fig. 48.2). It is a snap-shot of the wave shape.

The **speed** of the wave is the speed of any one of the crests in the direction of travel. It is also called the **wave velocity** and it is measured in metres per second.

The speed of a wave, its wavelength and its frequency are related to one another:

wave speed = frequency × wavelength
(c) (f) (l)

In Fig. 48.3 the sea-gull counts nine crests go past in a second. So the frequency of these waves is 9 Hz. The sea-gull noticed that the ninth crest travelled just the length of the moored boat, 18 m, in a second. You can see the nine wavelengths equal 18 m, so one wavelength is 2 m. You can check this using the formula:

velocity = frequency × wavelength
18 m/s =   9 Hz   ×   2 m

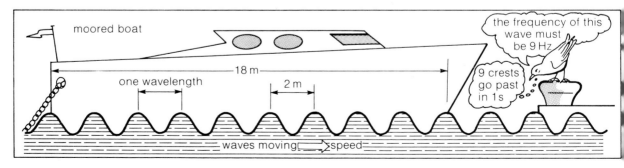

Fig. 48.3 The sea-gull learns that: wave speed = frequency × wavelength.

49 Waves bounce

If you throw a ball at an angle to the floor, it will bounce away at an angle similar to that at which it hit the floor. If you send a karate chop **pulse** along a length of rubber tubing stretched tightly between two walls (Fig. 49.1), it will bounce back from the further wall. It is **reflected**.

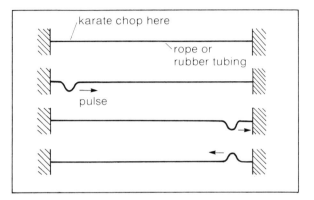

Fig. 49.1 A karate chop pulse reflected at the far end of a rope. On which side is the pulse reflected?

REFLECTION OF PLANE WAVES

Solid barriers in a ripple tank reflect the ripples. In Fig. 49.2 plane waves are shown by lines drawn along each wave crest. These lines, like the waves, are parallel to the vibrating rod or source. The straight barrier reflects these plane waves as plane waves, but in a new direction. As with rays of light falling on a plane mirror (Fig. 58.4 on p. 106), the angle of reflection equals the angle of incidence.

REFLECTION OF CIRCULAR WAVES

Figure 49.3 shows circular waves from a vibrating point source striking a straight barrier. The waves are reflected as circular waves but are turned inside out. They seem to spread out from a point behind the barrier. This point is the **mirror image** of the point source. The pattern is **symmetrical**, the same on both sides. So the image is just as far behind the barrier as the source is in front.

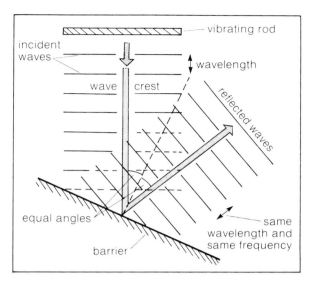

Fig. 49.2 Reflection of plane waves at a barrier in a ripple tank.

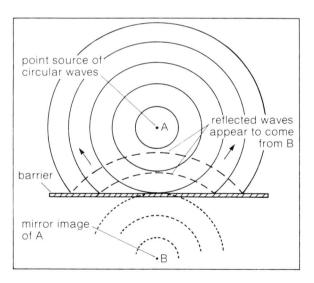

Fig. 49.3 Reflection of circular waves at a barrier in a ripple tank.

50 Waves that bend and overlap

WAVES THAT BEND

Waves travel at different speeds in different materials. You can make the waves in the ripple tank travel slower by making the water shallower (Fig. 50.1). You do this by placing an extra piece of glass on the bottom of part of the tank. The vibrations of the bar are still at the same rate so the frequency does not change. As the wave is travelling slower over the shallower water it will not get so far in the time of one vibration as it does over deeper water. It must have a shorter wavelength. The top view of Fig. 50.1 shows the faster waves striking the boundary dead square on. They keep going in the same straight line, only more slowly and closer together.

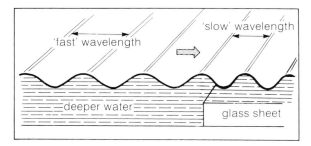

Fig. 50.1 The ripples travel slower over shallow water. What happens to their wavelength?

If they strike at some other angle, their direction changes as they cross the boundary (Fig. 50.2). This change of direction is called **refraction**. The wave crests are dragged round because they do not travel so fast when over the boundary. What will happen to the waves if they move on over deeper water?

WAVES THAT OVERLAP

If two similar waves come together, they add together. If they are exactly in step, or exactly one or two wavelengths out of step—you cannot tell the difference!—they give a wave of double amplitude (Fig. 50.3). If they are half a wavelength, or one-and-a-half wavelengths, out of step, the troughs and crests cancel out; that is, they add to give no wave. This is called **interference**, and what you see is an **interference pattern** (Fig. 50.4).

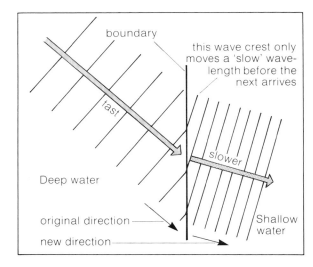

Fig. 50.2 Ripples dragging round as they cross the boundary from deep to shallow water.

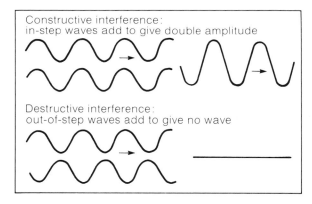

Fig. 50.3 Two similar waves going in the same direction at the same place interfere.

Fig. 50.4 Two dippers vibrating together produced this interference pattern on the water surface.

51 Waves spread round corners

BARRIERS WITH DIFFERENT GAPS

Try sending plane waves in a ripple tank so that they go through a hole in a barrier. Figure 51.1 shows what happens with a hole several wavelengths wide. The plane waves go through. When the hole is reduced to three wavelengths wide (Fig. 51.2) the waves spread round the corners to about 45°. The smallest hole is one wavelength wide. Now circular waves spread out over the whole area (Fig. 51.3). This is called **diffraction**.

Fig. 51.1 Plane waves moving up the page and passing through a hole several wavelengths wide.

Fig. 51.2 Plane waves spreading out from a hole about three wavelengths wide.

Fig. 51.3 Plane waves spreading into circular waves after passing a hole just one wavelength wide.

OBSTACLES OF DIFFERENT SIZES

Figure 51.4 shows plane waves in a ripple tank arriving at a large obstacle, several wavelengths wide. There is a wave shadow behind it. When the obstacle is three wavelengths wide, spreading of the waves round the edges can be seen (Fig. 51.5). With a small obstacle only one or two wavelengths

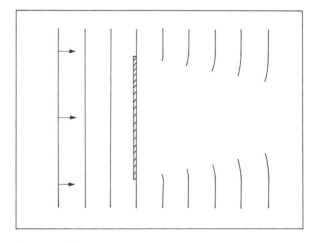

Fig. 51.4 Plane waves spreading a little into the shadow behind a large obstacle.

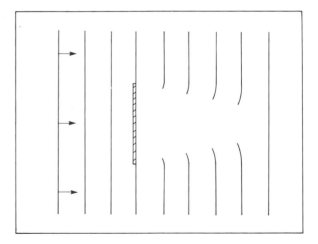

Fig. 51.5 Behind a smaller obstacle, about three wavelengths wide, the waves spread further into the shadow.

wide, the waves soon join up behind it
(Fig. 51.6). It has no wave shadow at a distance
from it.

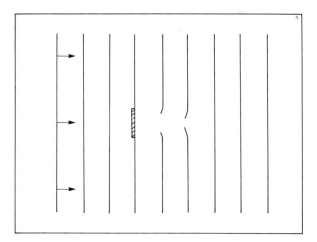

Fig. 51.6 Behind an obstacle about one wavelength wide,
the waves soon join up again, leaving no shadow.

WHY DO PEOPLE SAY LIGHT IS A WAVE?

You have seen that ripples on water can be
reflected or bounced, refracted or bent,
diffracted or bent round an obstacle. They also
travel with a fixed speed in any one medium.

Light too can be reflected (p. 105) and
refracted (p. 109). It has a fixed speed in any
one medium. If you knew it could be diffracted
or bent round an obstacle to produce patterns
like those in the ripple tank, you would believe
that light behaves as waves do.

Figure 51.7 shows how light has spread
round the edges of a razor blade to produce an

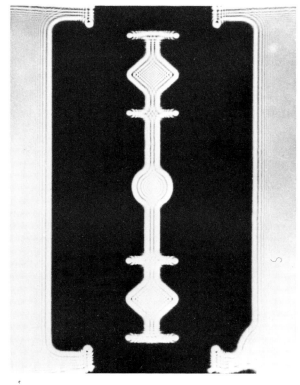

Fig. 51.7 The diffraction of light around a razor blade.

unexpected pattern. You can see a similar
pattern for yourself if you look at a distant
bright street lamp with your eyes half-closed
or through a pocket handkerchief.

These are the reasons why you can say that
light behaves as a wave. Light is one of a
whole range of **electromagnetic waves** which
have different frequencies and wavelengths
but the same speed.

52 Electromagnetic waves

The wavelengths of electromagnetic waves range from very, very short in gamma- and X-rays to very long indeed in long radio waves (Table 52). Their frequencies go from very, very high in gamma- and X-rays to quite low in long radio waves. Electromagnetic waves all travel at the same speed in empty space (a vacuum). This is the speed of light, 300 000 km/s. They are transverse waves (p. 89), but are much more complicated than waves on water.

In electromagnetic waves, electric and magnetic fields vibrate at right angles to the direction of travel.

You need a special **detector** for each wave: your eyes for visible light, a radio set and aerial for radio waves, a photo-film for X-rays as well as light, a Geiger—Müller tube for gamma-rays (p. 199) and so on.

Remember, sound is *not* one of these waves. It is a longitudinal wave that travels in air at about 330 m/s.

Table 52 Properties of electromagnetic waves

Radiation	Wavelength (m)	Sources	Detectors	Uses
Gamma-rays	10^{-12}	Cosmic rays, radioactive substances	Geiger counters, bubble/cloud chambers	Checking welds, killing cancer cells
X-rays	10^{-10}	X-ray tubes	Photographic film, fluorescent screens	Medical/dental inspections, analysis of crystal structure
Ultraviolet	10^{-8}	Mercury vapour lamps, the sun	Fluorescent screens/dyes	Forgery detection, sun lamps
Light	10^{-6}	Hot bodies, lasers, fluorescent screens	Photographic film, photodiodes	Chemical spectral analysis, fibre optics
Infra-red	10^{-4}	Warm bodies, the sun	Blackened thermometers, thermocouples	TV remote control, light vision sights, radiant heaters
Radio	$10^{-2} - 10^{4}$	TV and radio transmitters	Aerials	Radio telescope, radar, communications links

---

SUMMARY: WAVES

- Waves are repeated vibrations carrying energy.
- Each part of the wave passes its energy on to the next.
- In transverse waves the vibrations move across the direction in which the wave is going.
- In longitudinal waves the vibrations move in the direction the wave is going.
- Matter does not move along with the wave.
- Amplitude is the maximum movement, from the central position to a crest or a trough.
- Wavelength is the distance from a crest to the next crest.
- Frequency is equal to the number of crests that pass a fixed point in 1 s.
- Speed is equal to frequency multiplied by wavelength.

- A plane wave reflects from a straight barrier as a plane wave. Its angle of reflection equals its angle of incidence.
- Refraction is the bending of the direction of a wave's travel due to a change of speed.
- Constructive interference of two waves in step gives a wave of double amplitude.
- Destructive interference of two waves out of step gives no wave.
- Diffraction is the spreading of waves round corners.
- Gamma-rays, X-rays, ultraviolet radiation, visible light, infra-red radiation and radio waves are all electromagnetic waves. These are in order of decreasing frequency and increasing wavelength.
- All electromagnetic waves travel in a vacuum at the speed of light: 300 000 km/s (3×10^8 m/s).

Light Goes Fast and Straight

53 Light travels fast carrying energy

THE SPEED OF LIGHT

Light is our name for the electromagnetic waves we can see. The colours red, orange, yellow, green, blue and violet have different frequencies and different wavelengths. In a vacuum, e.g., out in space, they all travel at the same high speed—the speed of light. This is the fastest anything can travel: 300 000 000 m/s (three hundred million metres per second or 3×10^8 m/s).

At this speed, a flash of light or a radio wave—a type of electromagnetic wave—could go eight times round the world in 1 s (Fig. 53.1). It takes light 500 s, that is just over eight minutes, to reach us from the sun.

MEASURING SPACE IN LIGHT-YEARS

Space is so vast that to measure it astronomers need large units such as the **light-year** (Fig. 53.2). This is the distance a ray of light travels if it keeps going for one year: 9 500 000 000 000 000 m (nine-and-a-half million million kilometres or 9.5×10^{12} km). The nearest star to the earth, apart from the sun, is *Proxima Centauri*, which is at a distance of 4.25 light-years. Its light takes 4.25 years to get here.

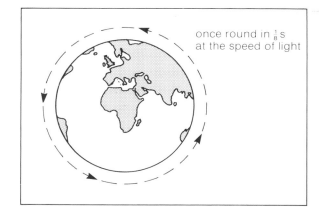

Fig. 53.1 A flash of light can travel a distance equal to going round the earth eight times in 1 s.

Fig. 53.2 This galaxy is so far away that the light takes 10 million years to reach us.

Fig. 53.3 TV cameras in use.

LIGHT WAVES CARRY ENERGY

All sources of light give out light energy. Your eyes convert this into electrical energy to pass to your brain (p. 117). A television camera does a similar job (Fig. 53.3). It has a small light-sensitive plate, equivalent to the retina of the eye. The lens focuses the scene on to this plate. The energy in the light arriving at a spot on the plate is converted to a tiny electrical charge at that spot. The cable carries these electrical charges as a current to the transmitter.

In **photography** light energy changes and blackens chemicals containing silver in the film. Thus a photographic negative has dark patches where the light parts of the scene were.

FOOD AND FUEL NEED LIGHT AND ENERGY

Photosynthesis is the process by which green plants use the energy of sunlight to build carbohydrate molecules like starch and sugars from carbon dioxide and water. All food for animals and humans starts in this way (Fig. 53.4). Without light energy there would be no food. Everyone in the world would starve! Nearly all our body fuel and all the wood, coal, oil and gas we use start from photosynthesis.

Fig. 53.4 The farmer with his horses is cutting grain. This grain can be used to make bread or even feed the horses.

54 Sources of light

Out of doors, during the day, all the light comes from the sun. The sun is a very hot glowing ball; it gives out light all the time. It is **luminous**. Things that emit or give out light are called **light sources**. Candle flames are luminous. Specks of carbon from the wax are heated white-hot and emit light.

Ordinary light bulbs used in your home have **filaments**, which are thin coiled-up wires (Fig. 54.1). These filaments get white-hot when the electric current passes through them. Then they emit light. The filament is made of the metal tungsten. Tungsten has a very high melting point, 3380 °C. If the glass bulb was full of air (containing oxygen) the tungsten would **oxidise** or burn as soon as it became hot. That's why the bulb contains some gas that doesn't let the tungsten burn.

Fluorescent tubes have mercury vapour (gas) inside them. When an electric current flows through the vapour the mercury atoms give out ultraviolet radiation. But your eyes cannot see with ultraviolet, so there is a thin layer of powder on the inside of the glass tube. This powder glows brightly in the ultraviolet light with white light that you can see. This is called **fluorescence**. Fluorescent tubes give four times as much light as filament lamps for the same amount of electrical energy. They are more efficient; they save energy (p. 52).

Other gases emit different colours when an electric current passes through them. Sodium vapour gives yellow light. Mercury vapour gives blue-green. Both are used in street lamps. Neon gives red light. Small neon lamps are often fitted to electric irons, cooker panels and switches to show whether they are on or off. Larger and longer neon lamps are used in advertising signs (Fig. 54.2).

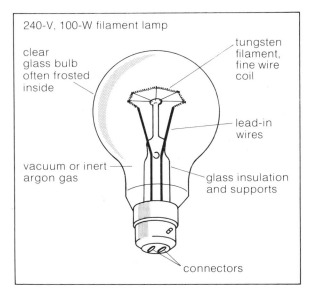

240-V, 100-W filament lamp
clear glass bulb often frosted inside
tungsten filament, fine wire coil
lead-in wires
vacuum or inert argon gas
glass insulation and supports
connectors

Fig. 54.1 What is inside an electric light bulb?

Fig. 54.2 Light for fun.

55 Seeing

You see things when light comes from them to your eyes (p. 117). Look at a lighted lamp. You see this luminous object with light that comes straight from the lamp to you (Fig. 55.1). A very bright lamp could hurt your eyes; you would need some protection to **absorb** or take in some of the light. The sun is so bright that you should never look at it.

SEEING NON-LUMINOUS OBJECTS

Most of the things you see everyday are **non-luminous**. They don't give out light in the way that a lamp does. They are themselves lit by light from the sun or a lamp. They absorb or take in some of that light, but some bounces off in all directions. This is called **diffuse reflection**. When some of the diffusely reflected or **scattered** light enters your eye, you see the non-luminous object from which it was reflected (Fig. 55.2).

Pale colours reflect most of the light that strikes them. Darker colours reflect less light; they absorb more light. A black surface reflects very little and absorbs nearly all the light that falls on it. The light that is absorbed gives energy to the surface and it warms up slightly. Green plants are able to use this energy to build up foodstuffs in the process of photosynthesis (p. 97).

The earth's moon, the other planets and their moons (satellites) are all non-luminous (Fig. 55.3). We see them by the sunlight they reflect back to us.

Like the sun, stars are luminous. They are suns of all sizes, some far larger than our own sun. They seem so small because they are a very long way away.

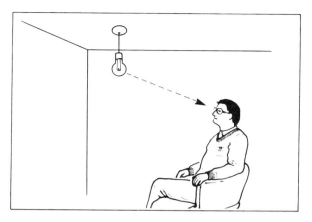

Fig. 55.1 A light bulb seen directly.

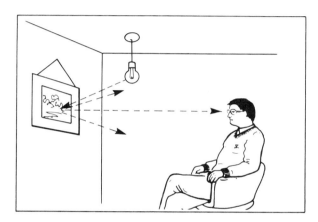

Fig. 55.2 This picture is seen because light is scattered from it to your eye.

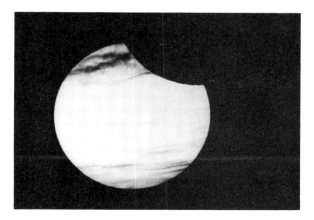

Fig. 55.3 The moon, which is non-luminous, is about to eclipse the luminous sun.

56 Light travels in straight lines

Look at the photograph on p. 96. You can see straight beams of light. You can see the beams because dust particles in the air scatter some of the light into the camera.

In Fig. 56.1 you cannot see light from the lamp. To see the lamp you must move board C so that the three holes are in a straight line. Look along the straight edge to check it. You would do the same when planting a row of trees. If the trees look to be in a straight line, they are! But, remember, on a very small scale, light does bend a very small amount (p. 109).

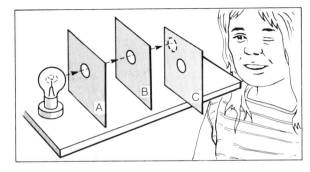

Fig. 56.1 When can you see the lamp through the three holes?

LIGHT RAYS AND LIGHT BEAMS

A **ray of light** is the thinnest line of light you can get. It is drawn as a straight line with one arrowhead on it (Fig. 56.2).

Three groups of rays travelling together are shown in Fig. 56.3. Parallel rays are like the lines on writing paper; always keeping the same distance apart. Converging rays come together eventually.

A **beam of light** is a broad bundle of many rays going in the same or nearly the same direction. To draw a beam of light you need only draw the two outermost rays.

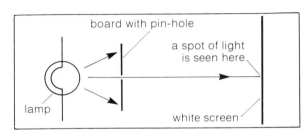

Fig. 56.2 How to get a single ray of light.

LIGHT RAYS HELP TO MAKE ACCURATE MAPS

To make a map, surveyors measure the angles between lines to many distant points. They use a **theodolite** for this. This is a small telescope arranged so that the direction in which it is pointing can be read on a circular scale in degrees. Theodolites are fixed to concrete pillars you see on many high hills (Fig. 56.4). The surveyor relies on the fact that rays of light are straight.

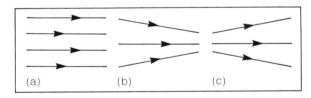

Fig. 56.3 Three ways in which rays are grouped in light beams. (a) Parallel. (b) Converging. (c) Diverging.

SHADOWS

Any opaque object in a beam of light has a **shadow** or dark area behind it. An **opaque** object is one through which light cannot pass. A **translucent** object is one that allows light to pass through it but the light is spread out so you cannot see things clearly through it. Tracing paper and frosted glass are translucent. Window glass is **transparent**; you can see distant things clearly through it.

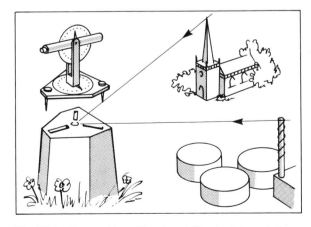

Fig. 56.4 Map-making with a theodolite at a 'trig. point'.

SHARP-EDGED SHADOWS

An opaque object in light from a point source throws a shadow with sharp edges. A **point source** of light is a tiny speck giving out light in all directions. A very small, hot filament lamp acts as a point source. A large lamp can be used instead if you put a screen with a small hole in front of it. The hole becomes the point source. Figure 56.5 shows how sharp-edged shadows are constructed using the fact that light travels in straight lines.

Point sources are used in shadow theatres. A translucent screen can be used so the shadows of puppets, hands or actors can be seen from the other side.

FUZZY-EDGED SHADOWS

Look round a room with light coming in through large windows. There are shadows behind opaque objects in this room, but they have fuzzy edges, not sharp. Large light sources such as windows, fluorescent tubes and globe lampshades are **extended sources** and they give fuzzy-edged shadows. Figure 56.6 shows how these fuzzy-edged shadows are made of a dark area around which is an area that is less dark.

The area of full shadow where no light arrives is called the **umbra**. The **penumbra**—part-shadow—is the fuzzy-edged area. Every point in the penumbra gets light from some part of the extended source but not from all of it. Light from the whole source can reach the bright area outside the shadow.

SHADOWS IN THE OPEN

You can see both types of shadows out of doors. The sun is so far from us, that it acts like a point source and gives sharp-edged shadows.

If there are clouds, these scatter the sunlight on its way down to the ground. The clouds become extended sources of light. So when it is cloudy we see fuzzy-edged shadows.

SHADOWS IN ASTRONOMY
Day and night

In the daytime, our source of light is the sun. During the **day** we are on the bright side of the earth. During the **night** we are on the shadow half of the earth (Fig. 56.7).

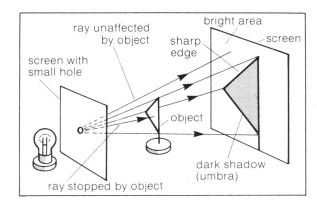

Fig. 56.5   A sharp shadow from a point source.

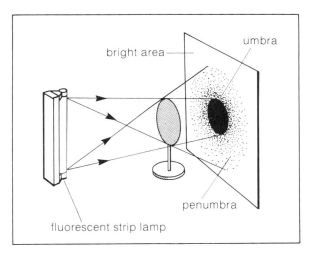

Fig. 56.6   A fuzzy shadow from an extended source—here a strip light.

Fig. 56.7   The earth seen from the moon. Day is the bright side.

The phases of the moon

The moon is non-luminous, it only reflects sunlight. The half of the moon facing the sun is bright. The other half is in shadow so it is dark. The dark half can't reflect light so your eyes cannot see it.

The moon goes round the earth once a month, a 'moon-th'. We get different views of the moon during the month. These different views are called the **phases of the moon**.

At full moon you see all the bright half of the moon. It is high in the sky at midnight. The sun is on the other side of the earth and directly opposite to the moon. A week later, you have a sideways view of the bright half and the dark half (Fig. 56.8), this is the **last quarter**. A week is a quarter of a month. After another week, **new moon** is at noon, midday. You see, or rather don't see, all the dark half. As the moon swings round the earth during the next week, the bit you see grows from a slim **crescent**, visible in daytime, to **first quarter**. Then in another week, you see full moon again.

Eclipse of the sun

To **eclipse** means to cut off light.

Every so often, the moon is exactly in line between the sun and the earth (see Fig. 55.3 on p. 99). The result is a **partial eclipse** of the sun. Partial means part-covered. A **total eclipse** happens if the moon blocks all of the sun's light, as seen from the earth.

You see a total eclipse if you are in the umbra of the moon's shadow (Fig. 56.9). If you are in the penumbra you see a partial eclipse. REMEMBER, NEVER LOOK DIRECTLY AT THE SUN.

Eclipse of the moon

A total eclipse of the moon occurs when it is in the earth's shadow. A partial eclipse occurs if the full moon is partly in the earth's shadow (Fig. 56.10).

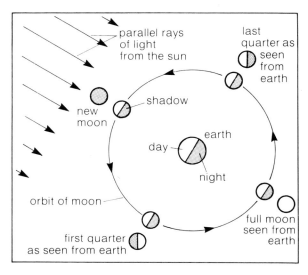

Fig. 56.8 As the moon goes round the earth, we see it as shown in the outer set of diagrams. (The drawing is *not* to scale.)

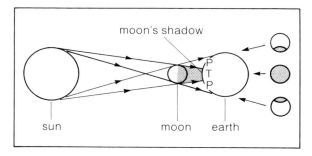

Fig. 56.9 An eclipse of the sun by the moon. At P you see a partial eclipse. At T you see a total one. (The drawing is not to scale.)

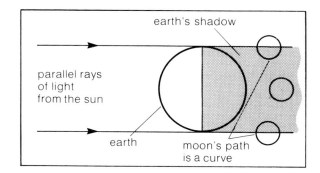

Fig. 56.10 The moon passing through the earth's shadow. (The drawing is not to scale.)

57 The pin-hole camera

LIGHT GOING STRAIGHT THROUGH A PIN-HOLE

A pin-hole camera (Fig. 57.1) works because light travels in straight lines. Rays from every point on a bright object go straight through the pin-hole to the screen. The screen is translucent so you can see what happens. The rays build up an **image** or picture on the screen. As the rays cross over at the pin-hole, the image is **inverted** or upside-down. The image is also reversed left-to-right.

BRIGHT OBJECTS AND REAL IMAGES

Light really does get to the image you see on the screen of your pin-hole camera. That's why we call it a **real image**. Real images can be caught on a screen. The light comes from a scene or **object**. This needs to be quite bright because only a little light can get through the small pin-hole. The image is quite faint.

IMAGES IN A PIN-HOLE CAMERA CAN CHANGE SIZE

The distance between the object and the pin-hole is called the **object distance**. As the object is moved nearer to the pin-hole, the image becomes larger and also fuzzier. If the camera is long enough you can arrange it so that the image is larger than the object. This image is **magnified**. When the object distance is large and the camera is short, the image is quite small, smaller than the object. It is a **diminished** image (Fig. 57.2).

Using lots of pin-holes

Make several pin-holes in your camera. You will find that each pin-hole produces its own image.

Using a pencil hole instead

Use a sharp pencil to make the pin-hole. You won't have a sharp image at all but a bright spot of light! To make this arrangement work you must use a lens (p. 112).

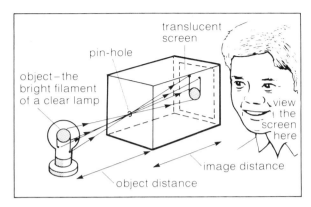

Fig. 57.1   A pin-hole camera gives an inverted, real image.

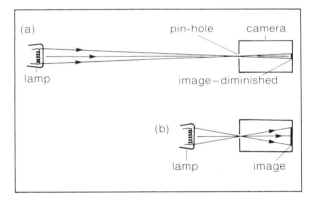

Fig. 57.2   A pin-hole camera can be used at almost all object distances. The nearer the object, the bigger the image.

PHOTOGRAPHY WITH A PIN-HOLE CAMERA

You can make a pin-hole camera (one hole only) light-tight—that is, light can only enter through the pin-hole. If a piece of photographic film is placed over the back of the box—this must be done in the dark—you can take a picture. You will have to uncover the pin-hole for several minutes and keep the whole thing perfectly still during that time. A pin-hole camera is not a very good camera to take away on holiday!

SUMMARY: LIGHT GOES FAST AND STRAIGHT

- Light waves carry energy.
- Light travels at a speed of 300 000 000 m/s (3×10^8 m/s) in a vacuum.
- Hot filaments, flames and the sun are typical sources of light.
- Sources of light are luminous, you see some of the light they emit.
- Non-luminous objects reflect or scatter some of the light that strikes them. You see a thing because light comes from it into your eye.
- Light travels in straight lines.
- An opaque object passes no light; a translucent one passes some light but not clearly; a transparent one passes light so you can see clearly through it.
- Point sources of light cast sharp shadows of opaque objects.
- Large, extended, light sources give fuzzy-edged shadows.
- No light reaches the umbra, the total shadow.
- Light from part of the source reaches the penumbra, the partial shadow.
- During an eclipse of the sun, the moon is in line between the sun and the earth.
- For safety, *never* look at the sun.
- During an eclipse of the moon, the earth is in line between the sun and the moon.
- A real image can be seen on a screen.
- When the object is moved nearer to the pin-hole of a pin-hole camera the image becomes larger.
- A small pin-hole gives a faint but sharp image; a larger pin-hole gives a brighter but fuzzier image; a large hole does not give an image.

SECTION 13

Light Bounces and Bends

58 Reflection in plane mirrors

Plane mirrors are flat mirrors. Look in a plane mirror and you will see an image of yourself. The mirror's job is to reflect rays of light. The rays of light bounce off the flat, shiny mirror surface. This bouncing off is called **reflection**.

THE IMAGE IN A PLANE MIRROR

Light from a lamp is reflected by a mirror into your eye (Fig. 58.1). You look along these rays of light and you see the image apparently behind the mirror. But no light gets behind the mirror. Because the light only appears to come from the image, it is called a **virtual image**.

WHERE IS THE IMAGE? HOW BIG IS IT?

The image of your face in a plane mirror is the same size as your face! It is the same distance behind the mirror as you are in front. The line joining you—the object—and the image is perpendicular (at right angles) to the mirror. Look at Fig. 58.2. The clear glass sheet stands on centimetre graph paper. It acts as a mirror. Count the squares between the object and the mirror; then count the squares between the image and the mirror. You find they are the same. When you look at yourself in a mirror, how far away from you is your image?

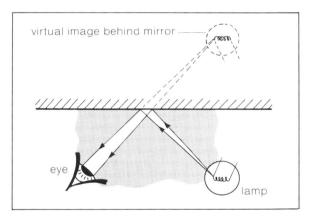

Fig. 58.1 Some light from the lamp is reflected by the plane mirror and enters your eye.

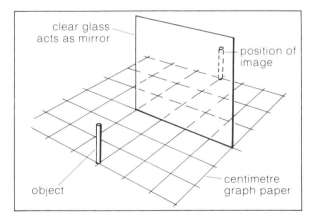

Fig. 58.2 Where is the image in a plane mirror?

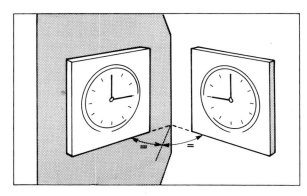

Fig. 58.3 Is it time for the 9 o'clock news or nearly tea-time?

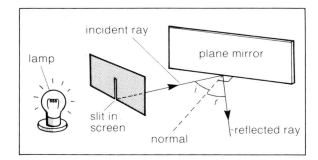

Fig. 58.4 How a ray is reflected from a plane mirror.

LATERAL INVERSION

In a mirror do you see yourself exactly as you are? Not quite! Close your right eye, your image closes its left eye. The image of your face is the correct way up, but its left and its right are swapped over. This effect is called **lateral inversion**, which means a side-to-side swap-over (Fig. 58.3).

LAWS OF REFLECTION

Look at Fig. 58.4. You see a single ray of light from the lamp falling on the plane mirror. This is called an **incident ray**. Between this and the reflected ray a line has been drawn which is at right angles to the mirror. This is called a **normal**. Measure the angle between the incident ray and the normal (**the angle of incidence**) and the angle between the normal and the reflected ray (**the angle of reflection**). You will always find them to be the same.

The **first law of reflection** states that: The incident ray, the reflected ray and the normal are all in the same plane—they can be drawn accurately on the same flat piece of paper.

The **second law of reflection** says that: The angle of incidence (i) equals the angle of reflection (r);

$$\angle i = \angle r$$

SOME USES OF REFLECTION

Periscope Two mirrors fixed as in Fig. 58.5 form a periscope, which lets you look over a crowd.

Multiple images Two parallel mirrors give many images of one object (Fig. 58.6).

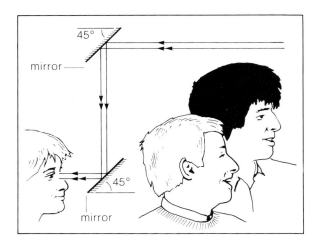

Fig. 58.5 How to see over other people's heads using two parallel mirrors.

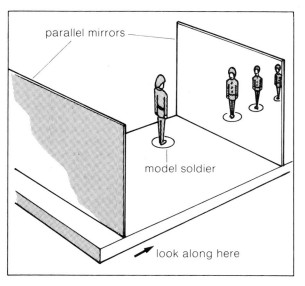

Fig. 58.6 One soldier or an army? (The image distances are not to scale.)

106

59 Reflection in curved mirrors

PARALLEL RAYS

When using such optical instruments as cameras, telescopes and microscopes people mention **parallel light** or **parallel rays**. Look at Fig. 59.1. Two rays from a point are falling on the eye to the right of the diagram. In (a) the point O is nearby. The two rays are certainly not parallel. In (b) O is further away. In (c) O is much further away—somewhere off the page to the left. In (d) it is so far away that the two rays are very nearly parallel to one another. So we say that rays of light from distant objects are parallel.

CONCAVE (CONVERGING) MIRRORS

Concave mirrors have the same shape as the inside of a sphere or a cylinder. Some people say they 'cave in'. They are also called **converging mirrors** because they can bring parallel rays of light together. If you arrange for parallel rays of light to strike a concave mirror, the light will be reflected and will converge to meet at the **principal focus (F)** (Fig. 59.2). The distance from the principal focus to the mirror is its **focal length** (*f*).

The **centre of curvature (C)** is where you would put your compass point to draw the curved mirror. The **radius of curvature** (*r*) is the radius you need to draw it. The focal length is half the radius.

REAL IMAGES FROM CONCAVE MIRRORS

A concave mirror can give a real image of a bright object, such as a distant window (Fig. 59.3). The screen on which the image appears is put near to the focus of the mirror. You can see that the image is smaller, inverted (upside-down and left-to-right) and in colour. It is a real image because it can be seen on a screen.

MEASURING THE FOCAL LENGTH OF A CONCAVE MIRROR

Fix a half-circle of tracing paper in a white card screen and light it from behind (Fig. 59.4). Move the concave mirror nearer or further

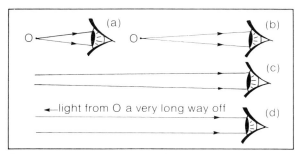

Fig. 59.1   What are parallel rays?

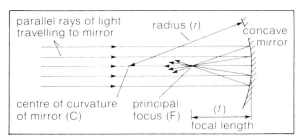

Fig. 59.2   This is what happens when parallel rays are reflected at a concave mirror.

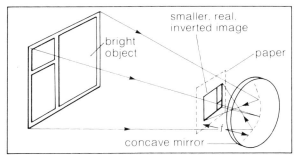

Fig. 59.3   An easy way to find the focal length of a concave mirror.

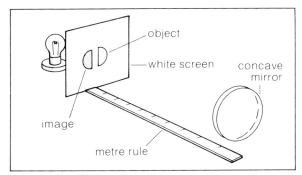

Fig. 59.4   A better way to measure the focal length of a concave mirror.

away to **focus** the sharpest image of the half-circle on to the white screen, right next to the half-circle itself. Both image and object are now at the centre of curvature of the mirror. They are the same size, the image is real and inverted. The distance from the mirror to the screen is its radius of curvature and the focal length is half of this.

USES OF CONCAVE MIRRORS

Reflecting telescope   Most large telescopes use concave mirrors, up to 2 m across (Fig. 59.5). They were invented by Isaac Newton. A small plane mirror turns the rays to one side, so that the real image can be viewed with a magnifying glass, the eyepiece.

Searchlights   The lamp is at the focus. Light reflected from the mirror comes out as a parallel beam (Fig. 59.6).

CONVEX (DIVERGING) MIRRORS

Convex mirrors have the same shape as the outside of a sphere or a cylinder. A shiny steel ball is a good example. They are also called **diverging mirrors** because they spread parallel light out or make it diverge. If you arrange for parallel rays of light to strike a convex mirror, the light will be reflected as if it were coming from a focus behind the mirror. This is a **virtual focus** (**F**) (Fig. 59.7). The light seems to diverge from this point. The distance from the virtual focus to the mirror is the **focal length** (*f*).

VIRTUAL IMAGES FROM CONVEX MIRRORS

A convex mirror always gives a virtual, upright, diminished or smaller image. This type of mirror is useful because it gives a wider field of view than that of a plane mirror and an upright image. Car driving mirrors and security mirrors in shops are convex mirrors (see the photograph on p. 105).

Fig. 59.5   The Isaac Newton telescope.

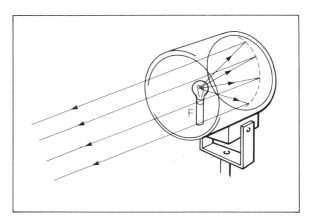

Fig. 59.6   Searchlights have a lamp at the focus of the mirror and the light comes out as a parallel beam. What other example of this arrangement can you think of?

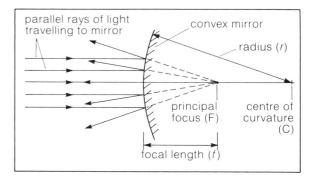

Fig. 59.7   This is what happens when parallel rays are reflected at a convex mirror.

60 Bending beams of light

Send a beam of light straight at a block of glass—along a normal. It goes straight on. But send it at an angle to the normal and it bends as it enters the glass. This is **refraction** (Fig. 60.1). If the light travels from, say, air into the glass, it bends towards the normal (the angle of refraction is smaller than the angle of incidence). But if it goes the other way, from glass into air, it bends away from the normal.

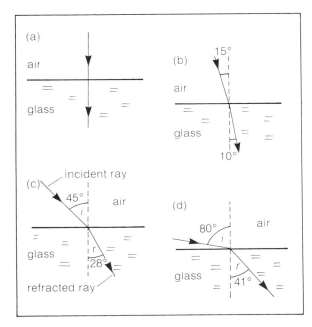

Fig. 60.1 Light bending at an air/glass surface. (a) A ray along a normal keeps straight on. (b)–(d) What happens to rays that make an angle with the normal?

You've seen this happen to ripples on water in a ripple tank (p. 92). So you know that the light must slow down when it goes from air into glass (Figs 60.2, 60.3 and 60.4).

THE LAWS OF REFRACTION

The ray that strikes the surface is the **incident ray**, angle *i*. The ray that leaves the surface is the **refracted ray** (Fig. 60.1(c)). The **angle of refraction** (*r*) is the angle between this ray and the normal.

The **first law of refraction** states that the incident ray, the refracted ray and the normal are all in the same plane.

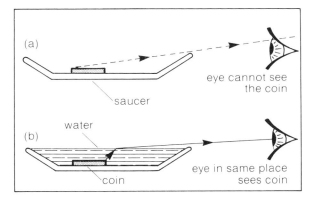

Fig. 60.2 Try this way to see round a corner. The penny appears when you pour water into the saucer because light from it bends away from the normal at the water/air surface.

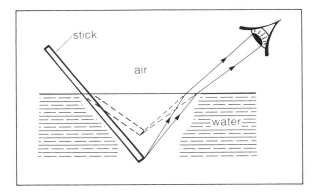

Fig. 60.3 Why does a stick seem to bend at an air/water surface? Use this diagram to find the answer.

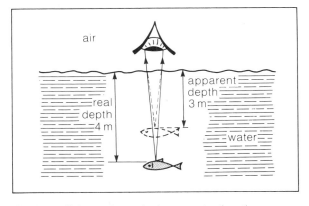

Fig. 60.4 Fish are always in deeper water than they seem to be. Divide the real depth by the apparent depth to find the refractive index of water.

The **second law of refraction** says that if you divide the sine of the angle of incidence by the sine of the angle of refraction, the number you get is always the same for the same two materials. It is called the **refractive index, n**.

$$\frac{\sin i}{\sin r} = n$$

The refractive index of ordinary glass is about 1.5 and for water about 1.3.

REFRACTION BY BLOCKS AND PRISMS

Figure 60.5 shows a beam of light striking a parallel-sided block of glass. The light **emerges**—leaves the block—parallel to its original direction. But it is **laterally displaced**, or shifted sideways. Some of the light doesn't even get into the glass; it is reflected. A little of the light is reflected at the second surface. What happens to it?

Figure 60.6 shows a beam of light striking a block of glass with a triangular shape (a prism). This time the beam is deviated or turned through an angle called the **angle of deviation (D)**.

INTERNAL REFLECTION

Look again at Fig. 60.5. Some of the light is reflected back into the glass at the far surface of the block. You can find out more about this light using a semi-circular glass block (Fig. 60.7). Ray 1 strikes the flat surface along the normal and goes straight on. Rays 2, 3 and 4 are refracted out into the air along 2′, 3′ and 4′ although a little is reflected; 4′ goes just along the surface of the glass block. Rays 5 and 6 do not leave the glass at all. Instead they are reflected **internally**, inside the glass, to 5′ and 6′. This is **total internal reflection**.

The **critical angle ($\angle C$)** is the angle of incidence inside the glass, or other medium such as Perspex or water, for which the angle of refraction in the air outside is 90°.

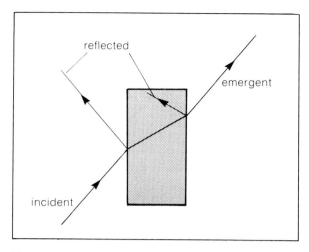

Fig. 60.5 Beams of light and a glass block. Which one is the incident beam?

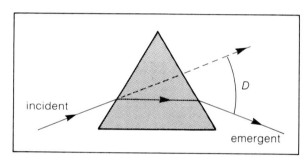

Fig. 60.6 A prism can turn a ray of light through an angle. *D* is the angle of deviation.

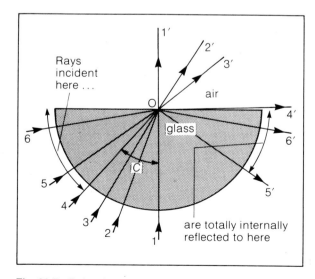

Fig. 60.7 Refracting and reflecting rays at a glass/air surface.

Total internal reflection can only occur if:

1 The light is travelling from glass, Perspex or water towards air.
2 The angle of incidence of the ray is greater than the critical angle for the material.

The critical angle and the refractive index are linked by the equation:

$$\text{sine of the critical angle} = \frac{1}{\text{refractive index}}$$

$$\sin C = \frac{1}{n}$$

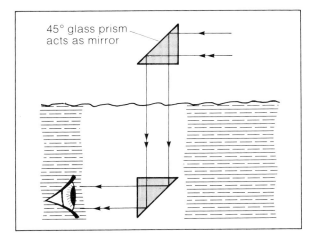

Fig. 60.8 How a pair of prisms can be used in a periscope.

HOW BIG IS THE CRITICAL ANGLE?

For glass and also Perspex it is 42°. A glass or Perspex prism with angles of 45°, 45° and 90° can act as a perfect mirror. Look at Fig. 60.8. The rays of light hit the inside surface at an angle just larger than the critical angle of 42°. They cannot get out into the air. They are reflected—totally. Prisms like this are used in periscopes, binoculars and vehicle reflectors (Fig. 60.9).

OPTICAL FIBRES

Light that enters the end of a solid glass rod hits the inside surface at angles that are always bigger than the critical angle. The light is trapped inside the rod. It is reflected from side to side until it gets to the far end where it can escape (Fig. 60.10). This happens whether the rod is straight, bent or even tied in a knot. Light captured like this can be piped over long distances. Flexible bundles of thin glass fibres can carry images or can transmit information rather like a telephone cable can carry information.

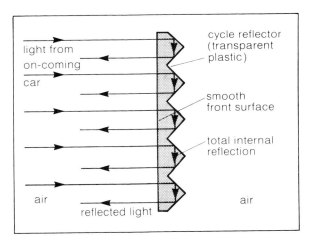

Fig. 60.9 A cycle reflector. Each little plastic prism reflects the light twice, sending it back towards the oncoming car.

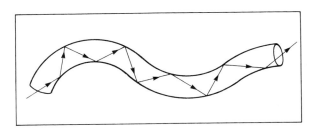

Fig. 60.10 Light travelling along a glass fibre.

61 Lenses

CONVERGING LENSES

The pin-hole camera is not a very good one (p. 103). To make a better camera you need a lens, to converge the light. Set up the pin-hole camera again. Make lots of pin-holes so that you see lots of images of, say, a lamp filament. Slide a suitable lens in front of the pin-holes and watch all the images come together to form a single bright one. Now poke your finger through all the pin-holes so that you have just one large hole and use the lens in front of it. Now you have a far better camera. Why? To answer that, look carefully at the lens. What shape is it? Fatter or thinner in the middle than at the edge? It is fatter. It is a **convex** or **converging lens**.

HOW CONVERGING LENSES WORK

Convex lenses bring light together; they converge the rays (Fig. 61.1). The fattest is the most powerful—it converges light the most. The **meniscus-convex lens** is often used in spectacles—why do you think this is?

Send parallel rays of light on to a convex lens. They will come to a **focus** (**F**) (Fig. 61.2). The distance between the focus and the centre of the lens is its **focal length** (*f*). Focal length is measured in metres or centimetres. There is a focus on each side of the lens. A slim lens is less powerful than a fat one. It bends the light rays less and it has a longer focal length.

MEASURING THE FOCAL LENGTH

The approximate focal length of a converging lens can be found by focusing a sharp image of a distant bright object on to a white screen (Fig. 61.3). Rays of light from each point of the object come to their particular focus on the screen. As the image is **real** it can be seen on a screen. The image is **diminished**—it is smaller than the object—and **inverted** (upside-down and left-to-right). If the object is far enough away for light from any point on it to be almost parallel when it reaches the lens, the sharp image is at the principal focus of the lens. The distance from the lens to the screen is then the focal length.

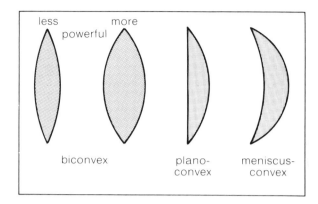

Fig. 61.1 Some convex (converging) lens shapes.

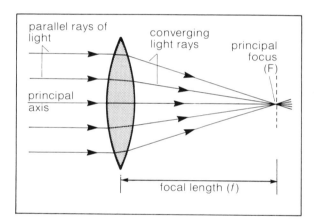

Fig. 61.2 A convex lens converging parallel light to the principal focus.

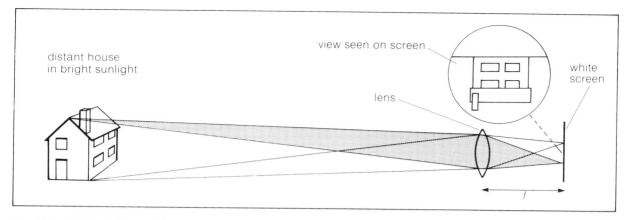

Fig. 61.3 A distant object and its real image on a screen. The distance from the lens to the screen is nearly equal to the focal length of the lens.

MAGNIFICATION

The **magnification** (*m*) tells us how many times the image is larger than the object.

USES OF CONVERGING LENSES

Converging lenses are used in telescopes, microscopes, cameras, in spectacles to correct long sight (p. 118), as magnifying glasses and so on.

DIVERGING LENSES

A **diverging lens** spreads out rays of light. They are thinner at the middle than at the edges. Diverging lenses are often called **concave lenses** because of their shape (Fig. 61.4). The **meniscus-concave lens** is often used in spectacles as it gives room for the eyelashes to move.

A diverging lens makes parallel rays of light spread apart as if they are coming from the **virtual focus** (**F**) behind the lens (Fig. 61.5). The distance between the focus and the centre of the lens is its **focal length** (*f*). To show that the lens diverges light, its focal length is written with a minus sign. There is a virtual focus on each side of the lens. The more curved the lens the shorter its focal length and the more powerful it is.

USES OF DIVERGING LENSES

Diverging lenses are used in opera glasses, Galilean telescopes and in spectacles to correct short sight (p. 118).

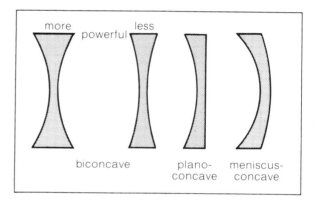

Fig. 61.4 Some shapes of diverging lenses.

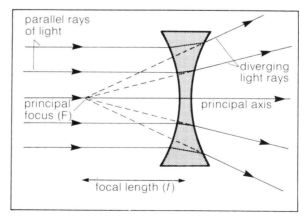

Fig. 61.5 A concave lens diverges parallel light from the principal focus.

13 Light bounces and bends

HOW TO DRAW RAY DIAGRAMS

1 Draw a line XY across the paper to act as your principal axis (Fig. 61.6).
2 Mark the position of your lens by a vertical line drawn across the principal axis. The rays of light will bend at this line and nowhere else.
3 Mark the two principal foci F_1 and F_2. These are at equal distances on either side of the lens.
4 Draw in an object OA.
5 Draw one ray of light from the top A of the object straight through the centre of the lens.
6 Draw a second ray from the top of the object parallel to the axis XY as far as the lens. This ray bends down towards the principal axis at F_1 if the lens is convex and up from F_2 if the lens is concave.
7 The image of the top of the object is where these two rays meet. Draw the image here. If you have to draw a ray against the direction of the light show this with a dashed line as in the diagram for the concave lens.

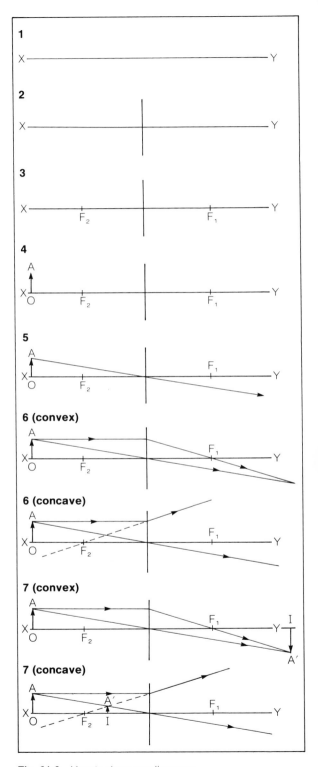

Fig. 61.6 How to draw ray diagrams.

114

62 Some converging lenses in use

FILM OR SLIDE PROJECTOR

When a bright object is between one and two focal lengths from the converging lens of the projector (Fig. 62.1), a magnified, inverted, real image is produced on the screen. As it is inverted, the film or slide has to be put in upside-down and left-to-right. The real image is then the right way up. A lot of light must pass through the small film frame—the object—so that the picture—the image—on the screen is bright enough. A small powerful lamp provides this light. Two condenser lenses, converging plano-convex, converge this light and direct it through the film so the projected image is bright.

PHOTOCOPIER

If a bright object is exactly two focal lengths ($2f$) from a converging lens, the real image is the same distance the other side, and the same size. This is useful when exact copies are needed; they are inverted, but you just turn them round.

LIGHTHOUSE

The object is a powerful lamp placed at the focus of a large converging plano-convex lens (Fig. 62.2). Rays of light from the lamp are sent out parallel after passing through the lens. In a lighthouse each lens is bigger than you are, so they are not made from lumps of glass. The lens is cut into many small sections, each with the correct curvature. These lenses are quite thin and light. They are called **Fresnel lenses**. There may be one in the overhead projector. A concave mirror (p. 107) is placed behind the lamp to send more light through the lens.

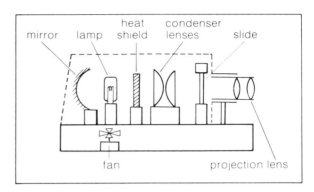

Fig. 62.1 A slide projector. Why is a concave mirror placed behind the lamp? How far is the lamp from the mirror?

Fig. 62.2 The lens in a lighthouse.

MAGNIFYING GLASS OR SIMPLE MICROSCOPE

The simple microscope is a converging lens of short focal length (Fig. 62.3). The object is placed just inside the focal length. You move your eye to see the best image. It is virtual, upright and magnified.

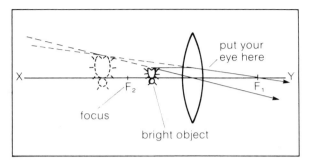

Fig. 62.3 What sort of image does a magnifying glass produce?

A CAMERA

When you added the simple convex lens to the pin-hole camera (p. 112) it formed a real, inverted, diminished image on the screen. This is exactly what happens even in the best of cameras. You can bring the image into sharp focus on the photo-film at the rear of the camera by adjusting the distance of the lens from the film. Usually you turn the lens mount on a fine screw thread with distance markings

on the mount. These markings tell you when an object at a particular distance is focused sharply.

The lens is fitted with a **diaphragm**, like the iris of your eye. This controls the amount of light the lens will let through. A big opening means a lot of light, fine for dull days. The film is exposed to the light by opening the shutter for a fraction of a second. The shutter is like a sliding door that opens and then shuts again. This controls the exposure time.

AN ASTRONOMICAL TELESCOPE

Not all astronomical telescopes use mirrors (see Fig. 59.5 on p. 108). Some use two converging lenses. You can easily make one. You will need one convex lens with a long focal length (called the **objective lens**) and another convex lens with a short focal length (the **eyepiece**). Fix the objective lens so that it forms an image of a distant scene on a scrap of translucent paper (p. 100). The image is real, inverted and diminished. Fix the piece of paper. Now look at the image with the short focal length lens used as a magnifying glass. Adjust the distance to give the best image and immediately take the scrap of paper away. And there, through the eyepiece, you will see a magnified, inverted but virtual image of the scene (Fig. 62.4). Astronomers don't have to worry about the image being inverted!

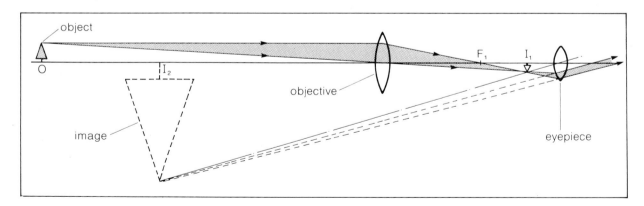

Fig. 62.4 How the light rays form a virtual image when they pass through a telescope.

63 Your eyes

Your eyes (Fig. 63.1) work like a camera (Table 63). Each eye has a **lens** made of a hard jelly-like material. Special muscles, the **ciliary muscles**, can change the shape of the lens. Your eye can focus on nearby objects or on distant objects.

The eyeball is black inside. The inside lining of the back wall is the **retina**. This is a wall of light-sensitive nerve cells. These cells turn the light energy they receive into electrical signals. These electrical messages are carried to the brain by the **optic nerve**. Since there aren't any light-sensitive cells where the optic nerve leaves the retina, you have a **blind spot** there. The space between the lens and the retina is filled with a clear watery jelly.

The front of the lens is covered by the **cornea** or outer surface of the eye. This is transparent and curved. It refracts the light coming in quite strongly. The light has been converged quite a lot before it strikes the lens. Behind this window a hole called the **pupil** lets light into the eyeball through the lens. The amount of light let in is controlled by a coloured ring called the **iris**. The size of the iris changes with the amount of light coming into the eye. There is a clear watery liquid between the cornea and the lens.

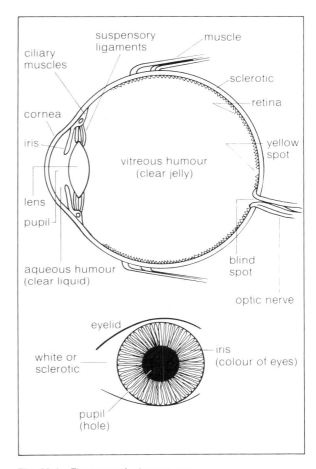

Fig. 63.1 The parts of a human eye.

Table 63 A comparison of the eye and the lens camera

Characteristic	Eye	Camera
Lens	Cornea surface/ converging 'jelly' lens	Converging glass lens
Accommodation		
How	Lens shape altered	Lens moved
Near object	Lens gets fatter	Lens is further from film
Far object	Lens gets slimmer	Lens is nearer to film
Image		
Type	Real, inverted, smaller	Real, inverted, smaller
Detector	Retina	Photographic film
Effect	Electrical messages sent to brain along optic nerve	Chemical development
Light intensity		
Light opening	Pupil	Aperture
Changed by	Iris/involuntary reflex nerves	Diaphragm/operator
Light barrier	Eyelid	Shutter

The light is bent first by the cornea and then by the eye lens. The ciliary muscles allow the eye lens to change its shape and power. To focus light from an object nearby it gets fatter; to focus light from a distant object the muscles relax and the lens gets thinner. This is called **accommodation**. A normal eye can focus light on the retina from objects as far away as the moon and as near as 25 cm.

DEFECTS OF VISION

Long sight (hypermetropia)

Someone with long sight can see distant objects clearly (Fig. 63.2(a)). But the ciliary muscles cannot squeeze the lens fat enough to focus light from a near object to form an image clearly on the retina. For these near objects a sharp image would be behind the retina; a hazy picture is seen (Fig. 63.2(b)). The lens in the eye is not powerful enough. Long sight is corrected by a suitable converging lens, which adds to the eye lens' power (Fig. 63.2(c)).

Short sight (myopia)

Someone with short sight can see near objects clearly (Fig. 63.3(a)). But even when the ciliary muscles are completely relaxed the lens in the eye is too fat for it to focus light from a distant object. The light rays from a distant object are brought to a focus in front of the retina (Fig. 63.3(b)). An out-of-focus picture is seen. The lens in the eye is too powerful. Short sight is corrected by a suitable diverging lens, which reduces the eye lens' power (Fig. 63.3(c)).

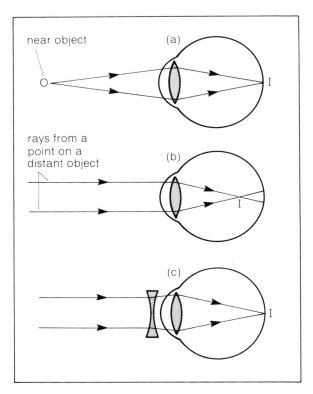

Fig. 63.3 A short-sighted person can focus (a) near objects, but distant objects (b) are out-of-focus. (c) What type of lens is needed to correct myopia?

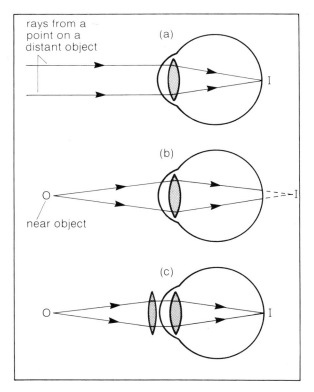

Fig. 63.2 How a long-sighted person sees (a) a distant object and (b) a near object. (c) What sort of lens would you use to correct hypermetropia?

Lenses correcting these and other defects are worn as spectacles or as contact lenses (Fig. 63.4).

Fig. 63.4 A contact lens.

SUMMARY: LIGHT BOUNCES AND BENDS

- The image in a plane mirror is (i) virtual; (ii) the same size as the object; (iii) the same distance behind the mirror as the object is in front; (iv) upright; and (v) reversed left-to-right.
- In reflection at a plane mirror the angle of incidence equals the angle of reflection.
- Concave mirrors converge light; they bring parallel rays together at a real focus.
- The distance from the focus to the mirror is the focal length. It is half the radius of curvature of the mirror.
- Objects placed outside the focus of a concave mirror give real images; objects inside the focus give magnified, upright, virtual images.
- Convex mirrors diverge light; they spread parallel rays out as if they were leaving a focus.
- A convex mirror always gives a virtual, upright, diminished image. This type of mirror gives a wider field of view than that in a plane mirror.
- The bending of a ray at the surface between two transparent materials is called refraction. Refraction is due to the different speeds of light in the two materials.
- Refractive index is equal to sine (angle of incidence) divided by sine (angle of refraction).
- With a parallel-sided glass block, the emergent ray is parallel to the incident ray, but displaced sideways.
- Total internal reflection occurs when a ray is passing from glass, Perspex or water into air and when the angle of incidence is greater than the critical angle.

- Refractive index is equal to the reciprocal of the sine of the critical angle.
- Forty-five degree prisms and optical fibres are perfect reflectors.
- Convex lenses converge light; they bring parallel rays together at a real focus.
- The distance from the focus to the centre of the lens is the focal length.
- The fatter the lens the shorter its focal length and the more powerful it is.
- Objects placed outside the focus of a convex lens have real images; objects inside the focus have a magnified, upright, virtual image.
- Diverging lenses spread parallel rays as if they come from a focus.
- Diverging lenses always give a virtual, upright, diminished image.
- A construction ray through the centre of a lens keeps straight on.
- A construction ray parallel to the principal axis is bent by a lens to pass through the focus. The image is found where the construction rays cross.
- The eye lens varies its fatness to focus clear images on the retina of objects at different distances.
- The camera is similar to the eye, but its lens must be moved to and fro to focus objects at different distances.
- Long sight is corrected with a converging lens.
- Short sight is corrected with a diverging lens.

SECTION 14

Seeing in Colour

64 Colours from white light

THE SPECTRUM

In a rainbow, white light from the sun is split into the **visible spectrum** of colours; red, orange, yellow, green, blue, violet. If you send a ray of white light through a glass prism (Fig. 64.1), you will see the same **spectral colours** (Fig. 64.2).

Each spectral colour covers a particular range of wavelengths (pp. 90 and 95). These have slightly different speeds in glass. Red light is the fastest and violet the slowest. So violet light, at the blue end of the spectrum, is refracted (bent) most by a prism. This spreading out of the colours in white light by a prism is called **dispersion**.

Fig. 64.2 The spectrum of white light.

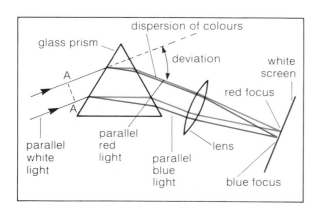

Fig. 64.1 Making a spectrum of white light with a prism.

120

Fig. 64.3 A stained-glass window.

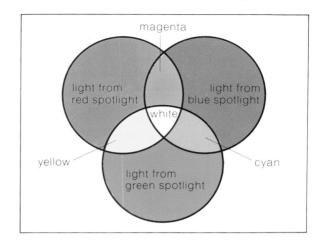

Fig. 64.4 Adding coloured lights on a white screen.

COLOUR FILTERS

Colour filters have been in use for centuries in stained-glass windows (Fig. 64.3). They are also used in stage and disco lighting.

Colour filters work by absorbing some colours and letting other colour(s) through. The light energy they absorb warms them up very slightly. A pure green filter, placed in the path of the light passing through the prism in Fig. 64.1, will allow only green light to pass. It absorbs all other colours.

MIXING COLOURED LIGHTS

Try sending three strong beams of light from three spotlights on to a white screen. Put a good green filter on one spotlight, a good blue filter on another and a good red filter on the third. You will probably have to reduce the brightness of the red and green spotlights but you will be able to light the screen up with white light. The three colours, red, blue and green, can add up to white. They are called **primary colours**. The process is one of **addition**; the colours are added together on the screen (Fig. 64.4).

Now switch off the red light. The screen is lit with blue and green light. The colour you see is called **peacock blue** or **cyan**. You might call it white minus red! Try blue and red together. The colour you get is **magenta** (minus green). Finally, add red and green. Now you get **yellow** (minus blue). If you arrange for the three light beams to overlap you will get white light.

SEEING COLOURED THINGS

Why does a red bus look red by daylight? Because the red paint reflects any red light back to your eyes and absorbs other colours.

Hold a piece of red cloth in the overlapping beams of your three spotlights. The cloth looks red in the red beam and in the magenta. But in the green, blue and cyan areas it looks almost black. There is no red to send back to you.

MIXING COLOURS BY SUBTRACTION

Take three filters: one cyan, one magenta and one yellow. Look at the sky through them in pairs. The cyan and yellow filters share green and that is the colour they let through. Try yellow and magenta. This time you see red, which is the colour they share. What will you see if you use cyan and magenta filters together? Finally, try all three filters in a sandwich. No light gets through. This process is the **subtraction** of colours from white light and it is the basis of painting, colour printing, dyeing and so on. In this process the three primary colours are cyan (usually called blue), yellow and magenta (usually called red).

COLOURS OF THE SKY AND THE SUN

When white sunlight passes through the atmosphere, the blue light in it is scattered more than the red. This is why the sun, early and late in the day, appears to be red

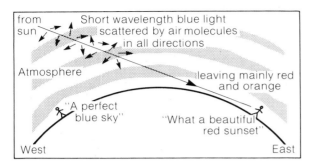

Fig. 64.5 Why is the sky blue and a sunset red?

(Fig. 64.5). During the day **scattered** blue light enters your eyes from directions away from the sun; so you see the sky.

COLOUR VISION AND COLOUR-BLINDNESS

Your eye can see a great range of colour and brightness. Scientists think that there may be three types of cells in the retina (p. 117) which detect red, green or violet and the colours next to them. For instance, both red- and green-sensitive cells are triggered by pure spectral yellow light. Red light plus green light (with no yellow light in it) gives the same sensation of yellow. This effect occurs because these two colours trigger the red- and green-sensitive cells equally, as pure spectral yellow does.

Some people cannot see much difference between certain shades of red and green. They are **colour-blind**. This is due to one of their sets of sensitive cells not working efficiently. Colour-blindness occurs mainly in males.

VARYING THE LIGHTING

The sodium (yellow) and mercury (blue) lamps used on main roads give objects very different appearances. Even white light has a slightly different balance of colours depending on its source. Average daylight is just a little bluish. Light from filament lamps has a yellowish tinge. Fluorescent lamps give several different shades of white. This is why, when you want to check the colour of something before buying it, you go outside the shop, or to a window to look at it in normal daylight.

COLOUR TELEVISION

By varying the amounts of the primary colours, red, green and blue, a colour television tube can give all the colours we see normally. The process is addition.

ARE THERE ANY OTHER SPECTRAL COLOURS?

Newton tried the experiment of passing a spectrum from a prism (Fig. 64.1) through another prism. No more colours were seen, only the familiar spectral ones. He then tried turning his second prism round as in Fig. 64.6. What do you think he saw on the screen?

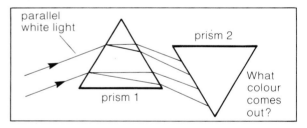

Fig. 64.6 Newton's double-prism experiment.

SUMMARY: SEEING IN COLOUR

- White light can be split into the spectrum (rainbow), which includes red, orange, yellow, green, blue, violet—the spectral colours.
- Dispersion is the spreading out caused by a prism, as the spectral colours travel in glass at slightly different speeds.
- Colour filters work by absorbing some colours and letting others pass.
- Filters are warmed slightly by the energy of the light they absorb.
- Mixing coloured lights is an additive process.

- Primary-coloured lights—red, blue and green—cannot be made by mixing other coloured lights.
- Surfaces are seen to be the colour of the light that they reflect to us.
- A white surface reflects all colours equally.
- A coloured surface is named by the colour it reflects in white light.
- Overlapping filters and pigments work by colour subtraction.
- The spectral colours can be recombined to give white light.

Sound

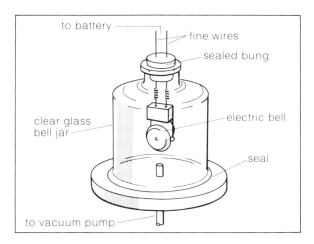

65 Production of sound

Anything you hear is **sound**. There are many different sources of sound. In all of them something happens to make the sound. The source vibrates. You can see the vibration of a guitar string if you watch closely as it is played.

Strike a tuning fork on hard rubber to make it vibrate and it will emit sound. When it is making a sound it will knock away a light ball on a thread which just touches it. It cannot do this when it is not vibrating and not making a sound. Press the stem of the vibrating tuning fork on the table and you hear a louder sound. The vibrations of the fork make the table vibrate. This makes more air near the table vibrate, so a louder sound is heard.

Sound cannot travel through a vacuum. Sound has to have a **medium** or material to travel in. You can show this by doing the experiment in Fig. 65.1. When you switch on the electric bell and slowly remove the air from the bell jar with a vacuum pump, the sound will fade away. You can see the hammer vibrating on the bell but you cannot hear it.

Sound travels through liquids and solids as well as through gases. Try the experiment shown in Fig. 65.2. You will hear clear sounds of the spoon or fork ringing if you press the top end of the string to your head near your ear.

Fig. 65.1 A good way to show that sound cannot travel through a vacuum.

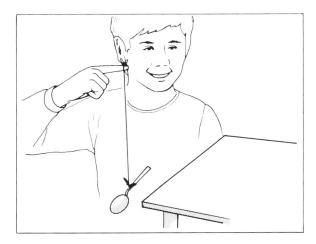

Fig. 65.2 Can you hear anything?

123

66 Sound travels

You have seen a longitudinal wave travelling along a slinky-toy (see Fig. 47.5 on p. 89). Some coils of the spring closed up as you pushed at one end; they moved apart when you pulled. The **compression,** where the coils were close together, travelled down the spring followed by a **rarefaction,** where the coils were a little further apart.

When a loudspeaker gives out a single note, it alternately pushes and pulls on the air in front of it. A longitudinal sound wave travels through the air in front of the speaker. Air molecules vibrate to and fro in the direction in which the wave travels; compressions and rarefactions follow one another through the air (Fig. 66.1). When these changing pressures reach your ear-drum, the compressions push the drum in a little. Normal pressure allows it to relax. The rarefactions let the air inside the ear on the other side of the drum push the drum outwards a little. Your ear-drum is forced to vibrate with the same frequency as the loudspeaker is vibrating.

Remember, frequency is the number of vibrations in a second. It is measured in hertz. Each hertz (Hz) is one vibration per second. The human ear can hear sounds that vibrate as slowly as 20 times a second (20 Hz) and as quickly as 20 000 times a second (20 kHz).

HEARING

A longitudinal sound wave in the air makes your ear-drum vibrate. This drives three little bones inside the ear, which are called the **hammer,** the **anvil** and the **stirrup** (Fig. 66.2). These pass the vibration through a window, which is another drum, to the liquid in the coiled-up **cochlea.** Special sensory cells in the cochlea pick up the vibration. They pass the information about frequency and loudness along the auditory nerve to the brain as electrical signals.

RESONANCE

If you push your small brother or sister on a swing you can build up a big swing, one with a large **amplitude.** You do it by giving lots of small pushes at just the right time. The swing, like anything else that vibrates, has its own

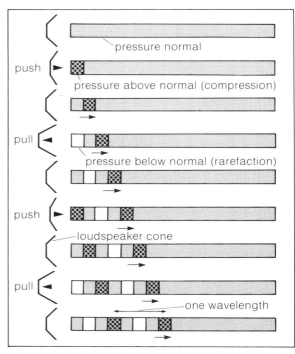

Fig. 66.1 How a vibrating loudspeaker cone makes a sound wave.

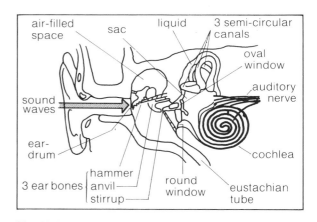

Fig. 66.2 A human ear.

natural frequency. This is the frequency at which it vibrates if left free. Building up the size of the swing by giving a lot of small pushes at the natural frequency is called **resonance**.

The sensory cells in the cochlea of your ear respond to particular frequencies using resonance. Resonance is used in musical instruments to build up the sound of the vibrating string or reed.

67 Pitch and frequency

A musician knows the notes on a piano key-board by their **pitch**. High pitch means high frequency.

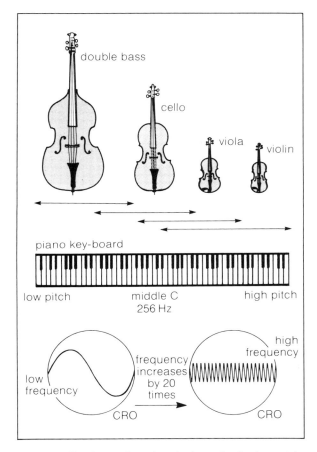

Fig. 67.1 The longer the string, the lower the fundamental frequency.

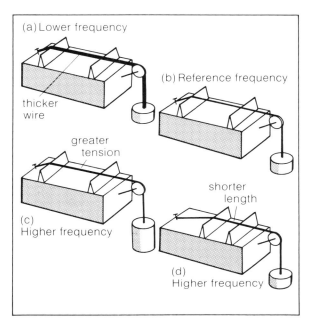

Fig. 67.2 Spot the item that is different in each of these sonometers.

FREQUENCY OF VIBRATING STRINGS

Guitars, violins, double basses, pianos and other musical instruments use strings that vibrate to make their sound (Fig. 67.1). You tune guitars and other string instruments by adjusting the **tension** in the strings. The tension is the force stretching the string. In a violin this force is about 40 N. When the instrument is tuned the natural or **fundamental frequency** of each string is adjusted to give exactly the right pitch. Then you can shorten the vibrating or sounding length of the string by moving a finger along it without changing the tension. This raises the frequency and thus the pitch of the note heard. You can use a **sonometer** to study these changes in a string (Fig. 67.2).

Changing the length with tension constant

A longer string gives a note of lower frequency. That's why a double bass is so much taller (longer) than a violin. Doubling the length halves the frequency or lowers the pitch **an octave**.

Changing the tension with length constant

Greater tension gives a note of higher frequency. To raise the pitch one octave (or to double the frequency) you have to increase the tension by four times.

Changing the thickness of the string

A thicker, more massive string gives notes of lower frequencies than a thinner one of the same length and at the same tension. This explains why the low-note strings on all stringed instruments are thicker and bigger than the high-note strings. Look at the piano strings in Fig. 67.3. Doubling the thickness halves the frequency or lowers the pitch by an octave.

RESONANCE IN STRINGS

A standing wave pattern or stationary waves can occur on a stretched string or wire (Fig. 67.4). Vary the driving frequency at the end of the string until a standing wave with clear loops forms. The lowest note giving a single loop is the fundamental frequency of the string. Its wavelength is twice the length of the string. If you double the frequency, you will see a two-loop pattern. This frequency is called the **second harmonic**. Its wavelength, shown by the solid black line in Fig. 67.4(c), is the length of the string. These loops can be shown with a strobe lamp. Then you can make any position of the wire appear stationary. The points marked N are the nodes, where no displacement occurs. At points A and A', the antinodes, maximum displacement occurs. Driving the string harder does not alter the frequency. It merely increases the amplitude of the displacement at the antinodes.

RESONANCE IN PIPES

Blow across the top of a large bottle; you will hear a low-pitched note. Half fill the bottle with water or use a smaller bottle and you will hear a higher pitched note. Blow across the top of a pen (not in class please!) and quite a high frequency note is produced. These findings agree with what you know of the wind instruments; the shorter ones produce high notes and the longer ones low notes. You can see and hear this at the same time if you watch a trombonist play.

A vibrating column of air in a pipe that has nodes and antinodes also has resonance. Open pipes are open at both ends. The wavelength of their fundamental frequency is twice the length of the pipe (Fig. 67.5). Closed pipes, like trumpets, are closed at one end and the wavelength of their fundamental frequency is four times the length of the pipe (Fig. 67.6).

ULTRASOUND AND ULTRASONICS

The ultrasonic dog whistle uses ultrasound. The whistle is so short that the frequency it produces is above the range you can hear. But a dog can hear these high frequencies and will obey commands given on the whistle.

Fig. 67.3 Notice the thicker, more massive strings at the bass end of this piano.

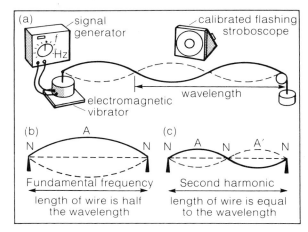

Fig. 67.4 Standing wave patterns on a string.

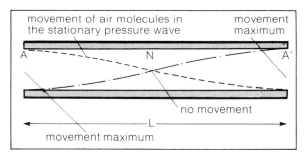

Fig. 67.5 The standing wave pattern for the fundamental frequency of an open pipe. The movement of the air molecules is a maximum at A and A' and zero at N.

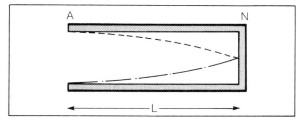

Fig. 67.6 A standing wave pattern in a trumpet (closed pipe).

68 Measuring sounds

If someone far away from you hits a ball with a bat, you hear the sound a short time after seeing the hit. Sound takes time to travel a distance.

THE SPEED OF SOUND IN AIR

You can work out the speed of sound if you know the time it takes sound to travel a measured distance. The time to cover a distance the length of three football pitches is about 1 s. If you use a longer distance it is possible to measure the time using a stop-watch. Start timing when you see the two bats (Fig. 68.1) clapped together and stop when you hear the bang. For example, the distance across a sports field measured 500 m and sound took 1.5 s to cross this distance.

$$\text{speed} = \frac{\text{distance}}{\text{time}} = \frac{500 \text{ m}}{1.5 \text{ s}} = 333 \text{ m/s}$$

The time measurement cannot be very accurate so we round off the speed of sound to 330 m/s. Why isn't the time measurement very accurate?

SPEED, WAVELENGTH AND FREQUENCY OF SOUND

You know that the speed of a wave is given by the equation

speed = frequency × wavelength

The frequency of the note called middle C is 256 Hz. Using 330 m/s as the speed of the sound in the air you find that the wavelength of the sound wave is 300 m/s/256 Hz, which is nearly 1.3 m. For a sound with a frequency one octave higher (512 Hz) the wavelength is 0.65 m.

SOUND IN LIQUIDS AND SOLIDS

Sound travels faster in liquids and solids than it does in air. Figure 68.2 shows an arrangement for measuring the speed of sound in metal rods. You need two rods of the same metal, one longer than the other. Make a single pulse of sound by tapping a hammer on one end of the rods. The time base of the cathode ray oscilloscope (p. 191) gives an accurate

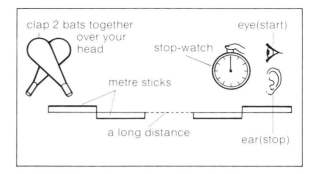

Fig. 68.1 A direct way to measure the speed of sound in air.

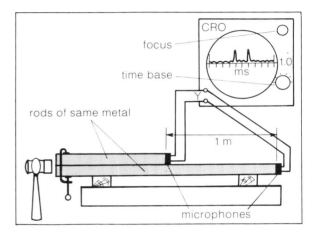

Fig. 68.2 How to measure the speed of sound in a metal rod.

method of measuring short time intervals. The two microphones send electrical signals to the oscilloscope when the sound reaches them. The positions of the two blips on the screen give the time taken by the sound to travel between the two microphones. Read this time from the screen using the horizontal scale and the known speed of the time base. You could use this method for an accurate measurement of the speed of sound in air. You would fix the microphones a known distance apart.

THUNDER AND LIGHTNING

Thunder and lightning happen at the same time. But at a distance this does not seem so. Light from the flash travels a million times

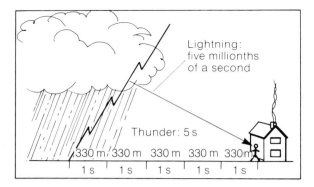

Fig. 68.3 If there is 5 s between seeing the lightning and hearing the thunder, the storm is about a mile away.

faster than the sound of the thunder (Fig. 68.3). Try counting the seconds between seeing the flash and hearing the thunder. For every second the flash is 330 m away. So for every 5 s it is about a mile away.

ECHOES AND REFLECTION OF SOUND

You can reflect sound waves (Fig. 68.4(a)). Buildings, walls and cliffs are good reflectors of sounds. **Echoes** are the reflected sounds you hear from them (Fig. 68.4(b)). Measure your distance from a cliff and double it. Then you can time how long a sound takes to travel there and back. In rocky caverns and cathedrals the sound is reflected a number of times so you get a repeated echo, or a ringing effect, called **reverberation**.

Echo-sounder

This machine uses accurate timing and the known speed of sound in sea water to show the depth of water under a ship (Fig. 68.4(c)). A strong pulse is sent out from the bottom of the ship. This is reflected from the sea bed and picked up by a receiver on the ship.

Example A pulse of sound returns to an echo-sounder half a second after it was emitted. Calculate the depth of the sea below the ship. (The speed of sound in sea water is 1500 m/s.)

distance travelled = speed × time
= 1500 m/s × 0.5 s
= 750 m

But the depth is half this because the signal travels down and then up. So the depth is 375 m.

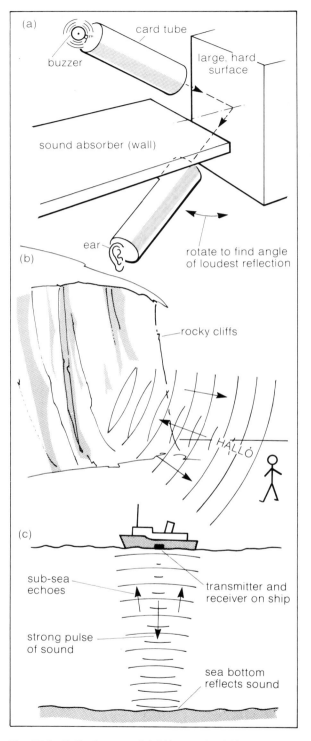

Fig. 68.4 Reflecting sound. (a) How to check if the angle of reflection is equal to the angle of incidence in the lab. (b) Echoes out of doors. (c) Echo-sounding at sea.

Table 68   Noise levels*

Noise	Level (dB)	Effect
	150	Ear damage
Nearby jet at take off	140	Not bearable
Shipyard riveting shop / Pop concert	130	Ear pain
Jet close overhead / Fire engine siren	120	Ear uncomfortable
Heavy hammering machine / Limit for new aircraft	110	Conversation impossible
Shouting in ear to talk	100	Working efficiency falls
Heavy diesel lorry / Pneumatic drill	90	Signs of ear damage / Ringing in ears
New limit for bikes and cars / Very noisy party	80	Annoying, if not involved
Motorway traffic nearby / School dining room	70	Well-being affected / Loud conversation
Vacuum cleaner	60	Disturbing
Light traffic / Hairdryer	50	Normal conversation
Room in house	40	Quiet
Soft whisper	30	Very quiet
Radio studio	20	
Rustling leaves	10	
Pin dropping	0	Limit of hearing

* The numbers are approximate and usually refer to the noisiest measured. In the danger sectors above 80 dB, ear protectors must be worn to prevent permanent ear damage.

LOUDNESS OF SOUND

You get a louder sound if you put more energy into the oscillator driving the sound waves. The waves have a larger amplitude. Loudness, or **intensity**, is measured in **decibels (dB)**.

The modern world is getting noisier every day (Table 68). We are learning that to stop us from becoming deaf, we must protect our ears from noises that are too loud. Transport produces a lot of noise. There are maximum noise levels that vehicles must not exceed. Measuring noise levels is now easy; a microphone is connected to a meter scaled in decibels.

Ear-plugs and ear-muffs are worn by workers in noisy jobs, like those who work near aircraft at an airport (Fig. 68.5). Motorways often run in cuttings where they are near houses and you may see sound reflectors put up at the sides of embankments. Pneumatic road drills have been made much quieter by simply putting a sound-absorbing gaiter round all the noisy parts.

Fig. 68.5 In noisy surroundings you must protect your ears from sounds that can damage them.

69 Music and wave-forms

You will often see oscilloscope traces of musical sounds like the one in Fig. 69.1(a). Traces like this are really graphs of the pressures in the sound wave which the microphone picked up. That's why the traces look like transverse waves even though the sound waves are really longitudinal ones.

You can get a trace like Fig. 69.1(a) with a microphone and a cathode ray oscilloscope if the time base is running at a suitable speed. The trace shown was made with a signal generator or audio-oscillator set to vibrate a loudspeaker at 256 Hz. It is a **pure tone**. If you double the frequency to 512 Hz, the trace changes to the one shown in Fig. 69.1(b). The amplitude is kept the same. The pitch of the note has been raised by one octave. The wavelength has been halved.

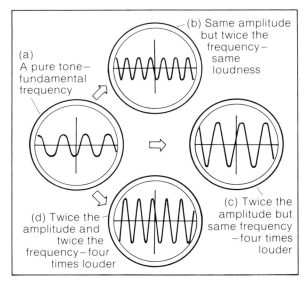

Fig. 69.1 Oscilloscope traces of musical notes. How do they compare with one another?

AMPLITUDE AND LOUDNESS

To make a sound louder you must put more energy into the vibrator. You bow a violin more strongly, you blow a pipe harder and so on. When the amplitude of the 256-Hz note (Fig. 69.1(a)) is doubled, the trace (Fig. 69.1(c)) is twice the height. But the note is four times as loud—not twice!

OVERTONES AND HARMONICS

You don't often hear a pure tone like the one from the loudspeaker and oscillator. That's because musical instruments produce several vibrations at any one time. If you play middle C (256 Hz) on a violin, the violin will sound a note of 256 Hz plus other notes at the same time. These other notes have frequencies that are two, three, four, etc., times 256 Hz; that is, one octave up, two octaves up, etc. So the wave-form (Fig. 69.2) is much more complicated than for the pure tone (Fig. 69.1(a)).

The lowest frequency heard is the **fundamental** or **first harmonic**. The others are the **overtones**; they are called the second, third, fourth, etc., **harmonic**. It is these overtones that make a musical instrument's notes interesting to listen to and which let us say which instrument is which.

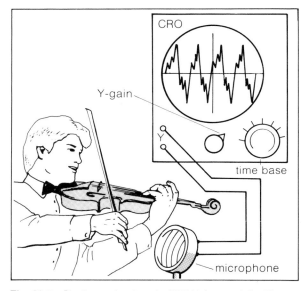

Fig. 69.2 Playing a steady note (256 Hz) on a violin. The microphone is connected to a cathode ray oscilloscope.

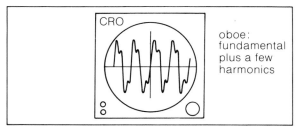

Fig. 69.3 The trace made by an oboe (256 Hz).

The **tone** or **timbre** of the note depends on these overtones. In Figs 69.2 and 69.3 you see the wave traces of the note middle C (256 Hz) played on a violin and an oboe equally loudly.

HEARING MUSIC AND SPEECH

Your brain can sort the signals coming from the cochlea of your ear into sets of fundamentals and harmonics which go together. So you can tell the difference between the notes of different instruments and you can sort out a number of sounds happening at the same time. It can tell you which of your friends is speaking. But before it can do this it must have learnt to sort out the many wave-forms used in spoken English (Fig. 69.4). It may be able to warn you before you suffer too much noise (Fig. 69.5).

By comparing the amplitudes of the waves received by each ear, the brain can tell you the approximate direction of a source of sound. Sounds from different directions arrive at each ear at slightly different times and your brain uses this information to tell you about the directions.

High-fidelity reproduction of sound aims to repeat the wave-forms you hear exactly as they were in the original performance. A lot of sound measurements are made in an **anechoic**

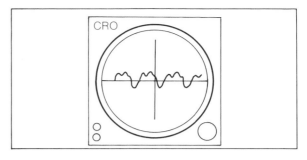

Fig. 69.4 A spoken vowel sound—say AHHH.

Fig. 69.5 Noise—random frequencies, random amplitudes, random harmonics.

chamber: *anechoic* means no echo. Sounds hitting the walls are absorbed by the fibre wedges so that echoes do not affect the accuracy of the measurements.

SUMMARY: SOUND

- Sound is anything that you can hear.
- To produce sound the source must vibrate mechanically.
- Sound can travel in solids, in liquids, in gases, but not through a vacuum.
- Sound travels as a longitudinal pressure wave.
- In the wave, compressions and rarefactions follow each other alternately.
- The ear can hear frequencies in the range of about 20 to 20 kHz.
- An oscillator will vibrate at its natural frequency if left free.
- Resonance is the increase in amplitude when an oscillator is driven at its natural frequency.
- Higher frequencies come from shorter, tighter, thinner, less dense strings.
- The fundamental is the lowest frequency sounded by a particular string or pipe.
- For a string, the wavelength of the fundamental is equal to twice the length of the string.

- Echoes are reflected sounds.
- The vibrations of strings are transverse.
- A pure note of single frequency produces a trace which is a sine curve.
- Harmonics are simple multiples of the fundamental frequency.
- Harmonics give musical instruments their characteristic tone.
- Sound waves are not electromagnetic waves.
- Musician and physicists use different terms:

Musician	Physicist
Pitch of note	Frequency of fundamental
Loudness	Intensity
Tone, timbre, quality	Wave-form, quality
Overtones	Harmonics
Octave higher	Frequency doubled
Octave lower	Frequency halved

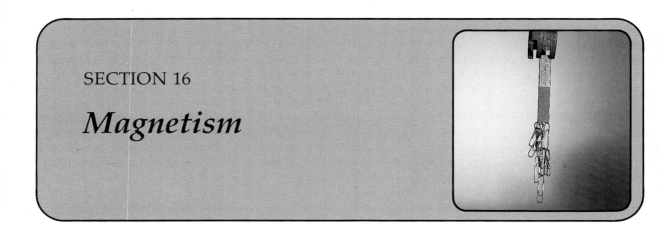

Magnetism

70 Magnets and magnetic poles

You may have seen a horseshoe-shaped magnet. There are also magnets shaped like round pencils—cylindrical magnets. Ring magnets are shaped like large Polo mints. Disc and bar magnets are often used in magnetic latches. A fairly strong bar magnet can hold several steel paper-clips close to its ends (Fig. 70.1). But it will hold fewer paper-clips at other places along its length. This shows where the pull of the magnet—its **magnetic attraction**—is strongest. The pull is strongest near the ends of the bar magnet. These two places are the **poles** of the magnet.

Suspend a bar magnet by a thread and it will point approximately north—south. One pole is called the **north-seeking pole**, the other the **south-seeking pole**. These names are usually shortened to north pole and south pole.

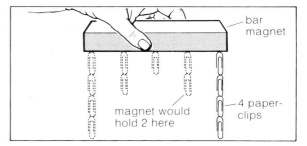

Fig. 70.1   Where are the poles of this bar magnet?

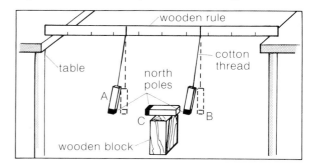

Fig. 70.2   Before C was put in position, magnets A and B were hanging straight down.

WHAT SUBSTANCES ARE ATTRACTED TO A MAGNET?

A magnet attracts iron, cobalt and nickel, and many alloys based on these metals. An **alloy** is a mixture containing mainly metals. Steel, which is an alloy of iron and carbon, is attracted to magnets. So is iron oxide. These are all **magnetic materials**. A magnet attracts them and magnets can be made from them. Some sound-recording tapes contain magnetic iron oxide (p. 185); all video and sound-recording tapes have a thin layer of a magnetic material on a plastic film.

BRINGING TWO MAGNETS TOGETHER

Try bringing a pole of one magnet close to a pole of another magnet. Figure 70.2 shows that the south pole of magnet C attracts the north pole of magnet B. But the north pole of C pushes away, or **repels**, the north pole of magnet A. Therefore we say: Like poles repel, unlike poles attract.

71 Making and unmaking magnets

NATURAL MAGNETS

Lodestone, a kind of rock, is a natural magnet. It is made of magnetic iron oxide, Fe_3O_4. Pieces of lodestone are only weak magnets (Fig. 71.1).

Fig. 71.1 A piece of lodestone is a weak magnet.

MAGNETIC INDUCTION

If you bring a magnet close to a piece of iron the iron becomes a magnet. If you take the magnet away again the iron loses its magnetism. This temporary magnetism is called **induced magnetism**. Making a temporary magnet this way is an example of **magnetic induction**. Magnetic induction works best if the piece of iron touches the magnet. A material like iron, which is easy to magnetise, but which loses its magnetism easily, is called a magnetically soft material (Fig. 71.2). Soft refers to its magnetism, and is nothing to do with the hardness or softness to the touch. The magnets you use in the laboratory are magnets all the time. They are called **permanent magnets**. Permanent magnets are made of magnetically hard materials.

In Fig. 71.3 the poles of the induced magnet, the **induced poles**, are labelled n and s. N and S are the poles of the permanent magnet. The attraction between the pole of the permanent magnet N and the induced pole s is the force that pulls the iron towards the magnet.

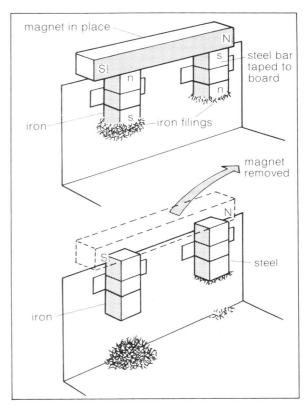

Fig. 71.2 Iron is easier to magnetise than steel, but it loses its magnetism more easily.

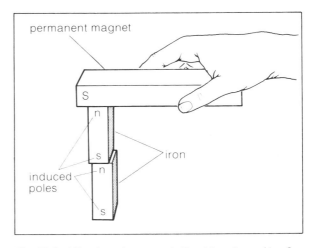

Fig. 71.3 Why does the magnet attract the piece of iron?

MAGNETISED AND UNMAGNETISED

You have already seen that magnetic materials can be made into magnets. If such a material has been made into a magnet it has been **magnetised**. If it has not been made into a magnet it is **unmagnetised**.

MAKING PERMANENT MAGNETS

If you stroke one pole of a permanent magnet many times along a piece of steel in one direction the steel becomes magnetised (Fig. 71.4). It becomes a stronger magnet than one made just by touching the steel with the magnet. You can magnetise a steel darning needle this way and then use it as a compass. But there are much better ways of making magnets than this.

Most magnets are made by an electrical method. Put the piece of magnetic material which is going to be magnetised inside a coil of wire (Fig. 71.5). Then pass a large, direct (one-way) current through the coil for a short time. The magnetic effect of the current (p. 168) magnetises the material, which becomes a permanent magnet.

Ceramic magnets look like black pottery. Powders containing iron and a plastic are heated and squeezed into shape and, as they harden, are magnetised. Ceramic magnets can be very strong magnets, but they break or chip if you drop them.

DOMAINS—WHAT HAPPENS WHEN AN IRON BAR IS MAGNETISED?

An iron bar contains lots of iron atoms. Each of these atoms contains moving electrons, which are tiny negatively charged particles (p. 187). The moving electrons in each iron atom make the atom a magnet. This atomic magnet is very small and weak. But millions of atoms arrange themselves in groups with their atomic magnets all pointing the same way. These groups are called **magnetic domains** and each single domain is a strong magnet. In the unmagnetised bar these magnets all point in different directions and cancel each other out.

If you put the bar in a coil like that in Fig. 71.5 the domains pointing the right way grow when the current flows. The other domains shrink (Fig. 71.6). When the growing and shrinking have gone as far as they can the magnet is at its greatest possible strength. It has reached **magnetic saturation**.

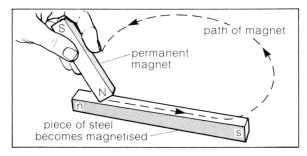

Fig. 71.4 How to magnetise a piece of magnetic material using a permanent magnet.

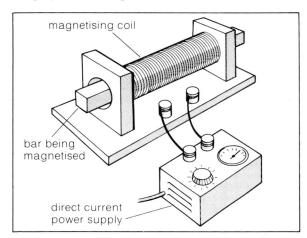

Fig. 71.5 How to magnetise a piece of magnetic material using an electric current in a coil.

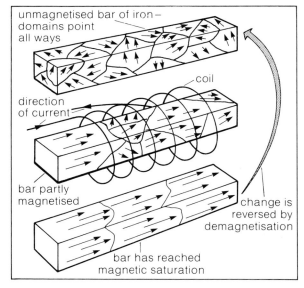

Fig. 71.6 Magnetic domains growing during magnetisation. The tiny arrows show the direction of magnetisation—and the domains are much smaller than shown here.

CUTTING A MAGNET INTO PIECES

Cut a thin sheet steel magnet in two (Fig. 71.7). Test the two halves. You have two complete magnets. The domains in the pieces are still arranged as they were in the unbroken magnet.

KEEPING MAGNETS STRONG—USING KEEPERS

A strong steel bar magnet slowly loses its magnetism if it is just put away by itself. At B (Fig. 71.8) the north poles of one domain are attracted by the south poles of the next domain. This keeps the direction of magnetisation of the domains in line. But at A and C there are no opposite poles to hold the domains in line. The directions of magnetisation slowly spread out, as shown in the diagram. This weakens the magnet.

If you put magnets nose-to-tail using soft iron **keepers**, the keepers become induced magnets (Fig. 71.9). The induced poles prevent the spreading out and both magnets stay strong.

DEMAGNETISATION

Sometimes you want to destroy the magnetism in an object. This process is called **demagnetisation**. Anything that changes the uniform—all one way—direction of magnetisation of the domains will work. There are three ways of demagnetising magnets.

1 **Hitting them**   If you hammer a magnet the vibration disturbs the neat pattern of the domains; even banging a magnet down on a bench weakens it.
2 **Heating them**   When a magnet becomes red-hot, all its atoms vibrate more vigorously and this disturbs the domains. If you magnetise a strip of steel and then heat it until red-hot in a bunsen flame for a few minutes, it will lose its magnetism.
3 **Electrically**   Put the magnet into a coil (see Fig. 71.5) and pass **alternating current** (p. 178) through the coil. This type of current flows first one way and then the other, changing many times a second. Everything magnetic in the coil is magnetised first one way, and then the opposite way, then the first way again, etc. If you make the alternating current smaller and smaller, the magnetisation is weaker each time the current reverses. After a few seconds of reversing and decreasing the current the magnet will be demagnetised.

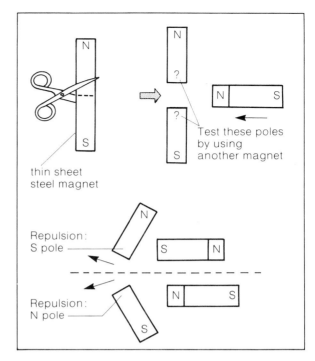

Fig. 71.7   Cutting a thin magnet gives you two small ones.

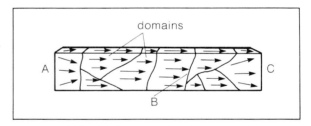

Fig. 71.8   This magnet is slowly demagnetising itself.

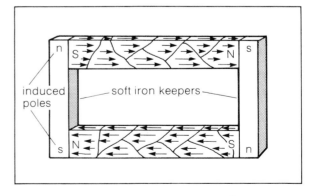

Fig. 71.9   How do the soft iron keepers work?

72 Magnetic fields

You can detect a magnetic effect in the space around a magnet. There is a **magnetic field**. You can map the field using a **plotting compass** (Fig. 72.1). This is a small magnet that can swing freely on a pivot inside a case. A compass needle shows the direction of the magnetic field. The lines you draw showing the direction of the field are called **lines of magnetic force** or **magnetic field lines**. Arrows on the lines show which way the north-seeking end of the compass points. The field is stronger where lines are closer together (Fig. 72.2). The further away you go from the magnet the weaker the field becomes.

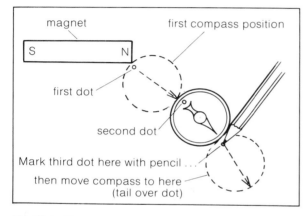

Fig. 72.1 How to map the field of a bar magnet with a plotting compass.

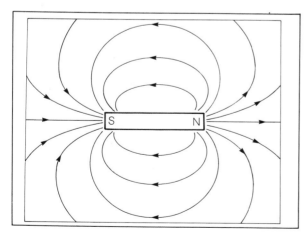

Fig. 72.2 The completed map of the magnetic field. The arrows show the direction in which the compass needle's north pole pointed.

OTHER WAYS OF MAPPING MAGNETIC FIELDS

You can use iron filings to show the direction of the lines of force in a magnetic field. Put a sheet of stiff plastic, card or even glass on top of a magnet. Sprinkle the filings on the sheet. Each filing becomes magnetised by induction (p. 133) and acts like a little compass. When you tap the sheet gently the filings move. Then they resettle along the lines of force. The magnet's field is not just flat, in the plane of the card. The field fills the space round the magnet—it is three-dimensional.

THE FIELD MADE BY TWO MAGNETS

If the north poles of two magnets are close together there is a place between them where their fields are equal, but in opposite directions. This place, where the fields cancel out, is called a **neutral point** (Fig. 72.3). Two south poles can also produce a neutral point, but two unlike poles can't (Fig. 72.4).

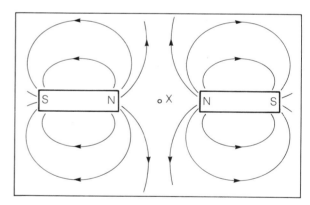

Fig. 72.3 The magnetic field between two like poles. X is a neutral point.

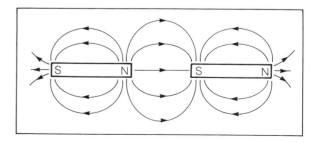

Fig. 72.4 The magnetic field between two unlike poles.

73 The earth as a magnet

The earth is turning all the time—one turn a day. It doesn't turn on a rod, as a wheel turns on an axle, but it is often helpful to imagine that it does. The places where that rod would come out of the earth's surface are the **geographic north** and **south poles.**

If you hang a bar magnet in a paper sling by a thread (Fig. 73.1), it will come to rest pointing in a certain direction. The magnet of a compass and a magnet floating on a flat cork will also point the same way. The swinging magnets point along the earth's lines of magnetic force. They are pointing from the **magnetic south pole** of the earth to the **magnetic north pole**. The ends of the magnets pointing to the magnetic north pole are called north-seeking poles (p. 132).

MAGNETIC DECLINATION

Although the needle of a compass points towards the geographic north pole (true north), it does not point exactly at it. The needle points to the magnetic north pole, which is in northern Canada. The angle between true north and magnetic north is called the **angle of declination** or the **angle of variation**. This angle varies from place to place. In Britain in the 1980s the needle points about 8° west of true north (Fig. 73.2). But this angle is slowly getting less. You can find what it is in your area by looking at the notes on an Ordnance Survey map.

THE ANGLE OF DIP

If you hold a small compass needle so that it can move in a vertical plane, the magnet points down into the earth. In Britain now it dips at about 70° below a horizontal plane. This **angle of dip** varies from place to place.

THE EARTH'S MAGNETIC FIELD

The needle of a compass points along the lines of the earth's magnetic field. These lines show that the earth behaves as if it had magnetic poles at A and B (Fig. 73.3). There cannot be a magnet inside the earth as the high temperature would demagnetise any magnets there. Scientists now think that electric currents in liquids flowing deep inside the earth cause its magnetism. Note that pole A attracts north-seeking poles of compasses.

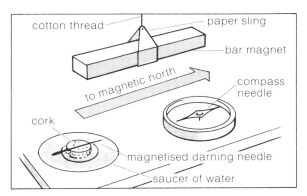

Fig. 73.1   The three magnets all point in the same direction.

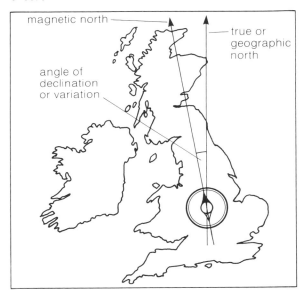

Fig. 73.2   A compass needle sets along a line joining magnetic south and north poles.

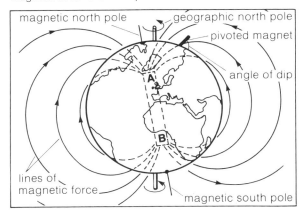

Fig. 73.3   The earth's magnetic field spreads out from points well inside the earth.

74 How are magnets used?

For several hundred years **magnetic compasses** have helped travellers find their way. A ship's compass is usually hung on rings and pivots, or **gimbals**. These keep it level when the ship rolls. The magnet is often fixed to a disc with directions (north, north east, east and so on) written on it. The disc and magnet move in a bowl of liquid, which helps stop the disc from wobbling (Fig. 74.1). In simpler compasses a magnet on a pivot swings over a card with the directions marked on it. Most aircraft and larger ships now have a gyro-compass as their main compass. This does not use magnetism.

Fig. 74.1 This mariner's compass is mounted so it can swing freely. Why?

MAGNETS PICK THINGS UP

You have probably seen a magnet used to pick up spilled pins. Sometimes pins picked up this way become permanent magnets, and it is hard to pick out just one from the pin box. A magnet also picks up drawing pins, which seems odd because brass (an alloy of copper and zinc) is non-magnetic. But the brass is only a coating on top of steel. It is the steel that the magnet attracts.

Small pieces of steel worn or broken from a car or motor-bike engine could harm the engine if they were pumped round with the oil. Putting a magnet into the oil drain plug collects these bits and prevents them from harming the engine. Electromagnets (p. 170) are also used for picking up things made of magnetic materials.

MAGNETS HOLD THINGS

Magnets can hold things made of magnetic materials in place. Magnetic tool racks hold steel tools and kitchen implements. A magnetic notice board is made of sheet steel; the plastic letters and figures contain a magnetic powder and stay in place when put on the board. A magnetic door catch has a strong ceramic magnet with an iron pole piece. The catch, screwed to the frame, attracts iron plates on the edge of the door. This attraction holds the door shut (Fig. 74.2). The magnetic refrigerator door sealing strip has a magnetic material in a rubber case (Fig. 74.3). When the door is shut the strip attracts the steel of the door seating. The seal stops cold air from leaking out of the refrigerator and the refrigerator is more efficient.

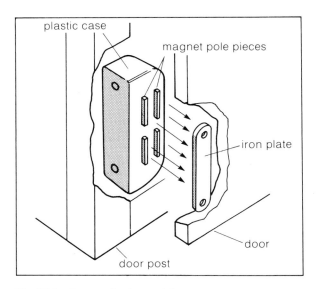

Fig. 74.2 A magnetic door catch.

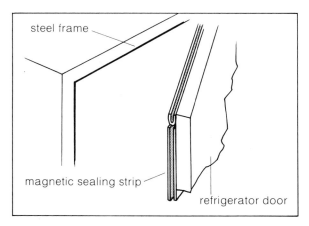

Fig. 74.3 Flexible magnetic strips are used to seal the door of a refrigerator.

MAGNETIC TOYS AND GAMES

Young children often play with magnetic fishing games. A magnet, hung from a string on a stick, hooks cardboard fish with steel staples through them. The aim of the fighting dog game is to get one plastic dog to sneak up on another from behind. This is impossible! The dogs contain magnets, and one always twists round as you bring up the other. One dog's nose has a north pole in it, the other a south pole. These attract and the dogs appear to rush at each other and fight. Travelling chess sets have plastic chess men with a magnet inside which holds them in position on a painted steel board.

MAGNETS MOVE THINGS

Some maximum and minimum thermometers have a steel index. This is reset ready to take a new reading by pulling it along the bore with a magnet (p. 69).

In a reed switch the reed is a springy piece of steel inside a glass case. The reed of the normally-open type does not touch the contact unless a magnet pulls it on to this contact (p. 212). Figure 74.4 shows a reed switch worked by a magnet on a sliding door. When the sliding door is shut, the magnet pulls the reed and closes the switch. This completes the circuit and lights the lamp.

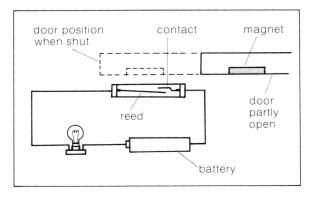

Fig. 74.4 How does this arrangement with a reed switch work?

OTHER USES

You may find permanent magnets in loudspeakers, ammeters and voltmeters, bicycle dynamos, some switches, small electric motors and so on. Moving magnets are used to generate electricity. Changing magnetic fields are used when sounds and pictures are recorded using tape and video recorders.

SUMMARY: MAGNETISM

- Iron, steel, cobalt, nickel and many of their alloys are magnetic materials.
- Like poles—N and N—repel each other.
- Unlike poles—N and S—attract each other.
- A magnetic material becomes an induced magnet when put near a permanent magnet.
- Permanent magnets are made of magnetically hard materials (like steel), which are hard to magnetise but keep their magnetism well.
- Permanent magnets are usually made by putting a magnetic material in a coil carrying a direct (one-way) current.
- A magnetic domain is a group of atomic magnets all pointing the same way.
- All the domains of a fully magnetised material are magnetised in the same direction.
- Keepers help to keep a magnet strong while it is being stored.
- A magnet can be demagnetised by hammering or dropping, by strong heating, or by putting it in a coil carrying an alternating current which is slowly decreased.
- Magnetic fields are mapped by using a plotting compass to trace the field lines.
- The field of a magnet is three-dimensional.
- The field of two magnets with like poles together contains a neutral point.
- Magnetic declination is the angle between the direction of true or geographical north and the direction of magnetic north.
- The angle which a freely pivoted magnet makes with the horizontal is the angle of dip.

SECTION 17

Electrostatics

75 Electric charges

Comb your hair on a fine, dry day; it tries to follow the comb. Try to wipe the dust off a record with a dry cloth and the dust sticks even harder to the record. A piece of plastic rubbed on your sleeve will pick up small pieces of paper. Walk across a nylon carpet and feel the shock when you touch the door handle. All these are effects of **static** (not moving) electricity. Electrostatics is the study of static electric charges.

POSITIVE AND NEGATIVE CHARGES

Rub a rod of Perspex and a rod of polythene on a woollen cloth. Each will attract small pieces of paper. They have become **charged**. Put a Perspex rod, which has just been rubbed on wool to charge it, through a folded piece of paper hanging on a length of nylon thread. Bring up another charged Perspex rod. The hanging one moves away (Fig. 75.1). It is **repelled**. Change the second Perspex rod for a charged polythene rod. The hanging rod will move towards the polythene one (Fig. 75.2). It is **attracted**. This is one of the basic laws of electrostatics. Charges exert forces on one another. **Like charges repel, unlike charges attract**. There are only two types of charge.

In the space round any electric charge we can detect an electric field. If you place a

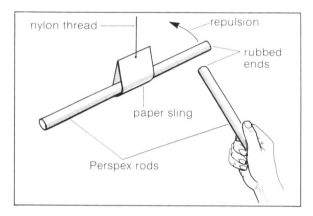

Fig. 75.1   Two similarly charged rods repel one another.

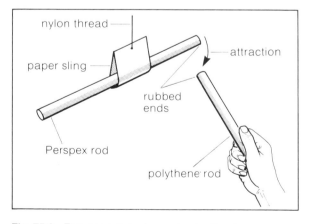

Fig. 75.2   Two oppositely charged rods attract one another.

negative charge in the field of another negative charge, the two charges repel one another. If you place a positive charge in the same field the two charges will attract one another. The electric field in the space round a charge, like the magnetic field round the pole of a magnet or even the gravitational field round the earth, gets weaker the further you go away.

CHARGES AND CURRENTS

Look at the experiment with the shuttling ball. This is a table tennis ball that has been coated to make it conduct electricity. The ball is held by a nylon thread between two insulated metal plates. These plates are connected to a power supply giving a few thousand volts. A sensitive ammeter is included in the circuit (Fig. 75.3).

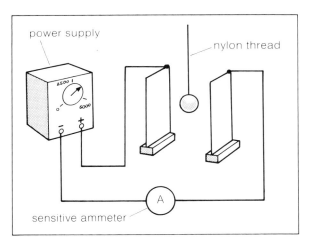

Fig. 75.3 In the shuttling-ball experiment, the ball carries the current between the plates.

When the power supply is switched on, the ball shuttles backwards and forwards between the two plates carrying negative charges one way and positive charges the other. The sensitive ammeter shows a small current. This is because when electric charges move, a small electric current flows.

CONDUCTORS AND INSULATORS

Materials that will allow electric charges to flow through them are electrical **conductors**. Materials that will not allow electric charges to flow through them are electrical **insulators** (Fig. 75.4). Metals, some forms of carbon and some liquids are good conductors. Plastics, rubber, dry air, etc., are examples of insulators.

Scientists believe that metals conduct electricity because the atoms of the metal contain electrons (p. 187), which are negative charges so weakly attached to them that the electrons are free to move around inside the metal itself. The tiny force of attraction from a nearby positive charge or of repulsion by a nearby negative charge can move these free or **conduction electrons** through the metal conductor very easily indeed. On the other hand, there are very, very few free electrons like this in an insulator.

76 Charging

CHARGING BY FRICTION

Have you ever heard a crackling sound when you undress? Try undressing in the dark; you will see sparks. Your clothes have been rubbing on each other and become electrically charged. When two objects rub together there is friction (p. 33). This causes electric charges to separate: one object becomes positively charged; the other becomes negatively charged. Friction produces equal and opposite charges.

When you comb your hair the comb becomes negatively charged. Your hair is positively charged.

You can become charged by walking about on a nylon carpet in plastic-soled shoes. Friction causes this charge. If you then touch a metal tap or door knob you will get a shock.

The outer skin of an aeroplane can be strongly charged by friction with the air. It has to be discharged, e.g., by contact with the ground, before anyone can touch the plane in safety.

CHARGING BY INDUCTION

Suppose you have a metal object—a conductor—mounted on a Perspex stand—an insulator. Electrons can move within the conducting metal but they cannot escape from it through the insulating Perspex. Bring a negatively charged rod near the conductor. Electrons move away because like charges repel (Fig. 76.1(a)). Now touch the conductor for a moment. The electrons can get even further away than the far end of the conductor by flowing to earth through you (Fig. 76.1(b)). This leaves an unbalanced positive charge on the conductor. Now take away the original charged rod. The positive charge spreads out over the conductor (Fig. 76.1(c)). It has been charged by **induction**. Note that the sign of charge on the conductor is the opposite to that on the charged rod.

You can explain the attraction of, say, uncharged pieces of paper to a charged rod using the idea of the separation of charges.

Rub a balloon on your clothes and stick the balloon to the ceiling. The rubbing charges the balloon by friction. It stays on the ceiling

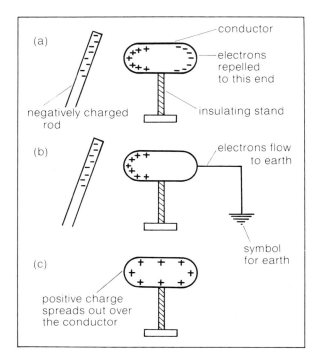

Fig. 76.1 How to charge a conductor by induction.

because it induces an opposite charge on the ceiling. This attracts the charge on the balloon and holds it there.

CHARGING BY CONTACT

A charged conductor will share its charge with another conductor when they touch. This will not happen to insulators because they do not allow charge to flow.

When a neutral conductor touches the charged one, some of the charge moves on to it. Both conductors then have a similar charge.

THE VAN DE GRAAFF GENERATOR

This electrostatic machine produces very energetic charges (Fig. 76.2). The lower set of points spray charge on to the belt. The motor moves the belt and the charge is carried along with it. The upper points draw the charge off the belt and it spreads out on the dome. The machine acts continuously, and so the charge builds up.

Big generators can produce large charges with high voltages. They are used in research (Fig. 76.3).

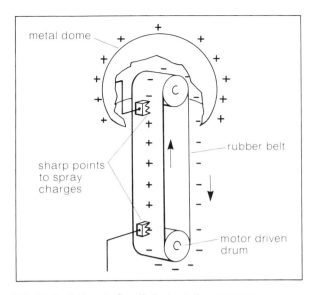

Fig. 76.2 A Van de Graaff electrostatic generator.

Fig. 76.3 This large Van de Graaff generator works in the same way as the one in Fig. 76.2.

THE LIGHTNING CONDUCTOR

Thunder clouds have a very large and energetic electric charge. This is discharged to the earth by lightning. The discharge is powerful enough to do a lot of damage to buildings. To prevent this, buildings are fitted with lightning conductors.

The lightning conductor discharges the cloud slowly so that the lightning is less likely to strike (Fig. 76.4). As the negatively charged cloud passes over, a positive charge is induced on the ground beneath it and on the points of the conductor. The charge on these points is so strong that electrons (p. 187) are stripped away from many nearby air molecules. This is called **ionisation**. The **positive ions** left in the air are pulled upwards by the negative charge on the cloud. So the charge is slowly neutralised. The electrons travel down the lightning conductor to the ground to neutralise its positive charge.

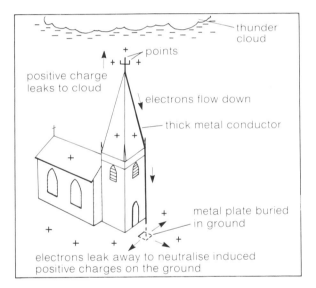

Fig. 76.4 How does the lightning conductor protect this church from damage?

SUMMARY: ELECTROSTATICS

- There are two sorts of electric charge—positive and negative.
- Normally, all the things we use have equal numbers of positive and negative charges. They are neutral.
- Charges exert forces on one another: like charges repel; unlike charges attract.
- Insulators such as Perspex or nylon can easily be charged by friction.
- Insulators hold their charges well because they don't allow charge to flow.
- Conductors such as metals allow charge to flow easily.
- Conductors can be charged by induction or by contact.

Electric Circuits and Measurement

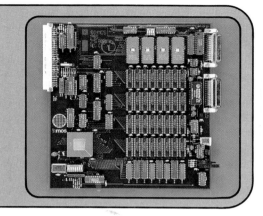

77 Electricity from chemicals

If a piece of silver paper touches one of your tooth fillings it hurts. This is because an electric shock passes to the nerve of your tooth. It is an example of electric charges being produced by chemical action. The effect was first put to use by Volta. He made the first electric cell by using a zinc and a copper plate separated by a piece of cloth soaked in brine (salt water). You can copy his experiment by using a copper and a silver coin with some brine between them. Test your cell with a **galvanometer**—a sensitive detector of electric current.

In the cell a chemical reaction separates positive charge from negative charge—chemical energy changes to electrical energy. In Volta's cell the zinc plate becomes negatively charged and the copper one positively charged. The plates are known as **electrodes** and the brine is an **electrolyte**.

THE SIMPLE CELL

This uses copper and zinc electrodes. The electrolyte is dilute sulphuric acid (Fig. 77.1). The chemical action of the acid on the metals takes negative charge from the copper electrode and puts it on the zinc one. This cell is not a very good one. It has two main defects.

1   Hydrogen gas is formed by the action of the acid on the zinc. This collects on the copper electrode and blocks the working of the cell. The cell is then unable to drive a current.

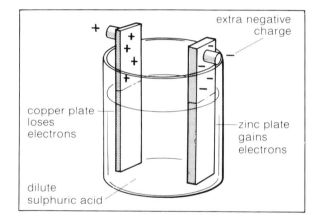

Fig. 77.1   A simple cell will drive a current, but not for long.

2   There are small pieces of other metals in the zinc. They form very small cells which dissolve the zinc even when the main cell is not in use. This is called **local action**.

These defects prevent the simple cell from providing a useful electric current for more than a few seconds.

THE DRY CELL

This is the cell used in cycle lamps, torches, portable radios, etc. (Fig. 77.2). The positive electrode is made of carbon. This is cheaper than copper, and it gives a bigger voltage, or more energetic charge. The electrolyte is a paste of ammonium chloride. This does not react with the negative zinc electrode when the cell is not in use. Around the carbon electrode is a **depolariser** (manganese(IV) oxide). This combines with the hydrogen and stops it collecting on the carbon rod. Some carbon powder is mixed with the manganese(IV) oxide to make it a better conductor. The dry cell is a **primary cell**. When the chemicals have been used up it is of no more use—you throw it away and buy a new one. A new cell provides 1.5 volts (p. 150). You may hear dry cells called **Leclanché cells**, after the man who first invented them.

THE LEAD-ACID ACCUMULATOR

This is called a **secondary cell** because it can be recharged and used over and over again (Fig. 77.3). The electrolyte is dilute sulphuric acid. Both electrodes are lead grids with an active paste pressed into them. A paste of lead(IV) oxide is used in the positive electrode. The negative electrode uses a paste made of small grains of lead.

The accumulator supplies 2 volts and can produce a large current. When in use it **discharges**. Both the active pastes take up sulphate ions and change to lead sulphate, and the acid becomes more dilute. You can **recharge** an accumulator using a battery charger (Fig. 77.4). You use it to pass a small, steady, direct current (p. 179) back through the accumulator to restore the sulphuric acid by breaking down the lead sulphate. With care you can use a lead-acid cell for a very long time. You must make sure that the acid level is above the active part of the plates. This means you must top up the cell with distilled (pure) water from time to time.

BATTERIES

A **battery** is a number of cells connected together. This gives a higher voltage. A very common form of battery is the 9-volt dry battery. This is used in some portable transistor radios. It has six small dry cells inside it.

Another common battery is the car battery. This contains six lead-acid cells. It provides 12 volts and can give very large currents. About 100 amperes (p. 149) flow through the battery for a very short time and this turns the starter motor. It is kept charged by the dynamo or alternator when the engine is working.

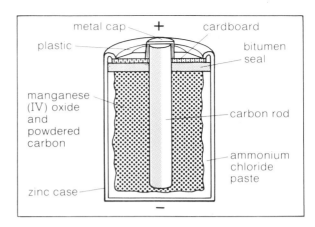

Fig. 77.2 A dry cell as used in a torch.

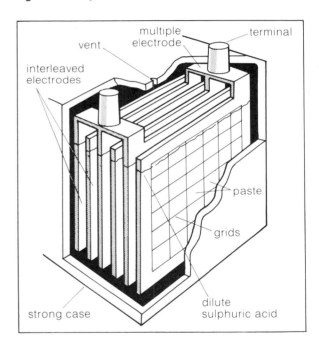

Fig. 77.3 A lead–acid accumulator.

Fig. 77.4 Recharging a car battery.

78 Circuits

Electric circuits are very important. You have many of them at home. They are essential for the working of all kinds of machines, trains, cars, aircraft and so on. Wherever you need to use electrical energy there will be a circuit.

An electric circuit has three essential parts:

1　Something to drive the electric charge round the circuit, e.g., a cell;
2　Something on which the moving charge can do a useful job, e.g., a lamp;
3　Conductors to join them together, e.g., copper wires.

The electric charge can only move when the circuit is complete.

WHY DOES CHARGE MOVE IN AN ELECTRIC CIRCUIT?

Take a cell. It has a positive charge on the positive electrode and a negative charge on the negative electrode. No chemical action is taking place. Connect the electrodes by metal wires to a switch and a lamp (Fig. 78.1). The switch is off. There are lots of free electrons in the connecting wires all ready to move. As soon as you close the switch:

1　Free electrons move away from the negative electrode because like charges repel;
2　Chemical action starts in the cell to replace the electrons that have moved off the negative electrode—chemical energy is converted to electrical energy;
3　The free electrons moving through the lamp filament make it hot—it glows and gives out light;
4　Electrical energy is converted to thermal energy and light in the filament;
5　Free electrons arrive at the positive electrode of the cell and are given more energy as they move across to the negative electrode;
6　And so on.

Charges flow in a complete circuit because like charges repel. The rate of flow of electric charge is called an **electric current**. The direction of flow of conventional current is from the positive electrode of the cell to the negative electrode.

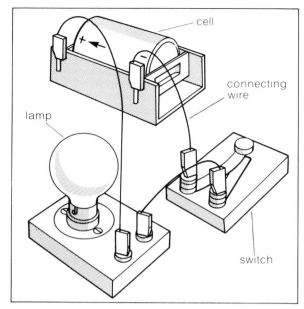

Fig. 78.1 Lighting a lamp.

CONDUCTORS AND INSULATORS

Conductors let the current flow round the circuit. Copper wire is the most common conductor, e.g., in household wiring. Carbon is sometimes used, e.g., in batteries and as brushes in electric motors. Some micro-switches are coated with gold for better contact.

You will not find many electric circuits with bare wires. The wires are insulated with a layer of rubber or plastic. This is for safety, to protect you from electric shock. It is also to stop the wires touching each other and causing a **short circuit** (p. 152). When this happens the current by-passes part of the circuit and may cause overheating and a fire.

A switch usually has a plastic base and cover. The conducting parts are inside; they are made of copper or brass. There is a moving part that joins the contacts when the switch is on. When the switch is off there is an air gap (insulator) in the circuit. This means that the circuit is not complete, so no current can flow.

CIRCUIT DIAGRAMS

When you plan or draw a circuit it is best to use symbols (Fig. 78.2). Other people can then recognise them. The symbols also save you the trouble of drawing the real things. The same circuit is shown in Figs 78.1 and 78.3. The diagram with symbols is easier to draw.

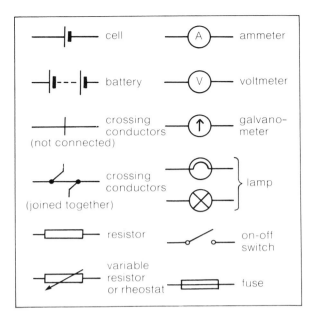

Fig. 78.2 Some circuit symbols.

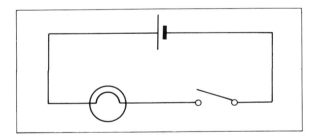

Fig. 78.3 Lighting a lamp.

SWITCHING CIRCUITS

Some simple circuits with batteries, lamps and switches are shown in Fig. 78.4.

Try the simplest—in (a). The switch can turn the lamp on and off. This is just like an electric torch circuit.

Now try (b) where there are two switches in the same circuit. This is called **series** connection. The lamp will only light when both switches are on. This is not the normal method of connecting switches. But it is useful where a safety switch is needed, e.g., in a school workshop. The teacher's master-switch must be on before you can switch on a machine.

Connect two switches in **parallel** as in (c). Each one is in its own circuit with the battery and lamp. The lamp can be switched on at either switch, but if one is on the other cannot turn it off. This method of connection is used when you have a doorbell, which can be rung from push-switches (p. 211) on both the front door or the back door.

In (d), a pair of **two-way** switches is shown. Switch S_1 joins X to either A or C. The circuit can be completed through wire AB or through CD. The diagram shows the circuit with the lamp on. If S_1 is moved so that X is joined to C, the lamp is off. The lamp could also have been turned off by changing S_2 instead of S_1, so that Y is joined to D. Draw a diagram to show this. Then moving either of the switches puts the lamp on again. This is useful for a light on the stairs. You can switch the light on or off from either switch, one at the bottom and one at the top of the stairs.

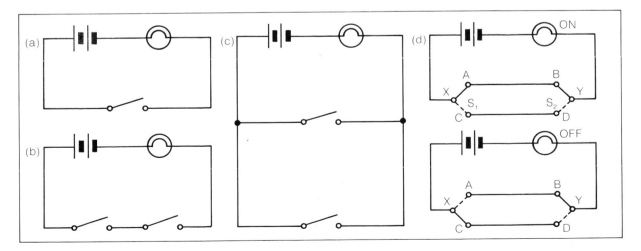

Fig. 78.4 Some simple circuits.

79 Series and parallel circuits

SERIES CIRCUITS

A series circuit has only one path for the current. The same current flows through everything in the circuit. In the simple series circuit in Fig. 79.1, close the switch—both lamps light. A break anywhere in the circuit will stop the current flowing. Take out one of the lamps—the other goes out. If one of the lamps breaks, both lamps go out. This is why series connection of lamps is not a good idea—one out, all out.

You may have a set of Christmas tree lights that are in series. If they go out it is not easy to find the faulty one.

To get a higher voltage (p. 150) join the cells in series. Connect the positive side of one cell to the negative side of the next. The circuit shown in Fig. 79.2 will not work because the two cells have been joined so that they push against each other—they will cancel out.

PARALLEL CIRCUITS

Sometimes there is more than one path for the current. This is called a **branched** circuit. Parts of the circuit are in **parallel**. Figure 79.3 shows a simple branched or parallel circuit. When the switch is closed both lamps come on. The lamps are in parallel. Each lamp has its own branch of the circuit. The current from the battery divides at point C. Each lamp has a share of the current. These shares join together again at Y and flow back to the battery. If you take out one of the lamps the other one stays on. If one lamp breaks, the other is not affected. Most lighting circuits are in parallel, and so you can find which lamp is faulty when one breaks.

If you use two lamps and three switches (Fig. 79.4) you can make a circuit in which each lamp is controlled by its own switch. The third switch is a master-switch. It controls the whole circuit. Neither lamp can be switched on unless the master-switch is on. In everyday life, circuits are not so simple as these.

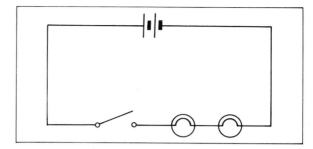

Fig. 79.1 What happens when one of the lamps is taken out from this simple series circuit?

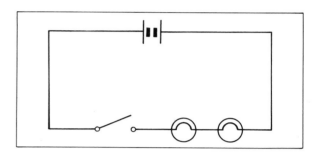

Fig. 79.2 Why doesn't this circuit work when you switch on?

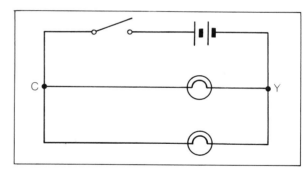

Fig. 79.3 What happens when one of the lamps is taken out of this simple parallel circuit?

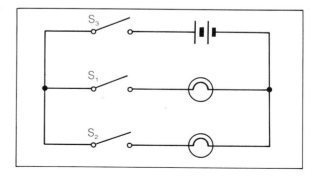

Fig. 79.4 What does each switch do?

80 Measuring electricity

Electrical measurements are very important. Electricity boards use meters to measure how much electrical energy has been supplied. Meters can also be used to find a fault in an electronic circuit. The instrument panel of some cars also has a meter to show when the battery is being charged.

MEASURING CURRENT

An electric current is a flow of electric charge (p. 146). In copper and other wires the moving charges are the free electrons. In a lightning flash they are **ions**, or charged atoms. In a cell or a battery positive ions go one way and negative ions go the other.

You cannot see a current but you know it is there by what it does. It may light a lamp, drive a vacuum cleaner, run a freezer, start a car or many other things.

You can measure current, that is the rate of flow of charge, with an **ammeter**. Just as you might say that the current of water down a river was so many cubic metres per hour, so you say that a current of electricity was so much charge per second. The unit of current is called the **ampere (A)**.

An ammeter is connected in the circuit so that the current flows through it. The red terminal on the ammeter should be joined to the positive side of the battery or supply unit. The pointer will show on the scale how many amperes are flowing.

CURRENT ROUND A CIRCUIT

Set up the series circuit shown in Fig. 80.1. All the ammeters show the same reading. The current is the same all the way round the series circuit; it is not used up. Therefore, you can put an ammeter anywhere in such a series circuit to measure the current.

Next set up the circuit shown in Fig. 80.2. Ammeter A_1 measures the current supplied by the battery. Ammeter A_2 measures the current through lamps L_1 and ammeter A_3 measures the current through lamps L_2.

What is the connection between the three currents? The current in ammeter A_1 is equal to the current in ammeter A_2 plus that in ammeter A_3.

What is the reading of ammeter A_4? When an electric current splits into two parts *no* current is lost. This is a very important result.

ENERGY AND ELECTRICITY

You pay for energy by paying your electricity

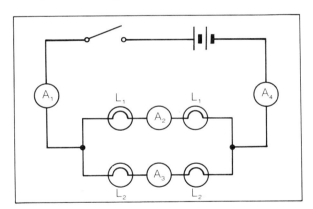

Fig. 80.2 Currents in a parallel circuit.

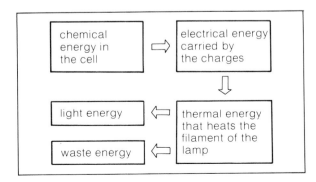

Fig. 80.3

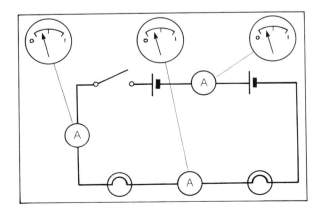

Fig. 80.1 Currents in a series circuit.

bill. Electricity boards sell energy in packets of 3 600 000 J (p. 165). We shall see why this number is chosen later. The cell you used in lighting the lamp (Fig. 79.1 on p. 148) gave the lamp the energy it needed to give light. The energy conversions are shown in Fig. 80.3.

The energy of the electric charges which light the lamp as they flow round the circuit is given by the **voltage** of the cell. The voltage is measured in **volts** (**V**). Some examples of voltage are listed below.

1 Charges from a 1.5-V dry cell are not very energetic.
2 Charges from 240-V mains electricity are quite energetic.
3 Charges from a 132 000-V overhead cable are very energetic.
4 Charges from a 10 million-V Van de Graaff generator are extremely energetic.
5 In a lightning flash the voltage might be as high as 100 million V!

The higher the voltage, the more energetic the charge. It's the volts that bite! Another name for voltage is **potential difference (p.d.)**.

MEASURING POTENTIAL DIFFERENCE

The potential difference of a battery or supply unit is measured with a **voltmeter**. This is connected across the battery. The red terminal of the voltmeter is joined to the positive side of the battery. Voltmeters and ammeters can look very much the same, so take care not to get them mixed up. They measure different things and are joined to a circuit in different ways (Fig. 80.4).

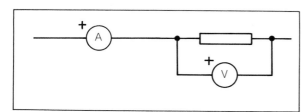

Fig. 80.4 How ammeters and voltmeters are used in circuits. Ammeters are always in series, but voltmeters are in parallel.

POTENTIAL DIFFERENCE ROUND A CIRCUIT

In Fig. 80.5 the voltmeters are measuring the potential differences of a series circuit. Voltmeter V_1 shows the p.d. across the battery. It will work whether the switch is open or closed. When the switch is closed the lamps will light. Voltmeter V_2 shows the p.d. across lamp L_1. Voltmeter V_3 shows the p.d. across lamp L_2. This will only be the same as the p.d. across lamp L_1 if the lamps are identical.

What do you notice about the voltage shown on the three voltmeters? The p.d. shown on voltmeter V_1 is equal to the p.d. shown on voltmeter V_2 plus the p.d. shown on voltmeter V_3. So the energy supplied by the battery is shared between the two lamps.

In Fig. 80.6 the voltmeter will show the p.d. across lamp L_1. It also shows the p.d. across L_2. They are both the same. Items joined in parallel have the same p.d. across them. The voltmeter also shows the p.d. across the battery.

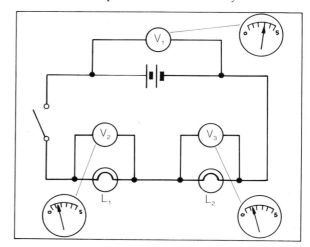

Fig. 80.5 Potential differences in a series circuit.

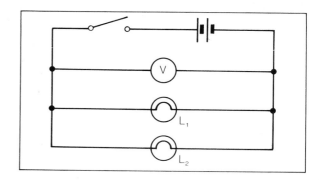

Fig. 80.6 Potential differences in a parallel circuit.

81 Resistance

There are different sorts of conductors in every circuit. Connecting wires are usually made of copper. Other components may be made of different metals, e.g., the filament of a lamp is made of tungsten. The same current flows through the copper wire and the tungsten filament in a series circuit. But the tungsten has a high **resistance**; that is, it resists the flow of current. This means that a lot of energy is changed to heat as the current flows through the tungsten.

All metals have some resistance. Those with low resistance, e.g., gold, silver, copper and aluminium, are used for connectors. They are made thick enough so they don't get hot when a current flows. Metals with a high resistance are used in all kinds of heaters, e.g., nichrome (an alloy of nickel and chromium) is used in the coils of an electric fire. Other materials such as carbon are used in the resistors used in electronic apparatus—radio and TV sets for example.

RESISTANCES IN CIRCUITS

In circuit (a) of Fig. 81.1 most of the resistance is in the lamp. Circuit (b) has another lamp and, therefore, has extra resistance. So the current is smaller and the lamps are dimmer. The lamps can be made bright again by adding another cell to the circuit. In circuit (c) the lamps are as bright as the lamp in circuit (a). The extra cell gives the extra energy needed.

You can control the current in a circuit by using a **variable resistor**, or **rheostat**. In one sort of rheostat you change the length of resistance wire connected in the circuit (Fig. 81.2). The wire is wound on a tube. When the rheostat is joined to the circuit at terminals A and B, the current flows through the wire between A and the sliding contact C. Then it flows through the rod from C to B. Moving C towards B increases the length of resistance wire in the circuit—the current gets smaller. You can make the current bigger by moving the slider towards A. Rheostats can also have a circular shape (see Fig. 112.3 on p. 209). Rheostats are used as volume controls on radios, tape-recorders and TVs.

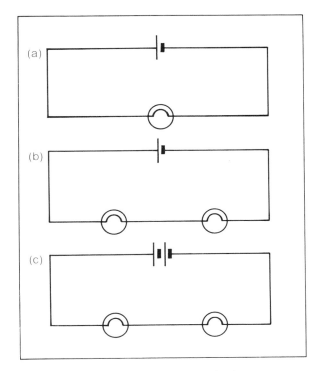

Fig. 81.1 The brightness of lamps in a circuit.

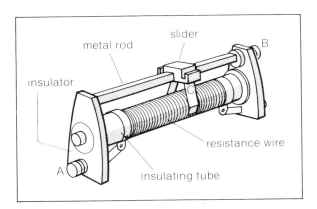

Fig. 81.2 A variable resistor or rheostat.

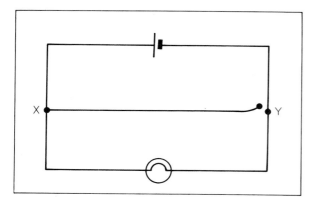

Fig. 81.3 A short circuit. When X and Y are joined the current in XY (with small resistance) is large. The lamp goes out.

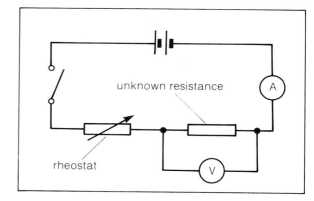

Fig. 81.4 How to measure a resistance.

SHORT CIRCUITS

If you join X to Y (Fig. 81.3) with a short length of copper wire the lamp will go out. And the cell will last for a very short time! This is because the copper wire has very little resistance. The cell has to provide a large current and most of the energy is wasted. The lamp has been by-passed. This is called a **short circuit**.

Short circuits can occur in older mains wiring where rubber insulation has been used. As the rubber perishes, the wires may touch and make a short circuit. The wires may then get hot enough to start a fire.

Short circuits can also take place through the human body. If the mains wire were drilled into accidentally, the drill operator could form part of the short circuit. This is very dangerous. Always switch the mains supply off at the switchboard near the meter before working with or near the mains cables.

MEASURING RESISTANCE

The current flowing in a circuit depends on the potential difference and the resistance of the circuit. It is often important to measure the resistance of a circuit or part of a circuit. If you measure the current and the voltage then the resistance can be found by using the formula:

$$\text{resistance} = \frac{\text{voltage}}{\text{current}} \quad \text{or} \quad R = \frac{V}{I}$$

where R is the resistance, V is the potential difference and I is the current. Potential difference is measured in volts (V), current in amperes (A) and resistance in ohms (Ω).

The circuit in Fig. 81.4 shows a way of measuring resistance. It is an important circuit. It can be used to do many jobs as well. You should practise setting up this circuit so that you don't forget it. You measure current and voltage and use the formula above to calculate resistance.

Example Calculate the resistance of the element of an electric fire. The current is 5 A and the voltage is 240 V.

$$R = \frac{V}{I} = \frac{240 \text{ V}}{5 \text{ A}} = 48 \ \Omega$$

So the resistance is 48 Ω.

Example How much current would flow in the cigarette lighter of a car if the lighter has a resistance of 4 Ω? (A car battery provides 12 V.)

$$R = \frac{V}{I} \quad \text{or} \quad I = \frac{V}{R} = \frac{12 \text{ V}}{4 \ \Omega} = 3 \text{ A}$$

Therefore the current is 3 A.

Example A lamp has a resistance of 960 Ω. The current flowing is 0.25 A. What is the potential difference?

$$R = \frac{V}{I} \quad \text{or} \quad V = IR = 0.25 \text{ A} \times 960 \ \Omega = 240 \text{ V}$$

So the potential difference is 240 V.

RESISTORS IN SERIES

Lengths of wire with resistance are called **resistors**. Figure 81.5(a) shows three resistors

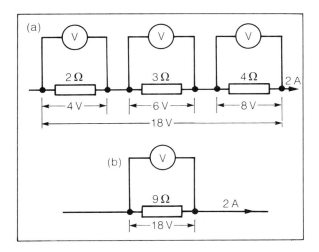

Fig. 81.5 Resistors in series.

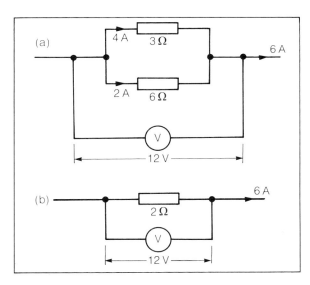

Fig. 81.6 Resistors in parallel.

in series. A current of 2 A flows through each of them. The potential difference across the first resistor is 4 V (2 A × 2 Ω). The potential differences across the other two are 6 V and 8 V. The total voltage is therefore 4 V + 6 V + 8 V = 18 V.

Figure 81.5(b) shows one resistor of resistance 9 Ω. With 2 A flowing through it the voltage across it is 18 V. You could put this one resistor in place of the other three and it would have the same effect.

Suppose we have three resistors of values R_1, R_2 and R_3 in series. If one resistor of value R is to be used to replace the three then

$$R = R_1 + R_2 + R_3$$

This equation tells us the total resistance of resistors joined in series. To find the resistance of resistors in series, add up the separate resistances.

Example Calculate the total resistance of two 6-Ω resistors and one 10-Ω resistor joined in series.

$$\begin{aligned} R &= R_1 + R_2 + R_3 \\ &= 6\,\Omega + 6\,\Omega + 10\,\Omega = 22\,\Omega \end{aligned}$$

Therefore the total resistance is 22 Ω.

RESISTORS IN PARALLEL

Resistances in parallel do not add up like those in series. This is because there is a different current in each resistor. Most current flows through the smallest resistance.

In Fig. 81.6(a) two resistors are joined in parallel. The voltage across each of them is 12 V. The current in the 3-Ω resistor is 4 A (12 V/3 Ω). In the 6-Ω resistor there is a current of 2 A. The total current is therefore 4 A + 2 A = 6 A.

In Fig. 81.6(b) one resistor carries a current of 6 A with a voltage of 12 V. Its resistance can be calculated:

$$R = \frac{V}{I} = \frac{12\,\text{V}}{6\,\text{A}} = 2\,\Omega$$

This is less than either of the two resistors. When resistors are connected in parallel, the total resistance is less than the resistance of the smallest one.

Suppose we have two resistors of values R_1 and R_2 joined in parallel. If one resistor of value R is to be used to replace the two then

$$\frac{1}{R} = \frac{1}{R_1} + \frac{1}{R_2}$$

This equation shows the total resistance of resistors joined in parallel. It can be used to check the result for the 3- and 6-Ω resistors in parallel.

$$\frac{1}{R} = \frac{1}{3\,\Omega} + \frac{1}{6\,\Omega} = \frac{2+1}{6\,\Omega} = \frac{3}{6\,\Omega}$$

$$R = \frac{6}{3}\,\Omega = 2\,\Omega$$

82 Is the resistance of a piece of wire a constant?

You can use the circuit in Fig. 82.1 to find the answer to this question.

1 Connect the wire into the circuit as the unknown resistance.
2 Alter the rheostat to change the current flowing.
3 Record pairs of values of the current through the wire and the potential difference (voltage) across it.
4 Work out the resistance each time using $R = V/I$. Here is a set of readings for a metre of wire:

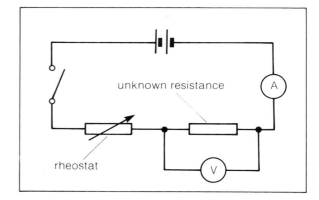

Fig. 82.1

Voltmeter reading (V)	0	3	6	9	12
Ammeter reading (A)	0	0.25	0.5	0.75	1
Resistance (Ω)		12	12	12	12

The resistance of the wire didn't change during the experiment.

This is true of all metal wires if you take care not to let them get warm. So long as the temperature of the wire stays constant, the resistance of the wire is constant. This is called **Ohm's law**.

To put it another way, the current flowing in a metal wire at constant temperature is directly proportional to the potential difference across the wire. The current goes as the potential difference. If you plot a graph of the current against the voltage you will get a straight line (Fig. 82.2).

You will get a different result if you let the wire get hot. Try using a small lamp instead of the special wire. The graph this time will be curved rather than a straight line (Fig. 82.3). The resistance of the lamp will increase as the filament gets hotter.

Only metals kept at a fixed temperature follow Ohm's law. Designers of electric circuits use many items or components that do not follow this law. Rectifiers, transistors, thermistors and many others are examples. So are electrolytes, the solutions that carry an electric current.

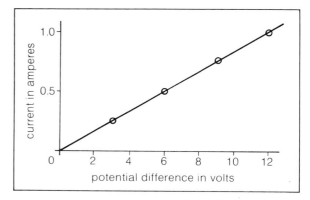

Fig. 82.2 A graph of current against potential difference for a wire at constant temperature. The wire follows Ohm's law.

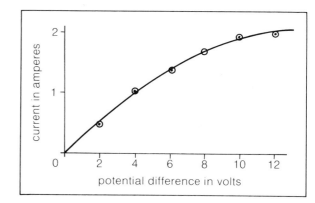

Fig. 82.3 A graph of current against potential difference for the filament of a lamp. As the filament gets warm its resistance increases.

Table 82 Electrical units

Current is measured in amperes (A)
Potential difference is measured in volts (V)
Resistance is measured in ohms (Ω)

If a potential difference of 1 volt makes a current of 1 ampere flow through a resistor, the resistor has a resistance of 1 ohm.

SUMMARY: ELECTRIC CIRCUITS AND MEASUREMENT

- In a cell chemical energy is changed to electrical energy and given to the electric charges.
- A cell has a positive and a negative electrode separated by an electrolyte.
- A dry cell has to be thrown away when it is used up. It cannot be recharged.
- A secondary cell—a lead-acid accumulator—can be recharged again and again.
- A battery is made of several cells joined together, positive to negative.
- A circuit connects a source of electrical energy—a cell—with something on which a useful job is done—a lamp—with connecting wires.
- A circuit must be complete if a current is to flow.
- A conductor allows electric charge to flow through it.
- An insulator does not allow electric charge to flow.
- A series circuit has only one path for the current. The current is the same all the way round.
- A parallel circuit has more than one path for the current. The current is different at different points.
- When an electric current divides no current is lost.
- A current is the rate of flow of electric charge. It carries energy from the source—the cell—round the circuit.

- Currents are measured with ammeters in units called amperes (A).
- An ammeter is connected so that the current it is measuring flows through it.
- Potential difference is the formal name for voltage. It is measured in volts (V).
- A voltmeter is connected across the potential difference it is measuring.
- The voltages in a series circuit add up to the total battery voltage.
- The voltage across components connected in parallel is the same.
- The resistance of a conductor is given by the equation $R = V/I$. This equation can be rearranged to give $V = IR$ and $I = V/R$.
- Resistance is measured in ohms (Ω).
- The total resistance of resistors joined in series is found by adding up all the separate resistances:

$$R_{total} = R_1 + R_2 + R_3$$

- The total resistance of resistors connected in parallel is less than that of any one of the resistors:

$$\frac{1}{R_{total}} = \frac{1}{R_1} + \frac{1}{R_2}$$

- Ohm's law states that the current flowing through a metallic conductor at constant temperature is directly proportional to the voltage across it: V/I = constant.

SECTION 19

Using Electricity

83 Some effects of an electric current

An electric current has three effects. It can cause heating, magnetic and chemical effects. These effects are used everyday by almost everyone.

HEATING EFFECTS

You have already seen that a resistance warms up when a current passes through it. This is because the supply has to do work (supply energy) as it pushes the current through the resistance. This effect is very useful in, say, an electric heater or cooker. It can also be a nuisance.

UNWANTED HEATING

When heating is not wanted, you use wires with low resistance; that is, very good conductors. It also helps if the wires are thick. The bigger the current flowing the thicker the wires used, e.g., the wires to a cooker in a house are much thicker than the wires of a lighting circuit.

Overhead aluminium cables supported by pylons carry a very big current. These cables are so thick that they cannot support their own weight. They have to be strengthened with a steel core (Fig. 83.1). And they still get quite warm.

USEFUL ENERGY

At home you may use a lot of heat produced from electricity. Try to add to this list: cooker, kettle, hairdryer, iron, water heater. In each of these objects there is just the right length of wire of high resistance to provide the energy you need. The resistance wire is sometimes wound in a coil, e.g., an electric fire. In other cases you can't see it, e.g., inside the heater of a kettle. The wires used are chosen from metals that will stand up to the temperatures needed, e.g., the wire in an electric fire element gets red-hot, but the wire inside the heater of a kettle remains just above 100 °C

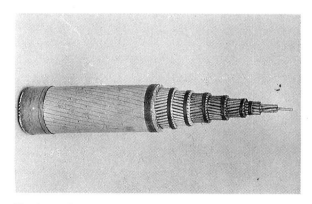

Fig. 83.1   This shows a cable from a 400-kV power line.

MAGNETIC EFFECTS

You may not find it so easy to name objects in your home that use the magnetic effect of a current. This is because it is not as obvious as the heating effect. In fact, anything that uses an electric motor uses magnetism. Electric drills, washing machines, vacuum cleaners, hairdryers and record-players are examples. The magnetic effect is also used in bells, tape and video recorders, telephones and many clocks. Most electrical meters also rely on the magnetic effect of a current. (See pp. 161−3.)

CHEMICAL EFFECTS

Chemical action can produce an electric current (Section 18). The reverse is also true−an electric current can cause chemical action. This process is called **electrolysis**.

An electrolyte is a solution that will allow a current to flow through it. It can do this because it contains ions. An ion is an atom or group of atoms (p. 196) that has gained or lost electrons. An ion is a charged particle: it is negative when electrons are gained and positive when electrons are lost. For example, copper(II) chloride exists as copper(II) ions, Cu^{2+}, which have lost two electrons, and chloride ions, Cl^-, which have gained one electron. There are twice as many chloride ions as copper(II) ions so that the whole solid or solution is neutral. In solution the ions are free to move; they carry the electric current.

ELECTROPLATING

In the circuit for copper plating shown in Fig. 83.2, the copper electrode joined to the negative side of the battery is called the **cathode**. This will attract positive copper ions. When they reach the cathode they gain electrons and become atoms. These atoms settle on the cathode so it becomes plated with pure fresh copper. At the positive side, the **anode**, copper atoms lose electrons and become ions. Thus the number of copper ions remains the same. The anode gradually dissolves away. This circuit can be used to make pure copper or to plate the cathode.

A large industrial electroplating bath is shown in Fig. 83.3. Electroplated nickel silver is marked EPNS. Chromium plating is done in the same way. The electrolyte contains the plating metal. The object to be plated is connected as the cathode.

FARADAY'S LAW OF ELECTROLYSIS

To study electrolysis you can use a circuit like that shown in Fig. 83.2. You will need to know the mass of the cathode before and after you pass a measured current and the time for which you pass the current. The increase in mass of the cathode depends on the current and the time.

Faraday's law of electrolysis states that: The increase in mass is proportional to the product of current and time.

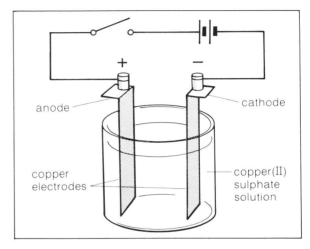

Fig. 83.2 Electroplating copper.

Fig. 83.3 Electroplating on a large scale.

84 Electricity in the home

Electrical energy is very useful. It is so easy to move from one place to another. All you need are cables connected to a **generator**. Then the energy is available at the press of a switch. It does not have to be stored like coal, oil or gas. It is clean and quiet and it can be easily changed into other forms of energy: light, heat, sound and mechanical.

HOUSE CIRCUITS

All house circuits start where the mains cable enters the house (Fig. 84.1). The cable is connected to the electricity meter. Then comes the **consumer unit**. This contains a mains switch with a fuse for each circuit in the house. A **fuse** is a thin piece of wire (Fig. 84.2(a)). Its thickness is chosen so that it melts if more than a certain current passes through it. Nowadays the fuse is often mounted in a small cartridge—a **cartridge fuse** (Fig. 84.2(b)). Each circuit in the house has three wires: **live** (shown brown), **neutral** (shown blue) and **earth** (shown green). The fuse is in the live wire. The mains potential difference is 240 V a.c. (p. 150) between the live and neutral wires. The earth wire is for safety.

 If there is a short circuit (low-resistance path) between the live and one of the other wires a large current flows. The fuse then gets hot and melts. This breaks the circuit and cuts off the current to stop overheating. This prevents fires and other damage to the wiring.

LIGHTING CIRCUITS

Many houses have one lighting circuit for each floor. Each circuit has its own fuse in the consumer unit. These are **rated** at 5 A. This means that the wire inside will melt if more than 5 A flows through it.

 The three-core cable is usually hidden above the ceiling. It is brought through the ceiling and connected to a **ceiling rose**. This has the light fitting attached to it. The wall switch is connected in the live wire (Fig. 84.3).

POWER CIRCUITS

These circuits join the 13-A sockets to the mains supply. There is usually one circuit for each floor of the house. Each circuit has its

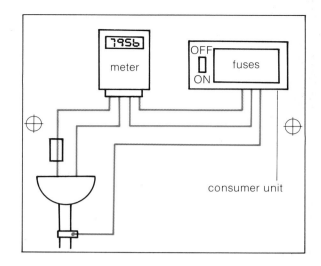

Fig. 84.1 How the electricity supply enters a house.

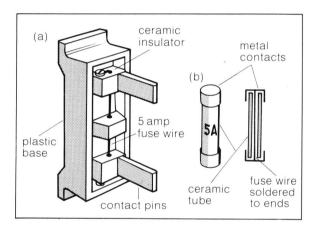

Fig. 84.2 Two sorts of fuse: (a) uses fuse wire and (b) is a cartridge fuse.

own 30-A fuse in the consumer unit. These are similar to the lighting fuses but have slightly different pins so that you cannot put them in the wrong place in the unit. Modern power circuits are joined in parallel as a **ring** (Fig. 84.4).

EARTHING

All appliances used in the home, e.g., kettle, iron, etc., should have a three-core flex (unless they have double insulation). The flex is connected to the plug as shown in Fig. 84.5. Each plug contains its own cartridge fuse (Fig. 84.2(b)). The rating of the fuse is slightly

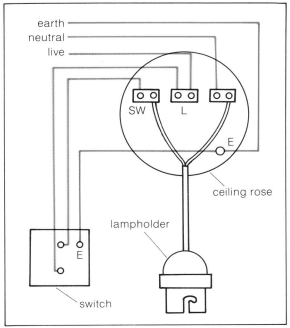

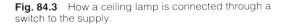

Fig. 84.3 How a ceiling lamp is connected through a switch to the supply.

Fig. 84.5 How a 13 A plug is connected. The earth pin is larger than the other two. It makes contact first and also opens the little shutters that have been closing the mains sockets.

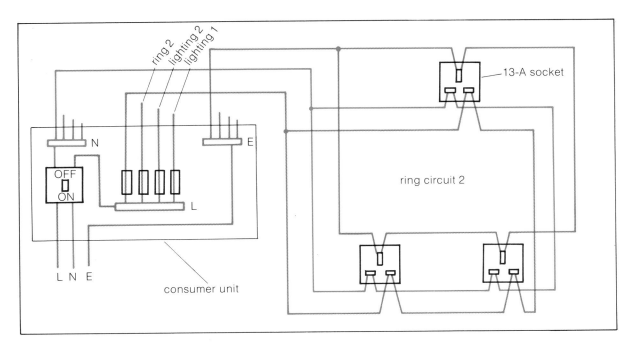

Fig. 84.4 How power supply sockets are connected in a ring circuit.

bigger than the current taken by the appliance (Fig. 84.6). The earth wire is joined to the metal case or outer frame of the appliance. This is called **earthing** the case. The part of the appliance needing the current is connected between the live and neutral wires. If the live wire accidentally touches the case there is a short circuit. The increase in current melts the fuse in the plug. This breaks the live-wire connection and protects the user, as well as the wiring. As long as the case is earthed you cannot get an electric shock from it.

HEATING CIRCUITS

Some of the appliances in your home need a lot of energy and so need large currents. For instance, cookers and immersion heaters each have their own circuit to a 30- or 45-A fuse.

The cable used in these circuits has to carry large currents. It is thicker than the other circuit cables so that it does not get hot when in use. The circuit usually includes a wall-mounted switch separate from the appliance itself.

CIRCUIT-BREAKERS

Some houses are fitted with **circuit-breakers** instead of fuses (Fig. 84.7). They are fitted in the consumer unit. Each house circuit has its own circuit-breaker. They do the same job as fuses. If there is an overload of current in a circuit the circuit-breaker switches off using either the magnetic or heating effect of the current. When you find out why the circuit-breaker switched off you can put the fault right. Then you reset the circuit-breaker by switching it on again.

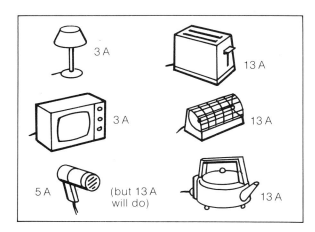

Fig. 84.6   Fuse values depend on the appliance used.

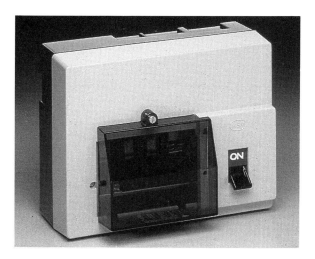

Fig. 84.7   (a) A consumer unit with fuses.

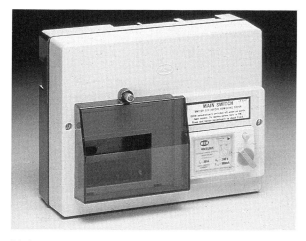

(b) A consumer unit with circuit breakers.

85 Electrical appliances

In your home many jobs are done by electrical **appliances**. Each appliance changes electrical energy to some other form. You need different appliances to dry your hair, play your records, heat your bath, cook your dinner, vacuum the carpet and so on.

HEATING APPLIANCES

All electrical heating appliances have a **heating element** inside them. Look at the element of an electric bar fire. The element is made of wire with a high resistance coiled round a fire-clay or silica tube. This wire is able to stand up to high temperatures. When the current flows the wire warms up. The rate at which the energy is converted to heat depends on the flow of current and the resistance of the element.

Electric irons   The heating element of an iron is wound on a thin sheet or former of insulating mica. This is bolted to the inside of the iron. The base is made of metal to conduct heat well and is chromium plated to make it smoother and stand up to wear better.

Irons are **thermostatically controlled**. A **thermostat** switches the current off when the iron is hot enough (p. 60). It switches the current on again when the iron cools below the temperature you have selected. The control knob moves the position of one of the thermostat contacts (Fig. 85.1).

Electric kettles   The heating element of a kettle is wound on an insulator and the whole thing is enclosed in a metal tube (Fig. 85.2). When a current flows the water round the element is heated by conduction. Then the energy is spread through the water by convection. You must have the heating element covered with water otherwise the element overheats. Most kettles have an automatic cut-out to prevent overheating, which would cause damage. The cut-out is either a circuit-breaker or a piston that springs out and pushes the connecting lead out.

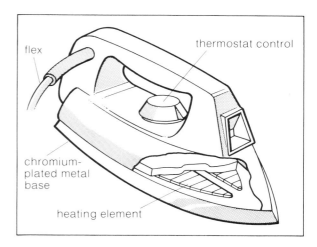

Fig. 85.1   An electric iron with its heating element exposed.

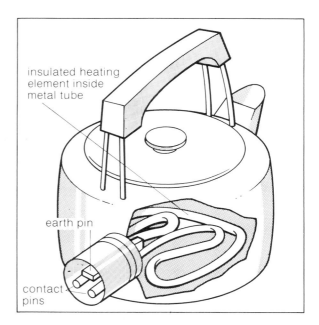

Fig. 85.2   Inside an electric kettle.

Immersion heaters   These are fitted inside the hot-water cylinder, usually inside the airing cupboard. Each heater has its own mains circuit and switch (Fig. 85.3). The element heats the water. You sometimes find a cylinder fitted with two heaters. The top one is used to heat the water in the top part of the cylinder— this is enough for washing-up, etc. The lower one is for heating all the water in the cylinder. It is switched on when you need a lot of hot water.

Hairdryers and fan heaters   These have a heating element and a motor-driven fan. The switch is made so that the heater will not come on until the fan is switched on. The cold air blowing through the heater stops overheating. Some hairdryers have slow and fast fan speeds.

Electric blankets   The heater of an electric blanket is very carefully designed. It is put on your bed and you are almost touching it. For this reason it must not overheat and it must be safe (Fig. 85.4). It has a good thermostat to keep its temperature at a safe level. It must be well insulated because there is no earthed case. Also the insulation must be waterproof. Some blankets have to be switched off before you get into bed. Blankets that go over you can be left on all night. Electric blankets are heat insulators like ordinary blankets. They should not be folded when hot.

Electric cookers   An electric cooker has its own circuit from the consumer unit. It takes a higher current than any other appliance in the home. The cooker point is a master-switch for the cooker. There are several circuits in the cooker, each with a separate control (Fig. 85.5).

The rings on top of the cooker are not thermostatically controlled. They do not overheat because they give heat to the saucepans on them. You should never turn a ring full on without standing a saucepan containing something on it. The oven temperature is thermostatically controlled. You set the knob to a certain temperature and when the oven reaches this temperature the thermostat switches off the current. When it cools, the thermostat switches the current on again to keep the oven temperature you have selected.

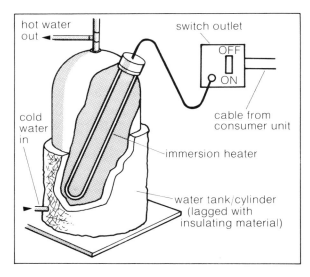

Fig. 85.3   How an immersion heater is connected. Why should the hot-water cylinder be lagged?

Fig. 85.4   Part of an electric blanket showing the heating element.

Fig. 85.5   Controls on an electric cooker. Where is the mains switch?

LIGHTING

Filament lamps   These are the most common of all electrical appliances and are found in every home. Smaller ones are used in torches. They may have different **power ratings** (p. 165) but they are all similar (Fig. 85.6). The filament is a coil of very thin tungsten wire. This is heated by the current until it is white-hot. Then the filament gives out light. Tungsten metal is used because it has a high melting point. The lamp contains the gas argon, which stops the filament evaporating. Argon is used because it will not let the tungsten burn.

Fluorescent tubes   These lamps are more efficient than filament lamps and, therefore, are cheaper to run. They can be made to give a light very like daylight. Also, they do not cast dark shadows because of their long shape. Fluorescent lamps are usually used in the kitchen or workshop. They are also very common in offices and public buildings.

Light is produced when a mixture of gases at low pressure conducts electricity. Some gas atoms are ionised. Positive and negative ions then carry the charge through the tube. The radiation from the gases contains ultraviolet radiation (p. 95) which is converted to blue-white light by the fluorescent coating inside the glass tube. Some fluorescent lamps require special fittings—a **starter switch** and a **choke** (Fig. 85.7).

Neon lamps   In the house you will find neon lamps used as pilot lights. These appear on appliances or sockets to show when they are switched on. They give a small red glow. Another common use for neon lighting is in advertising and display—neon lights are eye-catching.

Light is given off by the neon gas when it conducts electricity. The tube containing low-pressure neon can be made into any shape. A different gas inside the tube would give a different colour of light. For example, sodium vapour gives a yellow light and mercury vapour green-blue light. These two gases are often used in street lighting.

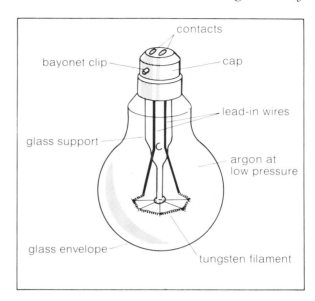

Fig. 85.6   Inside a filament lamp.

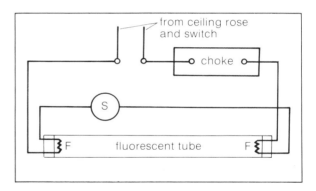

Fig. 85.7   The circuit for a fluorescent tube. The starter switch (S) controls the two heaters and switches these off as soon as the tube glows properly. The choke stops the tube from taking too big a current.

ELECTRIC MOTORS

There are many different sorts of electric motor working in different ways. All of them change electrical energy to mechanical energy. The motor usually makes something turn. Some electric motors, for example those in food mixers, hairdryers and electric drills, run off the mains (240 V). But others—model electric trains and car starter motors—run at low voltages.

Food mixers Two beaters turn together (Fig. 85.8). A switch on the mixer allows you to choose the speed you need.

Hairdryers The motor drives the fan which can drive a stream of air on to your head. The heater heats up the stream of air.

Electric drills These are very useful power tools. They can act as the source of power for many other tools—saws, planers, sanders, grinders, etc. In some drills the speed can be changed by the use of gears or by electronic means.

Model electric trains These have a simple motor which does not need to be very powerful. It uses a low voltage so that you don't hurt yourself if you touch the track. The track carries the electric current to the motor of the train.

Fig. 85.8

Car starter motors Every time someone starts a car an electric motor is used. It has to be powerful enough to 'turn the engine over'. It works on a low voltage because a car only has a 12-V battery. It takes a large direct current (p. 179).

86 Electrical energy and power

Energy costs money! Whatever fuel you use to give energy—coal, gas, oil, petrol, wood, electricity—you have to pay for it (Fig. 86.1). It is easy to measure how much coal or oil or gas you use. But not so easy to find out how much energy you have paid for. A coal merchant's bill doesn't tell you; but a gas bill does, if you read the fine print!

HOW IS ELECTRICAL ENERGY MEASURED?

The voltage of a supply tells you just how much energy is carried by the electric charge moving in a circuit (p. 146). A good example is an ordinary motor-car battery. When you buy one you know the voltage it will give you—almost always 12 V—and its **capacity**. That is the amount of electric charge it can give before you have to recharge it. A small one might give you 20 **ampere-hours** of charge. You could expect it to run an appliance taking a current of 5 A for 4 h (or 14 400 s). That is 72 000 **ampere-seconds** worth of charge. The ampere-second is usually called a **coulomb of charge (C)** for short.

The voltage tells you just how much energy each ampere-second or coulomb of charge carries. Charge from a 12-V battery carries 12 J for each coulomb. In fact:

1 volt is 1 joule per coulomb

The car battery will give you $12 \times 72\,000$ J; that is over 800 000 J.

Now let's think about a car headlamp. Suppose it took a current of 3 A. How much charge passes through it in each second? 3 C. The voltage is 12 V. So each coulomb carries 12 J of energy. The lamp must be converting electrical energy into heat and light at a rate of 12×3 J every second; that's 36 J per second.

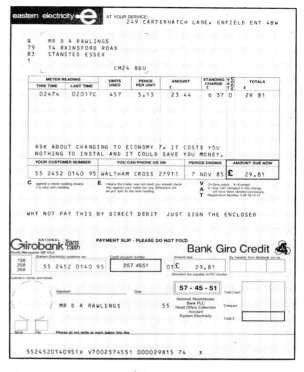

Fig. 86.1 Bills, bills, bills! How many energy units were used? What are they?

POWER AND POWER RATING

The **power rating** of an electrical appliance tells you the rate at which the appliance converts electrical energy to other forms. The car headlamp did this at a rate of 36 J per second. That is its power rating. As

1 watt (W) = 1 J per second

the power rating of the lamp is 36 W. To find the power we multiplied the potential difference (p. 150) across the lamp by the current passing through it. So

$$\text{power (in W)} = \text{potential difference (in V)} \times \text{current (in A)}$$

$$P = VI$$

A mains lamp may have a power rating of 60 W. This lamp will convert electrical energy into heat and light at a rate of 60 J per second, or 60 W. It is a 60-W lamp.

Some appliances convert energy very quickly and have much higher power ratings. A cooker or a heater is a good example. For these, a useful unit of power is the **kilowatt (kW)**.

$$1 \text{ kW} = 1000 \text{ W}$$

An electric fire rated at 1 kW converts 1000 J of energy every second.

Now you can work out the power rating of an electrical appliance. Here are some examples.

1   An electric iron works from the mains (240 V) and takes a current of 3 A. It has a power rating of 240 V × 3 A which is 720 W.
2   A TV set working at 240 V takes a current of 0.5 A. It has a power rating of 240 V × 0.5 A which is 120 W.

You can work out the current passing through an appliance if you know the power rating.

Example   What is the current in a 60-W lamp used on a mains supply (240 V)?

$$P = VI$$
$$60 \text{ W} = 240 \text{ V} \times I$$
$$I = \frac{60 \text{ W}}{240 \text{ V}} = 0.25 \text{ A}$$

So the current is 0.25 A.

Example   What is the current in a 250-V/ 1000-W electric fire?

$$P = VI$$
$$1000 \text{ W} = 250 \text{ V} \times I$$
$$I = \frac{1000 \text{ W}}{250 \text{ V}} = 4 \text{ A}$$

Therefore the current is 4 A.

In the second example you can use the voltage and the current to calculate the resistance of the heating element (p. 151):

$$R = \frac{V}{I} = \frac{250 \text{ V}}{4 \text{ A}} = 62.5 \text{ } \Omega$$

So the 250-V/1000-W electric fire has a resistance of 62.5 Ω.

ELECTRICAL ENERGY

Energy can be worked out from the equation:

energy (in J) = power (in W) × time (in s)

If you measure electrical energy in joules you get very big numbers; e.g., a 1-kW electric fire converts 3 600 000 J in an hour. To avoid large numbers the electricity board uses a bigger unit of energy—the **kilowatt-hour** or the **Board of Trade unit (kWh)**. Since one kilowatt-hour is the amount of energy converted by a 1-kW appliance in an hour, the equation can be written:

$$\frac{\text{energy}}{\text{(in kWh)}} = \frac{\text{power}}{\text{(in kW)}} \times \frac{\text{time}}{\text{(in h)}}$$

Example   Calculate the energy converted by a 2-kW boiler used continuously for 6 h.

$$\text{energy} = \text{power} \times \text{time}$$
$$= 2 \text{ kW} \times 6 \text{ h} = 12 \text{ kWh}$$

The energy converted is 12 kWh, or 12 units.

Example   Five similar lamps use 4 kWh in 8 h. What is the power rating of one lamp?

$$\text{power} = \frac{\text{energy transformed}}{\text{time}}$$
$$\frac{\text{energy}}{\text{transformed}} = 4 \text{ kWh}$$
$$= 4000 \text{ watt-hours}$$
$$P = \frac{4000 \text{ watt-hours}}{8 \text{ h}} = 500 \text{ W}$$

So the power of one lamp is 100 W.

If you know the cost of one unit of electrical energy you can work out how much it costs to run an appliance. For example, if electricity costs 6p per unit then the electric boiler in the previous example costs (12 kWh × 6p) = 72p to run for 6 h, or 12p per hour.

(b)

Fig. 86.2   Two different types of electricity meter. (a) Dial type. (b) Digital.

READING METERS

The electricity meter near your consumer unit at home measures the energy converted from electrical energy to other forms. It shows how many kilowatt-hours (units) you have used. There are two common types of meter (Fig. 86.2). Meters are usually read every quarter (three months). The dial type is read by noting the lower number nearest to each pointer (Fig. 86.3). The difference between this quarter's reading and the last is used to work out the electricity bill.

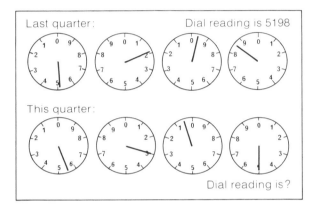

Fig. 86.3   How to read a dial-type meter. How many units does this householder have to pay for?

SUMMARY: USING ELECTRICITY

- An electric current has three effects—heating, chemical and magnetic.
- When a current passes through a resistance the resistance gets hot.
- Electrolysis may occur when a current passes through an electrolyte.
- Objects to be electroplated are connected to the negative side of the electricity supply.
- Household lighting circuits are separate from power circuits.
- Nowadays, houses are usually wired with ring main power circuits.
- The appliances used on a ring main have square pin plugs containing a suitable fuse.
- Fuses are safety devices that melt if too much current flows.
- Almost all appliances used at home have a safety connection to earth.
- Electrical appliances change electrical energy to other useful forms.

- The potential difference across an appliance tells you how much energy each unit of electric charge carries.
- The unit of electric charge is the ampere-second or coulomb (C).
- A potential difference of 1 V means that each coulomb of charge that passes through the appliance carries 1 J of energy.
- Power is the rate of conversion of energy. It is measured in joules per second or watts (W): 1000 W = 1 kW.
- Power is potential difference multiplied by current.
- Energy is power multiplied by time.
- Energy is measured in joules or kilowatt-hours (kWh): 1 kWh = 3 600 000 J.
- A kilowatt-hour is also called a (Board of Trade) unit.

SECTION 20

Magnetism from Electricity

87 Magnetic effect of an electric current

Even though you don't often notice it, all electric currents have magnetic effects. Sometimes these effects are very large. This section explains how good use can be made of them.

OERSTED'S EXPERIMENT

It all started in 1820 when a Dane called Oersted noticed that a wire carrying a current was able to turn a nearby compass needle (Fig. 87.1). When the compass is above a wire carrying a current towards the north, the north-seeking pole of the compass moves to the right. When the compass is below the wire the north pole moves to the left. If the current flows in the opposite direction, the compass needle swings the other way. The way the north pole moves is the direction of the magnetic field (p. 136).

FIELD SHAPES

Straight wires

Use a plotting compass to explore the magnetic field round a wire carrying a current (Fig. 87.2). The wire is vertical and the card is horizontal. When the lines of magnetic force (the field lines) are joined up they form circles, one inside the other. The wire is at the centre of the circles. The direction of the field is shown in Fig. 87.3. When the current is reversed the magnetic field reverses.

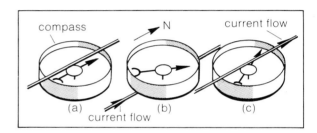

Fig. 87.1 Oersted's experiment. (a) No current in the wire: compass below it. (b) Current in the wire: compass above it. (c) Current in the wire: compass below it.

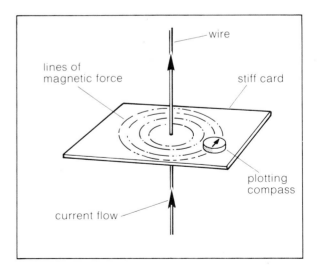

Fig. 87.2 Plotting the magnetic field round a straight wire carrying a current.

Maxwell's corkscrew rule

To find out the direction of a magnetic field you can use **Maxwell's corkscrew rule**. This states that: The direction of the lines of force round a current is the same as the direction in which you would turn an ordinary screw to move it forwards in the direction of the current (Fig. 87.4).

Flat coils

The shape of the field lines for a current in a flat coil of wire is shown in Fig. 87.5. You will notice that the fields from each part of each wire are in the same direction in the middle. This causes a strong field in the space inside the coil. If more turns are added the field becomes even stronger. You will also see that the magnetic field is at right angles to the plane of the coil.

Solenoids

A **solenoid** is a long coil with many turns of wire. It is usually wound on a cylinder called a **former**. Figure 87.6 shows a solenoid without a former. There is a stiff card through the middle of it. The field lines are drawn on the card. Their position could have been found using a plotting compass or iron filings (p. 136). The field is strong through the middle of the solenoid. The lines are also parallel showing that the field has the same strength along most of the solenoid.

The field outside the coil is just like the magnetic field of a bar magnet (p. 136). In fact, you could say that a solenoid has poles. End A acts like a north pole and end B like a south pole. There is a simple rule for finding which pole is which. Look at the coil end-on from the outside. If the current is anticlockwise that end acts like a north pole. If the current is clockwise that end acts like a south pole. You can remember which is which by pretending that the letters N and S have arrows on their ends. They go in the same way as the current.

If the current in the solenoid is reversed then the poles will change over. Note that the magnetic effect is due to the current not the wire. If the current is switched off then there is no magnetic effect at all. The larger the current the greater the effect.

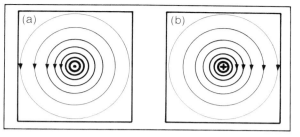

Fig. 87.3 Magnetic field lines round straight wires carrying a current are circular in shape. A dot in the middle tells you the current is coming towards you; the + sign tells you it's going away from you.

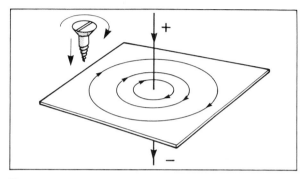

Fig. 87.4 Maxwell's corkscrew rule.

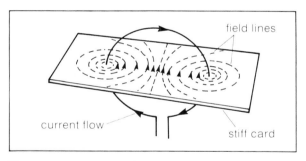

Fig. 87.5 The magnetic field of a current in a flat coil.

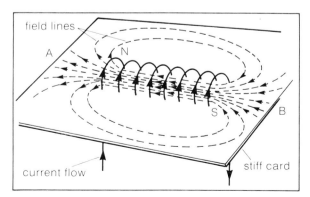

Fig. 87.6 The magnetic field of a current in a solenoid.

88 Solenoids at work

IRON CORES

An iron core inside a coil will increase the magnetic effect when the current is switched on. The magnetic field inside the iron is hundreds of times stronger than it is in the air. Strong electromagnets can be made using soft iron (p. 133).

All electromagnets have the advantage that the magnetism is switched off when the current is switched off. Electromagnets have many uses. Some large ones are used to lift steel scrap and separate it from non-magnetic metals (see the photograph on p. 168). Another sort is used in eye hospitals to remove steel fragments without damaging the eye. Some of the uses are given below; others are described elsewhere, e.g., telephone earpiece and tape-recorder (p. 184).

Electric bells   In the direct-current type (Fig. 88.1) when the bell-push is pressed the circuit is complete. Current flows from the battery through the solenoids in the bell. The solenoids magnetise the iron core. This attracts the iron **armature**, which moves towards the solenoids. As the spring bends it loses contact with the screw. The gap stops the current flowing and the core loses its magnetism. The armature is not attracted and the spring pulls it back. This makes the contact again and the whole process is repeated. The striker keeps hitting the gong for as long as the bell-push is pressed. The electric **buzzer** works in just the same way but has no gong.

Door chimes   These are used instead of a bell. When the bell-push is pressed a current flows through the solenoid (Fig. 88.2). This pulls the iron rod in and the wooden striker hits the right-hand chime—ding. When the bell-push is released the current stops. The spring pulls the iron rod back and the other striker hits the left-hand chime—dong.

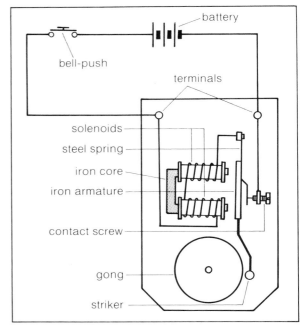

Fig. 88.1   A battery-operated electric bell. The electromagnet attracts the iron armature when a current flows.

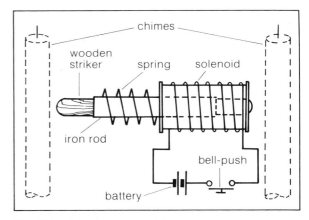

Fig. 88.2   A battery-operated door chime.

MAGNETIC RELAYS

A relay is a switch worked by an electromagnet. It is used when you want one circuit to operate another. This is done when large currents are in use. For example, it would not be sensible to pass the current in the motor of a lift through the control panel. The controls in the lift must use a small, safe current. This means that they cannot be in the same circuit as the motor. The control circuit and the motor circuit are linked by a relay.

Older telephone circuits use lots of relays (Fig. 88.3). A current from the control circuit passes through the coil. This makes the iron core into a magnet. The armature is attracted by the magnet and swings in at A while the other end D goes up. This pushes the two contacts B together. The second circuit is now switched on. In the new telephone exchanges the switching is done electronically.

Some relays have more than one set of contacts so that several circuits can be switched on together. Others have the contacts normally closed and a current in the coil opens them. This means that one circuit can be made to switch another off, e.g., for safety reasons.

REED SWITCHES AS RELAYS

These will do a similar job to the magnetic relay but need less current. They are also smaller and act more quickly (Fig. 88.4). A current through the solenoid makes the two iron reeds into magnets As they have opposite poles at the ends they attract each other, move together and make contact. When the current is switched off the reeds lose their magnetism. They spring back and switch off the current circuit. The ends of the reeds are coated with a thin layer of a good conductor, e.g., gold. An inert gas inside the solenoid stops the contacts oxidising.

THE CAR RELAY

This is used when starting a car. The starter motor needs a current of up to 100 A to start turning the engine. This is too big a current to have flowing through the ignition switch. When the ignition key is turned a small current of a few amperes flows through the solenoid (Fig. 88.5). The magnetic effect pulls the iron armature to the left and the copper plate joins the contacts. This completes the starter-motor circuit and a large current can

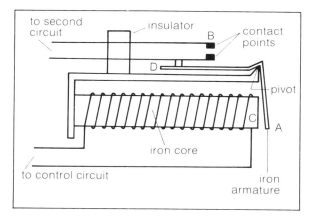

Fig. 88.3 A magnetic relay. The electromagnet C attracts the iron armature A. The other end D pushes the switch contacts at B together.

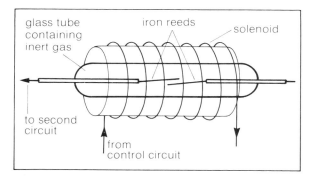

Fig. 88.4 A reed switch and solenoid can act as a relay.

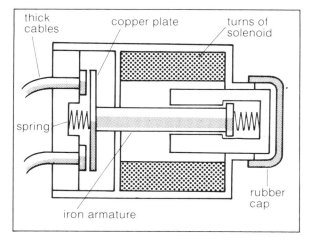

Fig. 88.5 A relay on the starter circuit of a car. If the relay fails you can close the switch by pushing on the rubber cap.

flow. When you release the key the armature springs back. The relay is in a safe place in the engine compartment.

89 The motor effect

A current in a wire has a magnetic field round it (p. 168). If the wire is placed in another magnetic field the two fields combine. A force is exerted on the conductor. You can see this quite easily if you place a wire between the poles of a strong horseshoe magnet. Switch the current on and the wire is flung to one side (Fig. 89.1). The direction of the force is given by **Fleming's left-hand rule** (Fig. 89.2): Hold the left hand with the thumb, first and second fingers at right angles. Point the first finger in the direction of the magnetic field, the second finger in the direction of the current and then the thumb shows the direction of the force. Electric motors use this force. So do moving-coil ammeters.

MOVING-COIL METERS

Current flows into and out of the coil through two springs (Fig. 89.3). The coil turns between the magnetic poles and a soft iron cylinder. The magnetic field in this space is even and in the same plane as the coil. It is called a **radial field**. The result is that the forces on the coil increase exactly in step with the current in the coil. The forces on opposite sides of the coil cause it to turn. It stops turning when the forces balance those of the springs. The pointer then shows the size of the current on the scale. The scale marks are evenly spaced because of the radial field.

   A moving-coil meter can be very sensitive. It is used as the basis of accurate microammeters, measuring in millionths of an ampere. It can only be used for direct current (d.c.; p. 179) and nearly all ammeters and voltmeters are of this type. If alternating current (a.c.; p. 178) is passed through the coil the force on it changes direction with the current. Because the coil is too massive to swing backwards and forwards with the current, it does not move and the pointer shows no current.

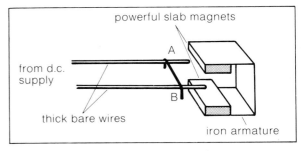

Fig. 89.1 The catapult effect. When the current is switched on the conductor AB moves sharply out of the field between the two poles.

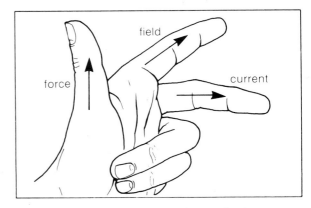

Fig. 89.2 Fleming's left-hand rule (motor effect).

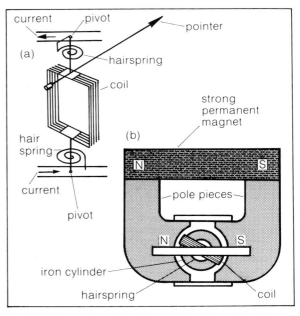

Fig. 89.3 A moving-coil meter: (a) shows the coil and its two hairsprings and (b) shows how the coil fits into the magnet system.

90 Electric motors

Electric motors change electrical energy to kinetic (movement) energy. You can now find out how they work.

THE SIMPLE D.C. MOTOR

This works on a direct (one-way) current. In its simplest form it has a single coil of wire (Fig. 90.1). This spins on an axle (shown as the dashed line AB) between a north and a south pole. The ends of the coil are connected to a split-ring called a **commutator** (XY). Each half of the ring is connected to one end of the coil. The commutator turns with the coil and rubs against two carbon **brushes** (P and Q). These are the fixed contacts between the coil and the battery.

The current flows from the battery through P and X, through the coil as shown and back to the battery through Y and Q. Both sides of the coil feel forces because of the field of the magnet. These forces are in opposite directions. Applying Fleming's left-hand rule (p. 172) you can see that the left-hand side of the coil moves down and the right-hand side moves up, so the coil starts to turn. When it is upright, the force on the upper side of the coil is vertically up; the force on the lower side is vertically down. These forces pull against each other. If nothing changes the coil will stay in this vertical position. This is the point at which the commutator becomes important. As the coil comes to the vertical position the half-ring Y loses contact with Q and touches P. Also, X moves from P to Q. This reverses the current in the coil and, therefore, the forces reverse. This keeps the coil spinning in the same direction. The direction of the current in the coil reverses each time the coil is vertical.

PRACTICAL MOTORS

Real motors are more complicated than the one in Fig. 90.1. The coil has many turns; and there is more than one coil. This means that the commutator has more than two sections. The coils are also wound on an iron rotor (Fig. 90.2). This strengthens the magnetic field, which is produced by an electromagnet.

Motors used with alternating currents are discussed on p. 179.

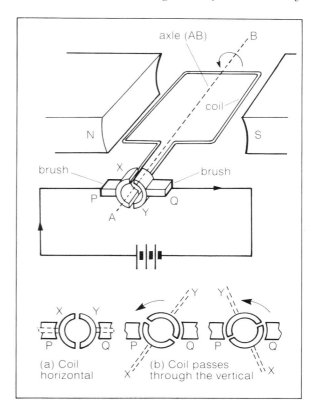

Fig. 90.1   The principle of a d.c. electric motor.

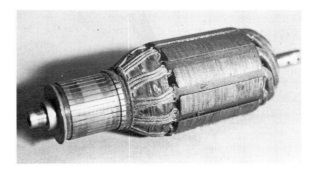

Fig. 90.2   The armature of a real electric motor. The commutator is on the left. The coils are wound on an iron core.

91 The loudspeaker

Here is another use of the motor effect. A loudspeaker changes electrical energy to kinetic (movement) energy and so to sound energy. The electrical energy is carried by an alternating current, which keeps on changing its direction. The current alternates at audio frequencies. These are frequencies you can hear (p. 124). The current comes from an amplifier connected to a microphone, radio, record-player, etc. To make audible sounds the current must make something vibrate.

The current flows through a coil wound on a thin former (Fig. 91.1). This is in the shape of a cylinder and fits in an air gap in a specially shaped magnet. The former is joined to a paper cone. There is a strong radial magnetic field inside the gap of the magnet. The turns of the coil are at right angles to this field. Applying Fleming's left-hand rule you can see that the coil will move. As the current changes direction so does the force and, therefore, the movement.

The alternating current causes the coil and the cone to move in and out of the magnet at the same frequency as the current. The

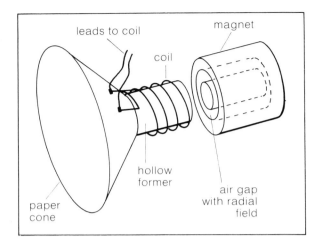

Fig. 91.1 How a loudspeaker works.

vibration of the paper cone moves a large volume of air. This causes a loud sound at the same frequency as the original sound which formed the current.

Loudspeakers come in various sizes. The large ones favour low notes and are sometimes called **woofers**. High notes are best produced by small speakers called **tweeters**.

SUMMARY: MAGNETISM FROM ELECTRICITY

- An electric current has a magnetic field round it.
- The shape of the field depends on the shape of the conductor carrying the current.
- Maxwell's corkscrew rule: the direction of the magnetic field round a straight current is the same as the direction in which you would turn an ordinary screw to move it forwards in the direction of the current.
- A solenoid has a magnetic field like that of a bar magnet.
- The polarity of a solenoid can be found from the direction of the current.
- An iron core increases the magnetic effect.

- The field of an electromagnet can be switched off with the current.
- Magnetic relays are magnetic switches linking two or more circuits.
- Reed switches can do similar jobs to relays.
- A current in a magnetic field experiences a force. The direction of this force is given by Fleming's left-hand rule.
- The moving-coil meter is used to measure direct currents and voltages.
- A d.c. motor needs a split-ring commutator.
- A loudspeaker converts electrical energy to sound.

Electricity from Magnetism

92 Faraday's experiment

Michael Faraday was the man who discovered how to make electricity from magnetism. Without that first discovery we would not have mains power at the flick of a switch. Yet his first experiments seem very simple to us now.

MAGNET AND COIL EXPERIMENTS

Connect the ends of a coil wound on a hollow former to a sensitive galvanometer. (Modern galvanometers are sensitive moving-coil meters with the zero in the middle of the scale.) When the pole of a magnet is moved into the coil a current flows. The galvanometer needle moves to the left (Fig. 92.1(a)). While the magnet is inside the coil, but not moving, no current flows (Fig. 92.1(b)). When the magnet is moved out of the coil the galvanometer needle shows a deflection to the right (Fig. 92.1(c)). This shows that a current is now flowing in the opposite direction.

This experiment shows that when the magnet moves near to a coil a current flows in the circuit. We call this an **induced current**. The name of the process is **electromagnetic induction**. The experiment also works if the magnet is held still and the coil is moved. Current is induced when there is relative movement between the magnet and coil.

Remember, the current only flows when the magnet (or coil) is moving. No movement of the magnet (or coil) means no current. The electrical energy comes from the energy of whatever it is that is moving the magnet.

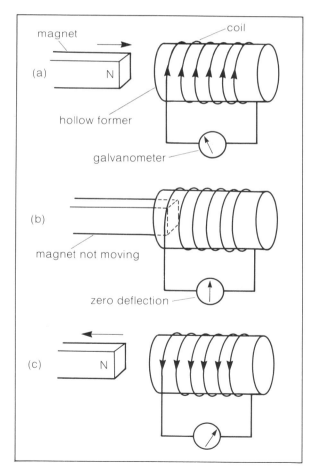

Fig. 92.1 Moving the pole of a magnet into then out of a coil induces a current in the circuit.

TWO-COIL EXPERIMENTS

Moving coils

Replace the magnet by a solenoid connected to the battery. This is called the **primary coil**. When the primary coil is moved towards the **secondary coil** the galvanometer needle is deflected to the right (Fig. 92.2(a)). When both coils are still there is no deflection. When the primary coil is moved away from the other coil the galvanometer needle is deflected to the left. This means that the current is now in the opposite direction. Keeping the primary coil still and moving the secondary coil gives the same results.

The primary coil has a magnetic field like that of a bar magnet (p. 136). Both experiments show that it is a moving magnetic field that induces the current in the secondary coil.

Stationary coils

Faraday finally found that he could cause a current to flow in the secondary coil without the coils actually moving. With both coils still he switched on the current in the primary coil. The galvanometer needle was deflected one way. An induced current was flowing in the secondary coil (Fig. 92.2(b)). When he switched off, a current flowed for a moment in the other direction. With a steady current in the primary coil no current flowed in the secondary.

When the current in the primary coil is changing its magnetic field is also changing. The changing field through the secondary coil induces the current in it. Moving the magnet was another way of changing the field through the coil.

Faraday also found that the induced current was much larger if the coils were wound on a soft iron former.

FARADAY'S FINDINGS

Faraday found that the induced current was much larger if strong magnetic fields moving very quickly were used. To induce a large current you must use a strong field and make it change very quickly. This is done either by moving the field very quickly, as in a dynamo (p. 178), or by changing the current direction quickly, as in a transformer (p. 180).

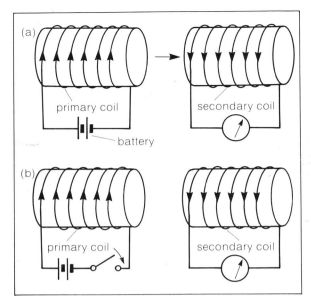

Fig. 92.2 The two-coil experiment. To induce a current either (a) move the primary coil towards the secondary coil or (b) change the current in the primary coil.

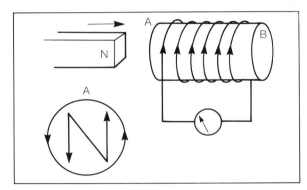

Fig. 92.3 Lenz's law.

LENZ'S LAW

There is one other law of induction. This is called **Lenz's law**. It states that: The induced current flows in a direction to oppose the change producing it.

You can see how this works by looking at any of the previous experiments (Fig. 92.3). As the north pole of the magnet approaches, the current flows as shown. This makes end A of the coil into a north pole. As like poles repel each other, the induced current in the coil is trying to stop the magnet approaching. It is opposing the change producing it. Try to explain the current direction in Fig. 92.1(c) and 92.2 by similar arguments.

93 Do-it-yourself electricity

You can generate some electricity with a magnet and a coil. All you have to do is provide the movement. Take a coil of about 100 turns and a strong horseshoe magnet. Connect the coil to a galvanometer (Fig. 93.1). Then pass the coil between the poles of the magnet. You will see a deflection. Pass it back again and you will see a deflection the other way. Move it more quickly and the deflection gets bigger. It does not matter whether the coil or the magnet moves.

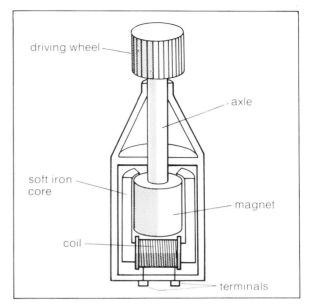

Fig. 93.2 How does this bicycle dynamo work?

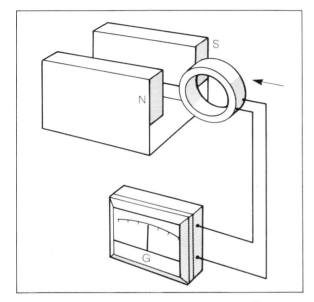

Fig. 93.1 Try generating some electricity yourself!

CYCLE DYNAMOS

These are a common form of do-it-yourself electricity. They save buying batteries and keep your lights working as long as the dynamo turns. One type is shaped rather like a bottle (Fig. 93.2). The coil inside is fixed and wound on an iron core. The driving wheel spins a permanent magnet. As this turns the magnetic field in the iron core changes. This induces a current in the coil. If the wheel moves fast enough the current is big enough to give quite a bright light. You may notice that it is harder to pedal when the dynamo is powering the lights. You will certainly find it becomes harder to turn a mounted cycle dynamo by hand when it is connected to a lamp (Fig. 93.3) and a current flows. The

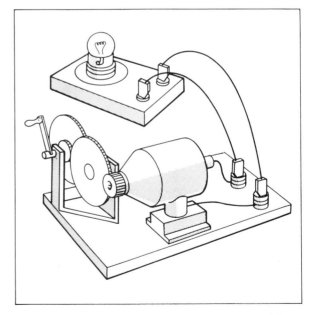

Fig. 93.3 When a lamp is connected to the dynamo, it is harder to turn the handle than when the lamp is not there.

electrical energy must come from somewhere. You provide the extra energy of movement by pedalling harder. The dynamo changes the kinetic (movement) energy to electrical energy.

94 Dynamos

There are two ways of making electricity for regular use. One uses chemicals, as in batteries (p. 145); the other uses magnetism and movement. Batteries are very useful to start petrol engines and for low-power jobs, e.g., running torches, transistor radios and calculators. But high-power jobs, e.g., heating and cooking, need more energy than batteries can give. This is where **dynamos** come in. If you need more power you use a bigger dynamo or turn the coils faster. There are two types of moving-coil dynamo.

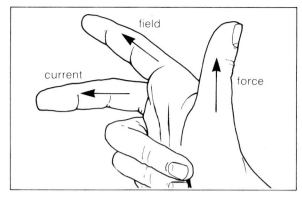

Fig. 94.1 Fleming's right-hand rule for dynamos.

A SIMPLE A.C. DYNAMO

This has a rectangular coil mounted on an axle between the poles of a permanent magnet. When the coil is spun round, the magnetic field through it changes. This induces a current in the coil. The direction of the current is given by **Fleming's right-hand rule** (Fig. 94.1): Hold the thumb and first two fingers of the right hand at right angles to one another. The first finger points in the direction of the magnetic field, the thumb in the direction of movement and the second finger shows the direction of the induced current.

Applying this rule to Fig. 94.2 you can see that the induced current in the left-hand side of the coil flows away from you. The current in the right-hand side is towards you. This current flows to the lamp through the two slip-rings. The two slip-rings (X and Y) each make sliding contact with a fixed carbon brush (P and Q). The current flows from Y to Q and from P to X.

When the coil has turned through 180° the sides of the coil will have changed places. The current flows from X to P and from Q to Y. Every time the coil turns through 180° the current reverses direction once. The current flows first one way in the circuit and then the other. This is called **alternating current (a.c.)**. The current changes its direction when the coil is vertical.

The graph of current against coil position (Fig. 94.3) is the trace you will see if you connect the output of the dynamo to an oscilloscope. If you turn the dynamo faster the amplitude of the trace gets bigger, so the voltage is bigger. The peaks also get closer together, so the frequency of the a.c. is higher.

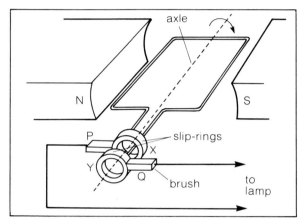

Fig. 94.2 A simple a.c. dynamo.

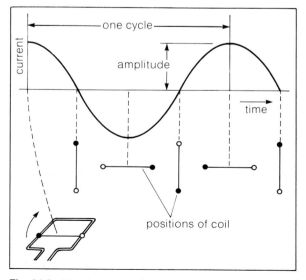

Fig. 94.3 How the current from a simple dynamo changes as the coil turns.

THE SIMPLE D.C. DYNAMO

For some purposes you need the current to be in one direction only. This is called **direct current (d.c.).** For example, d.c. is needed to recharge a car battery, a.c. will not do it.

To generate d.c. the dynamo has a commutator instead of the slip-rings. The rest of the dynamo is the same. In the split-ring commutator (Fig. 94.4) the ends of the coil are joined to two halves of a split-ring (XY), which turns with the coil. After turning through a half-circle (180°) X leaves P and contacts Q. At the same time Y makes contact with P. This means that the current in the coil changes direction at the same moment that the commutator changes over. These two changes simply cancel one another. The current flows out of Q and in at P all the time. It is direct current. The graph of current against coil position (Fig. 94.5) is not steady, but it is in one direction only.

Many modern motor-car dynamos (or generators) produce a.c. This is turned into d.c. by a **rectifier.** A rectifier is a one-way valve for electricity (p. 193).

PRACTICAL DYNAMOS

In practice dynamos are more complicated. They have an iron core called a **rotor.** This has one coil wound on it. The coil is fed with d.c. so that it becomes a powerful magnet. The rotor is rotated at a fixed speed inside three fixed coils called **stator coils.** Currents are induced in these coils and led directly away.

These big generators are very much like bicycle dynamos, which have one fixed coil and a rotating magnet.

USING A.C. TO DRIVE A MOTOR

Small a.c. motors are in common use. You will find them in refrigerators where they drive the pump, spin dryers and washing machines,

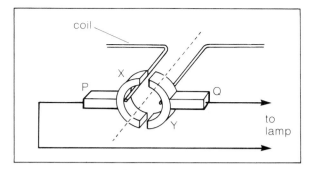

Fig. 94.4   A split-ring commutator.

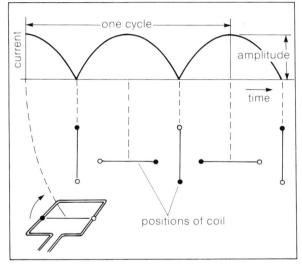

Fig. 94.5   How the current from a dynamo fitted with a commutator changes as the coil turns.

vacuum cleaners, electric drills and so on. They look just like d.c. motors. They have a rotating coil or armature wound on a soft iron former, a stationary electromagnet and a commutator with carbon brushes.

Mains clocks, record-players and tape-recorders use motors that are **synchronous.** This means that they move at a speed tuned to the frequency of the a.c. mains supply.

95 Transformers

Different voltages are needed for different jobs. Your doorbell probably works on a 6-V supply. The picture tube in your TV set needs several thousand volts. Transformers can supply all these different voltages from the mains supply (240 V).

THE TRANSFORMER PRINCIPLE

This is very much like Faraday's two-coil experiment (p. 176). Two coils linked by an iron bar (Fig. 95.1) are used. The iron bar makes all magnetic effects greater.

Connect the primary coil to a battery. Connect the secondary coil to a suitable lamp. When you switch on the current in the primary coil the lamp flashes once. The current in the primary coil and, therefore, the magnetic field grow from nothing to some value. A current is induced in the secondary coil. Once the current is steady in the primary coil no more changes occur and there is no induced current. The lamp does not light. What will happen if you now switch the current off in the primary coil?

If a.c. is supplied to the primary coil the lamp remains on all the time. As the a.c. is continually changing, the magnetic field it makes is, therefore, continually changing. A current is induced in the secondary coil by this continually changing magnetic field. An oscilloscope would show you that the output is also alternating. The frequency will be the same as that of the primary current.

A transformer is more efficient if the **magnetic linkage** is better. This can be improved by using a specially designed iron core (Fig. 95.2). The magnetic field is stronger when there is a closed loop of iron because many more field lines from the primary coil link the secondary coil.

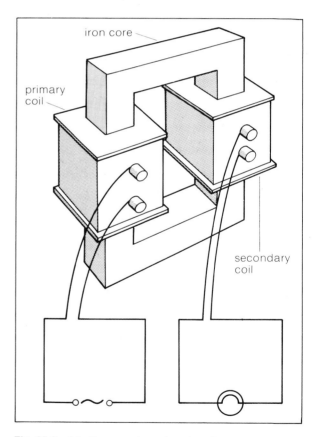

Fig. 95.2 A better core shape for a transformer.

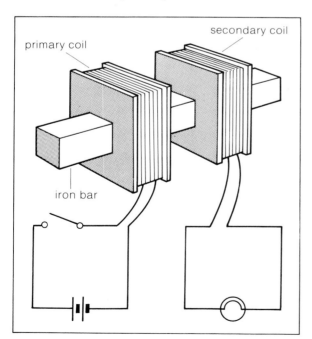

Fig. 95.1 A very simple transformer showing a primary coil (energy in), a secondary coil (energy out) and an iron bar.

EDDY CURRENTS

Although iron is a good electrical conductor no current flows between the iron and coils in a core. This is because the coils are insulated from the iron. However, the changing magnetic field induces currents in the iron core itself. These currents are called **eddy currents**. They flow in little circles round the field.

LAMINATED CORES

Eddy currents waste energy and make the transformer less efficient. To reduce eddy currents the resistance of the iron core must be increased. This is done by making the core out of sheets, or **laminae**, of iron. These sheets are insulated from each other and are bolted together to make a solid core.

The best shape for a **transformer core** is shown in Fig. 95.3. The coils are wound one on top of the other on the middle part. The magnetic field then has two loops of iron to pass through; and the **laminations** are too thin to allow large eddy currents to flow.

STEP-UP AND STEP-DOWN TRANSFORMERS

As an a.c. in the primary coil causes an alternating voltage across the secondary one, a transformer can be used to change voltages. This is done by having different numbers of turns on the coils. A **step-up transformer**, which has more turns on the secondary than on the primary, increases the voltage. A **step-down transformer** decreases the voltage by having fewer turns on the secondary than on the primary.

The following equation can be used to work out the secondary voltage:

$$\frac{\text{voltage of secondary}}{\text{voltage of primary}} = \frac{\text{number of secondary turns}}{\text{number of primary turns}}$$

$$\frac{V_s}{V_p} = \frac{N_s}{N_p}$$

N_s/N_p is called the **turns ratio**.

A model railway uses a step-down transformer. It changes 240-V mains to 12 V. The turns ratio is 12/240 or 1/20. This means that there is one turn on the secondary for every 20 turns on the primary.

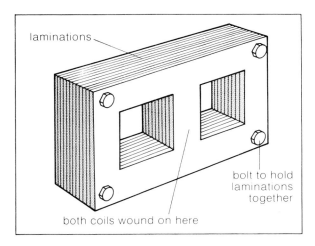

Fig. 95.3 The core of a transformer is built up from many thin sheets (laminae) of special iron.

POWER IN THE TRANSFORMER

The power that you get out of a transformer cannot be more than you put in. So, if you step up the voltage then the current is stepped down. Remember, power = voltage × current. If the voltage is stepped up 10 times then the output current will be at most one-tenth of the input current.

96 Mains electricity

You need energy to do jobs. Fuels such as coal, oil and gas transform energy when they burn. Some of this energy is used to produce electrical energy. This kind of energy is clean to use, is easily distributed, does not have to be stored and can be turned on and off. But it is difficult to store in large amounts. This unit is about the generation of electrical energy and how it gets to your home.

GENERATION

Electrical energy can only be made from another form of energy (Fig. 96.1). Most of our power stations use coal as fuel. But some use oil or nuclear fuels. Coal and oil have chemical energy which is changed to thermal energy or heat when the fuel is burned. The heat is used to produce steam under pressure. This steam has potential energy. When the steam turns the turbines the potential energy is changed to kinetic (movement) energy (Fig. 96.1). The kinetic energy is changed to electrical energy in the dynamo or **generator** (Fig. 96.2).

HYDROELECTRIC POWER

This is a form of natural power. It is available in a few places in Britain, e.g., Scotland. Water is collected high up, behind a dam. It is then allowed to run down steep pipes. This converts the potential energy to kinetic energy as the water turns the turbines, which turn the generators.

Electrical energy cannot be stored on any large scale. However, the demand for electricity changes through the day and night. At night, when the demand is low, surplus electrical energy can be used to pump water to a high level. During the day, when demand is high, the water flows down again to produce more electricity. This is called a **pumped storage system** (Fig. 96.3).

Scientists are also working on ways of using energy from the wind, the waves and the tides to generate electricity.

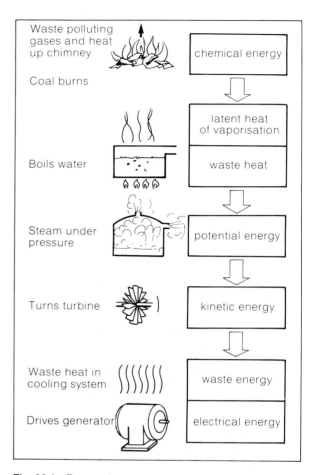

Fig. 96.1   Energy changes at a power station.

Fig. 96.2   A 660-MW turbine at Hinckley Point nuclear power station.

Fig. 96.3 The pumped storage system at Ffestiniog.

POWER TRANSMISSION

Electricity is generated as an alternating current so that the voltage can be stepped up or down by transformers. A mains electricity supply is connected to the generator at the power station. The circuit is not a simple one. There is a complex system of transformers, switches and cables. The system must be safe and it must not waste too much energy.

The generator at the power station works at around 25 000 V. A large turbo-generator (see Fig. 96.2) might produce energy at a rate of 660 MW (660 000 000 W). From p. 165:

$$\text{power} = \text{voltage} \times \text{current}$$
$$660\,000\,000 \text{ W} = 25\,000 \text{ V} \times \text{current}$$
$$\text{current} = 26\,400 \text{ A}$$

This is a very large current which requires very large cables if too much energy is not to be wasted as heat in the cables. If the voltage is increased to 400 000 V (that's 16 times larger) the current becomes 16 times smaller (1650 A). This would waste much less energy. But working at 400 kV requires a very well designed system.

THE NATIONAL GRID

Power stations produce a.c. at 25 000 V which is stepped up to 132 000 V (132 kV) or 400 kV. This high tension electricity is carried by cables you see on pylons (Fig. 96.4). The cables are held high up on large insulators for safety reasons. Before you use any of this energy the voltage must be stepped down. This is done in stages. The final stage (to 240 V) is done in local substations. You may find one near to where you live (Fig. 96.5). This system of sending electricity round the country is called the **National Grid** (Fig. 96.6).

Fig. 96.4 A 400-kV power line.

Fig. 96.5 A 400-kV sub-station on the National Grid.

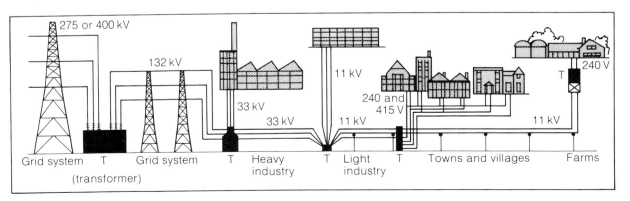

Fig. 96.6

97 Recording and playing

Sound recording and play-back is very popular. It uses the electric current. Sounds are changed into electrical signals and recorded. They can then be changed back when the recording is played.

THE MICROPHONE

All microphones do the same job. They change sound energy into electrical energy. A **carbon microphone** (Fig. 97.1) is used in telephones. Sound waves make a thin aluminium plate vibrate. As it moves backwards and forwards a carbon block moves with it. This squeezes **carbon granules** (tiny pellets of carbon) against a second carbon block. When they are pressed together the resistance of the carbon granules gets smaller. The current from the battery in the microphone circuit gets bigger. When the carbon block moves outwards the resistance of the microphone increases. This causes the current to get smaller. The current flowing in the microphone is a wavy d.c. (Fig. 97.2). It has the same frequency as the original sound.

THE TELEPHONE EARPIECE

When you talk on the telephone the current from your microphone goes to the listener's earpiece (Fig. 97.3). The earpiece has two coils on cores of iron. In front of these cores is a thin steel plate. When the current flows in the coils the magnetic force on the steel plate changes as the current changes. So the steel plate or **diaphragm** vibrates with the same frequency as the current. This sets the air vibrating. The listener hears a sound similar to that at the microphone.

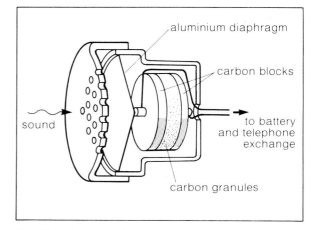

Fig. 97.1 A carbon microphone.

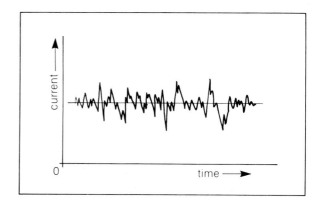

Fig. 97.2 The electric current from a carbon microphone has a wave-form something like this when someone is speaking.

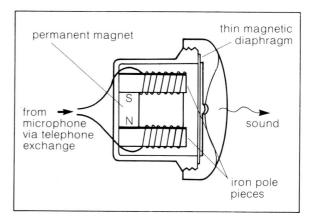

Fig. 97.3 A telephone earpiece.

RECORDING SOUNDS

The current from a microphone can be made bigger, or **amplified**. Then the amplified current can be used to make a recording of the original sound. The wavy current makes a needle vibrate. This needle cuts a wavy groove on a soft disc which is turning round (Fig. 97.4). A copy of this soft disc is then made in metal. This is the **master disc**. The records you buy have been pressed out in plastic from a master disc.

When you put a record on to the turntable of a record-player the needle, or **stylus**, of the **pick-up head** rests in the wavy groove. As the disc turns the needle vibrates in the wavy groove copying the original vibrations of the cutting needle. This vibration is turned into electrical signals by the pick-up. These signals are made bigger by an **amplifier** and fed to a loudspeaker. If the disc turns at the same speed as the original disc did, the sound you hear from the loudspeaker is like the original sound.

TAPE RECORDING

This is the most popular way of recording sound, and pictures too. It uses a plastic tape coated with tiny particles of a magnetic material. The current from the microphone is amplified and then flows to the **recording head** (Fig. 97.5). In this head the wavy current flows through a small coil wound on a specially shaped iron core. This causes a magnetic field which magnetises the magnetic particles on the tape as it moves past at a very steady speed. As the current changes so the recorded magnetic effect changes. The magnetic powder on the tape keeps its magnetism.

When you play the tape back, the tape moves past the head (now used as a **play-back head**) at the same speed and in the same direction as before. But now the coil in the head is connected to an amplifier. As the magnetised tape passes the coil in the head, a wavy current is induced in the coil. This current is a copy of the original recorded current. So the sound you hear from the loudspeaker connected to the amplifier is a copy of the sound first received by the microphone.

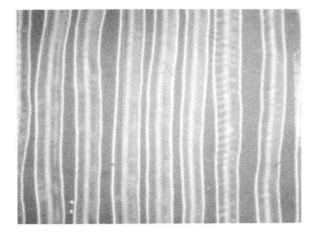

Fig. 97.4   A magnified view of the grooves on a gramophone record.

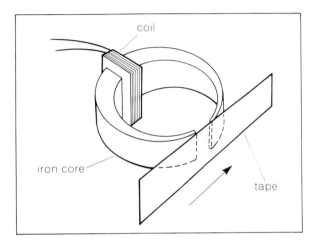

Fig. 97.5   Inside the head of a tape-recorder.

MAGNETIC PICK-UP

Some electric guitars use magnetic pick-ups (Fig. 97.6). They change the sound energy of the strings to electrical energy. The strings are made of steel. As they move up and down, the strength of the field in the iron core of the magnetic pick-up changes. This induces a current in the pick-up coils. An amplifier makes this current big enough to work loudspeakers.

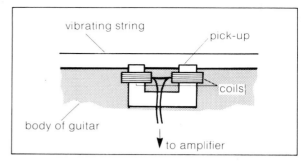

Fig. 97.6 A magnetic pick-up.

SUMMARY: ELECTRICITY FROM MAGNETISM

- A moving magnetic field can cause an electric potential difference and so an electric current in a circuit.
- The size of the induced electric potential difference and current depends on the rate at which the magnetic field changes in the circuit (Faraday's law).
- The induced potential difference or current will be in a direction that opposes the change that causes it (Lenz's law).
- To find the direction of the potential difference from the direction of the force and the field, Fleming's right-hand rule can be used.
- Dynamos or generators have rotating coils or rotating magnets.
- A small a.c. dynamo does not have a commutator; there are two slip-rings instead.
- A d.c. dynamo needs a split-ring commutator.
- Generators in power stations have the coils wound on a stator; the magnetic field is produced by a rotating electromagnet.

- The iron cores of transformers are laminated to reduce eddy currents.
- A transformer can step alternating voltages up or down. It will not work on d.c.
- In a transformer:

$$\frac{\text{secondary voltage}}{\text{primary voltage}} = \frac{\text{number of turns on secondary coil}}{\text{number of turns on primary coil}}$$

- Electrical energy is transmitted along the cables of the National Grid at high voltages. This reduces energy losses.
- Microphones convert sound energy to electrical energy.
- Sounds can be stored as patterns on plastic discs or on magnetic tape.

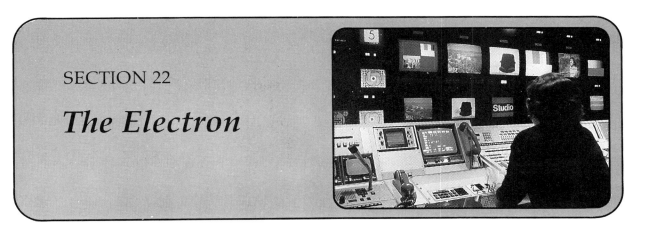

SECTION 22

The Electron

98 Charge, current and electrons

You know that some substances, e.g., such metals as copper and aluminium, are good **electrical conductors** (p. 141). Some other substances, e.g., air, polythene and other plastics, are very poor conductors. These are called **electrical insulators**.

Electrons are tiny negatively charged particles. They normally form a cloud round the nucleus of the atom (Fig. 98.1). The number of negative electrons equals the number of positive charges in the central nucleus of an atom; the atom is neutral.

Metals like copper and aluminium conduct electricity well. Their atoms can lose an outer electron easily, and these drift about inside the metal. These are **conduction electrons** (p. 141).

Electric currents in metals consist of large numbers of these electrons drifting round a circuit. They drift along because cells or generators repel electrons from the negative terminal and attract them to the positive terminal.

CAPACITORS

Imagine that you connect a cell to two metal plates with an air gap in between (Fig. 98.2(a)).

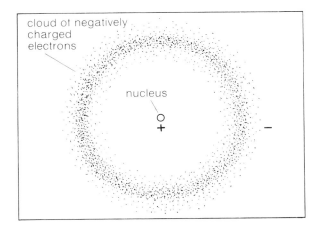

Fig. 98.1 A model of an atom. A cloud of electrons surrounds a central tiny positively charged nucleus.

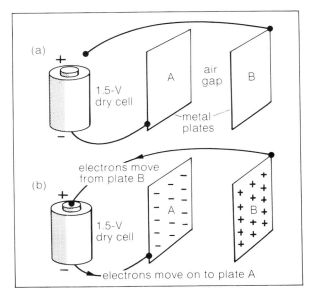

Fig. 98.2 Two insulated metal plates connected to a dry cell.

187

Electrons will be repelled from the negative pole of the cell and move along the wire to the metal plate A. They will collect there and stop any more electrons leaving the cell. The other plate B will lose just as many electrons to the positive pole of the cell. The two plates will have equal and opposite charges on them (Fig. 98.2(b)). The two plates and the air gap will store a little electric charge and a little electrical energy.

The larger the plates, the more charge they can store. The closer the plates are together, the more charge they can store. Two plates held apart by a good insulator like this make a **capacitor**. Capacitors store charges and small amounts of energy. They are found in all radio and TV sets. There are many different sorts. Three common ones are shown below.

Electrolytic capacitors   These have a large **capacitance** (ability to store charge) for their size because the insulator layer is very thin. They are formed by passing a current through a chemical solution in contact with the plates. You must connect electrolytic capacitors in a circuit the right way round. If they are connected the wrong way the insulator may be destroyed. The positive terminal is clearly marked.

Polyester capacitors   The conductors are sheets of aluminium foil (Fig. 98.3). The insulator is a polyester film rolled up to make it more compact. The capacitance is fixed.

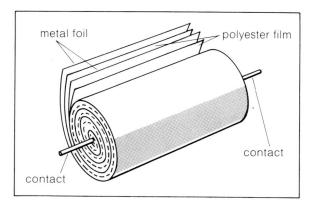

Fig. 98.3   Rolling up the metal plates in a polyester capacitor.

Variable air capacitors   These have two sets of metal plates (Fig. 98.4). The insulator is air. They are used in radio-tuning circuits. Turning the knob varies the overlapping area of the plates. This changes the capacitance of the capacitor.

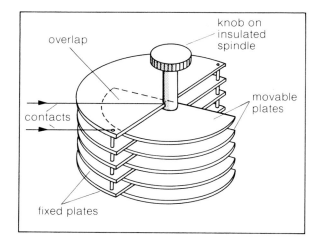

Fig. 98.4   A variable air capacitor.

THERMIONIC EMISSION

When a metal is heated in a vacuum electrons can escape. This process is called **thermionic emission**. The kinetic theory (p. 85) tells us that when materials get hotter, the particles in them move or vibrate faster. In a very hot metal wire the drifting conduction electrons rush about at high speeds. When the metal is hot enough, some of these electrons are moving so fast that when they reach the surface of the wire they keep going into the space outside it.

For each electron outside, there is one positive charge left behind on the nucleus of the metal. These positive charges attract the negative electrons back into the wire. So long as the metal wire is kept hot, electrons escape out, taking the places of those attracted back in. The average number of electrons in the space just outside the hot wire remains about the same.

99 Making electron beams

An **electron beam** is a stream of electrons all rushing along the same line through space. Electron beams are used in picture tubes of TV sets and in cathode ray oscilloscopes (p. 191).

AN ELECTRON GUN

To make an electron beam, the electrons are shot out of an **electron gun**. A filament of thin tungsten wire—the heater hh in Fig. 99.1—is sealed into one end of a glass vessel, the **envelope**, from which the air has been pumped out. The envelope contains a vacuum. A metal disc with a central hole is put just in front of the heater. (Most heaters operate from a 6-V supply.)

The heater is also connected to the negative pole of a supply giving about 100 V d.c. The metal disc is connected to the positive pole of this supply. This makes the heater a cathode and the metal disc an anode.

Electrons 'boil off' the glowing heater where thermionic emission takes place. They are immediately attracted to the positively charged metal disc or anode. As the electrons have so little mass they are accelerated to very high speeds. Some will come out of the hole in the anode and move into the space in the rest of the envelope. With 100 V between the cathode and the anode, these electrons will be moving at about 6000 km/s. These electrons make the electron beam, which crosses the vacuum in the rest of the envelope (Fig. 99.2).

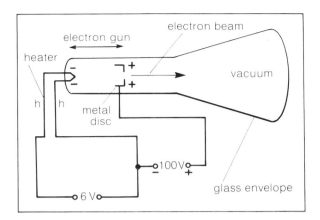

Fig. 99.1   An electron gun.

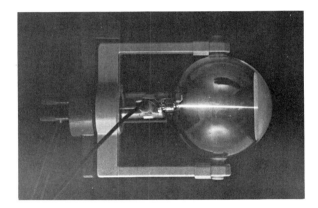

Fig. 99.2   An electron beam travelling straight.

100 How to bend electron beams

USING ELECTRIC FIELDS

Electric charges pull and push each other. There is an **electric field** in the space where these electric forces are. You know that unlike charges attract and like charges repel each other (p. 140). The electrons in the beam are negatively charged. Negative charges are attracted by positive charges and repelled by other negative ones. The fast-moving electrons in the beam will change direction a little as they pass the charged plate in Figs 100.1 and 100.2.

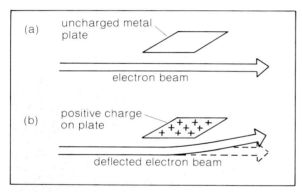

Fig. 100.1   (a) An electron beam and a metal plate. (b) If a positive charge is put on the plate, the beam is deflected upwards.

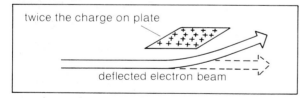

Fig. 100.2   Double the charge—and you double the deflection.

Two plates are usually used, one above the beam and another under it. These are given opposite charges so each moves the beam in the same direction (Fig. 100.3). Plates like these are used in the cathode ray oscilloscope (p. 191).

USING MAGNETIC FIELDS

Magnets and electric currents pull and push each other. There is a **magnetic field** in the space where these magnetic forces are.

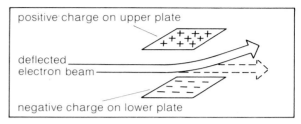

Fig. 100.3   Two plates, one positively charged and the other negatively charged, are even better.

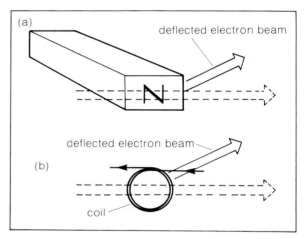

Fig. 100.4   (a) A magnetic field of a N pole causes the beam to bend. (b) So does a magnetic field due to a current in a coil.

A current in a wire is a flow of electrons. The flow of electrons in the beam is like a current in a wire. A magnetic pole placed beside (Fig. 100.4(a)) the beam will force the beam upwards or downwards. The beam will be bent, or **deflected**. The closer and stronger the magnet, the larger the deflection.

A current in a coil produces a magnetic field (p. 168). If the coil is placed beside the electron beam, the beam will be pushed upwards or downwards as before (Fig. 100.4(b)). Larger currents through the coil give bigger deflections. Reversing the current reverses the magnetic field and the deflection. In picture tubes of TV sets small permanent magnets are moved to centre the picture. Circular magnets focus the beam to give a clear picture. The deflections of the beam, which give the lines of the picture, are produced by currents in coils close to the tube.

101 The cathode ray oscilloscope

THE ELECTRON GUN

The beam of electrons is produced by thermionic emission from the filament or cathode. The anode operates at about 1000 V and is positively charged, so it attracts the electrons. However, many pass on in a straight line through the hole in the anode (Fig. 101.1).

THE DEFLECTING PLATES

Two sets of deflecting plates are used. One set is vertical called the **X-plates**. They deflect the beam and the spot on the screen to either side. The up-and-down movement of the beam and the spot is controlled by the **Y-plates**. The X and Y deflections are very like the X and Y axes of a graph. The oscilloscope can draw graphs.

THE FLUORESCENT SCREEN

This is a coating on the inside of the flat end of the glass tube. When an electron hits the screen, its kinetic energy is changed into a tiny flash of light. With many millions of electrons in the beam, these flashes add up to a bright spot.

THE TUBE

The electrodes (cathode, anode and plates) are fixed inside a glass envelope. Their connecting wires are sealed through the glass. All the air is taken out of the tube to make a good vacuum. The electrons can then move without being stopped by bumping into air molecules.

THE CONTROLS

Brightness   If all the electrons from the cathode strike the screen the spot may be too bright. You can stop some of the electrons by repelling them with a small negative voltage on a metal ring in front of the cathode. Varying this voltage varies the brightness of the spot.

Focus   If the electrons spread out too far they give a fuzzy spot. They can be pushed back into line with a small negative voltage on a focusing cylinder. You vary this negative voltage to get the sharpest point on the screen.

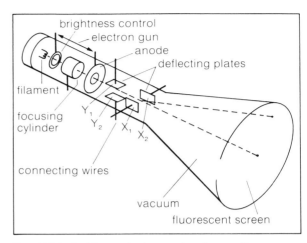

Fig. 101.1   Inside a cathode ray tube of an oscilloscope.

Fig. 101.2   A cathode ray oscilloscope.

X-shift, Y-shift   Small steady direct voltages are given to the X- and Y-plates to bring the spot accurately to the centre of the screen.

Y-gain   An amplifier makes the voltages larger before they are put on the Y-plates.

Look for these controls on the cathode ray oscilloscope shown in Fig. 101.2.

102 Jobs the oscilloscope can do

MEASURING STEADY VOLTAGES

Figure 102.1 shows what happens when you connect different numbers of dry cells to the Y-plates by the Y-terminals. The larger the number of cells, the bigger the voltage. The bigger the voltage, the more the spot is deflected. If you know the voltage and measure the deflection you can work out the deflection in millimetres per volt. Then you can use this result to measure an unknown voltage, if you don't change any control on the oscilloscope.

MEASURING ALTERNATING VOLTAGES

When you apply a small alternating voltage to the Y-plates, the spot traces out a vertical line (Fig. 102.2). The spot moves up and down at the same frequency as the alternating voltage. As the voltage increases to its maximum (positive), the spot moves to the top of the line seen on the screen. Then it moves to the bottom of the line as the voltage drops to its lowest value (negative). This is repeated so quickly that you see a vertical line on the screen. If the alternating voltage is from the a.c. mains, the line is traced out 100 times every second (50 times up and 50 times down).

You can measure the **peak** (maximum) **voltage** of this from the screen. Find the length of the line in millimetres from the centre and divide by the known millimetres per volt.

DRAWING GRAPHS USING THE TIME BASE

The electron beam can be made to draw graphs of voltage (vertical Y-axis) against time (horizontal X-axis). For this a **time base** is needed along the X-direction. A steadily increasing voltage moves the spot horizontally across the screen from left to right (Fig. 102.3). When it gets to the end, the spot flicks back to the start. It is made to disappear while it is flicking back. It keeps on repeating this at a speed you fix using the time-base control. The electronic circuits needed for this are fitted into the same case as the cathode ray tube and its controls. Some examples of its use are a.c. wave-forms (p. 178) and musical wave-forms (pp. 130 and 131).

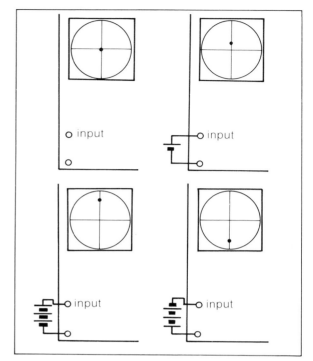

Fig. 102.1 The spot deflected by different steady voltages on the Y-plates.

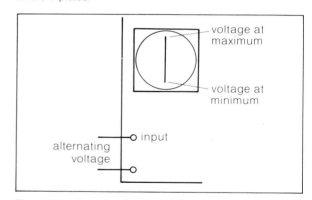

Fig. 102.2 The vertical line made by the spot when an alternating voltage is applied to the Y-plates.

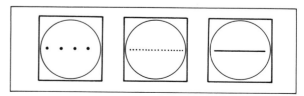

Fig. 102.3 How a time base works. The spot moves steadily from left to right.

103 How to rectify alternating current wave-forms

Connect a resistor across the Y-input of an oscilloscope and connect it to a low-voltage a.c. supply. Take this supply from the mains via a step-down transformer (p. 181). Adjust the time base carefully so that there are exactly two cycles of the signal on the screen (Fig. 103.1). The time-base frequency has to be 25 Hz for this to happen.

The graph drawn by the spot is shown in Fig. 103.1. It is called a **sine curve**. All the other graphs in this unit can be compared to this curve.

HALF-WAVE RECTIFIED A.C.

Add a **solid-state diode** to the circuit as shown in Fig. 103.2. In a diode, electrons can flow from a negative cathode to a positive anode but not the other way. No current flows when the anode is negative, as it then repels the electrons back to the cathode. A diode is a one-way street for electrons (p. 213).

The wave-form on the screen (Fig. 103.2) shows a half-cycle of the voltage when the current is flowing, followed by a half-cycle pause, the flat line. There is no current then because the electrons can't flow the other way. This is then repeated. The current flows all one way; it has been **rectified**. But it flows in jerks; half-cycle, nothing, half-cycle, nothing. It is called **half-wave rectified**.

SMOOTHED HALF-WAVE RECTIFIED A.C.

To reduce the jerkiness of the half-wave rectified current, connect a large capacitor in parallel with the resistor, which is called a **load resistor** (Fig. 103.3). The capacitor acts like a storage tank for electricity. It fills up with electrons when the voltage is high. It lets these electrons run out, into the circuit, when the voltage is low or zero. This keeps some current flowing in the half-cycles when the diode does not conduct. The ups and downs of the current are less; it has been **smoothed**.

FULL WAVE RECTIFIED A.C.

Connect four diodes in a diamond shape (Fig. 103.4). Every half-cycle of the a.c. can pass the same way through the load resistor. Diodes A and B conduct for half a cycle. Then diodes C and D conduct for half a cycle. This is called **full wave rectified**.

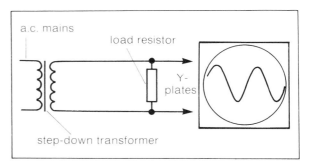

Fig. 103.1 The wave-form of the a.c. mains appears across the load resistor.

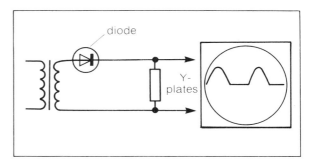

Fig. 103.2 Put a diode in the circuit and half the trace disappears.

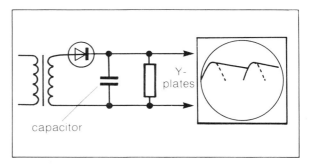

Fig. 103.3 Now add a capacitor to smooth out the wave-form.

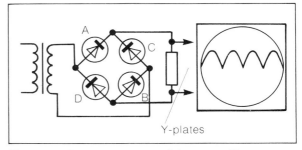

Fig. 103.4 Four diodes act as a full wave rectifier.

104 Semiconductors

A **semiconductor** is a material with conductivity between that of a conductor and an insulator. The two main semiconductor materials in use today are germanium and silicon. These materials are first made very pure. Then tiny amounts of different impurities are added to make the semiconductors. There are two types: **n-type** and **p-type**.

Semiconductor diodes are quite small: a diode only about 35 mm long can carry 26 A at mains voltage. A semiconductor diode has n-type and p-type material in the same crystal. The join between them is called a **junction**. If the p-type material is connected to the negative side of the battery in a circuit no current flows (Fig. 104.1). If it is connected to the positive side a current does flow. Thus a **p—n junction** acts as a diode (one-way device).

A **transistor** has three different regions. Either a sandwich of two p-type and an n-type in the middle (p—n—p transistor) or two n-type and a p-type in the middle (n—p—n transistor). The middle region is called the **base**. The other regions are called the **emitter** and the **collector** (p. 214). A transistor could be used in a simple circuit like that shown in Fig. 104.2. If a small current flows through the emitter and base a large current is allowed to flow through the whole transistor. The small current controls the larger one. This transistor acts as an amplifier. Many other components are needed to make the transistor do its job. Note that the transistor is only one little component; it is not a complete radio!

There are many other semiconductor components in use in electronics (see Section 24).

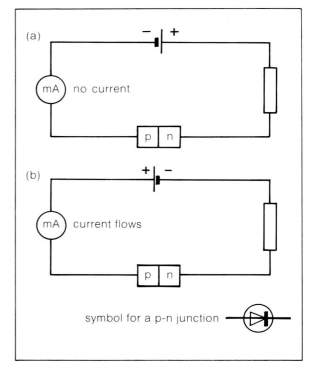

Fig. 104.1 A semiconductor diode.

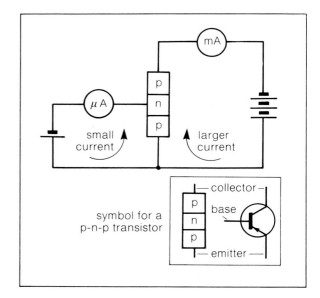

Fig. 104.2 A p—n—p transistor.

RECENT DEVELOPMENTS

Scientists have found ways of putting several transistors and other components into a very small space. These are called **integrated circuits** (IC; p. 216) (Fig. 104.3). As time has passed, more and more components have been crowded into smaller and smaller packages. The latest integrated circuits are often called **silicon chips**. The working part may contain thousands of components on a piece of silicon about the size of a pin-head. They form the hearts of computers and microprocessors.

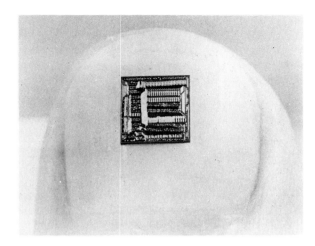

Fig. 104.3 An integrated circuit resting on a thumb nail.

SUMMARY: THE ELECTRON

- Electric currents in metals consist of very small negatively charged particles, called electrons, drifting round a circuit from the negative pole of a battery to the positive pole. We say that currents flow the other way.
- An electron carries a single negative charge.
- A capacitor can store small amounts of electric charge: the negative plate will have extra electrons and the positive plate will be short of the same number of electrons.
- Electrons may escape from very hot wires in a process called thermionic emission.
- Electrons can be accelerated in an electron gun to form a beam.
- Electron beams can be deflected by electric and magnetic fields.

- The electron beam in a cathode ray oscilloscope can be made to move up and down as well as from side to side.
- Oscilloscopes can measure both direct and alternating voltages.
- The time base of an oscilloscope makes the spot move from left to right at a known speed. This speed can be changed over wide limits.
- A diode will produce direct current from alternating current. This is called rectification.
- Semiconducting materials are used in such electronic components as diodes, transistors and integrated circuits.
- A transistor can be used either as an electrical switch or as an amplifier.

Radioactivity and Nuclear Energy

105 Atomic structure

We think that an atom has a nucleus with a cloud of electrons round it. The **nucleus** is made of **protons**, which have a positive charge, and **neutrons**, which have no charge. Protons and neutrons have about the same mass. Most of the mass of an atom is in the nucleus because the electrons are far less massive than the protons or neutrons. Remember,

Neutral
eutrons in
ucleus

Plus
ositive
rotons

Each electron has a negative charge. Electrons move about in the space round the nucleus at varying distances from it. This space is very much larger than the nucleus. The nucleus holds them because its positive charge attracts their negative charge. This theory of the atom is called the **Rutherford model**.

Imagine a scale model of an atom as big as a multi-storey car park with 10 floors. The nucleus would be about the size of a grain of rice. It would be in the middle of the model. The electrons would be much smaller than pin-heads. They would rush about the whole model.

SYMBOLS, MASS NUMBERS AND ATOMIC NUMBERS

Each kind of atom has a symbol. He stands for a helium atom, N for a nitrogen atom, U for a uranium atom and so on. The number of protons in a nucleus is its **atomic** or **proton number**. A helium atom (Fig. 105.1), which has two protons, has an atomic number of 2. The total number of particles in the nucleus is an atom's **mass number**. A helium atom with two protons and two neutrons has a mass number of 4. These numbers are sometimes written by the atom's symbol, e.g., $^4_2$He.

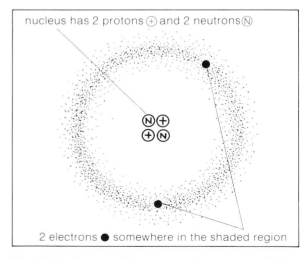

Fig. 105.1 One way of drawing a helium atom—but *NOT* to scale.

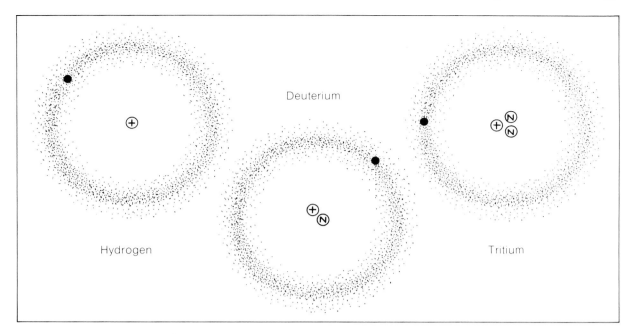

Fig. 105.2   The three isotopes of hydrogen.

ISOTOPES

All atoms of the same element have the same atomic number; that is, they all have the same number of protons in the nucleus. For example, all hydrogen atoms have a single proton in the nucleus; the atomic number is 1. But about three hydrogen atoms in every 20 000 have a neutron as well; and a very small number have two neutrons in the nucleus

(Fig. 105.2). Although all these types have the same atomic number (1), their mass numbers are different. The mass number for ordinary hydrogen is 1, that for heavy hydrogen (deuterium) is 2 and that for tritium is 3. These are called **isotopes** of hydrogen. Most elements exist as mixtures of isotopes (Table 105). Note in this table that carbon-14, for example, refers to carbon with a mass number of 14.

Table 105   Isotopes of hydrogen and carbon

Isotope	Atomic number	Mass number	Symbol
Hydrogen: 1 proton	1	1	$_1^1H$
Deuterium: 1 proton, 1 neutron	1	2	$_1^2H$
Tritium: 1 proton, 2 neutrons	1	3	$_1^3H$
Carbon-12: 6 protons, 6 neutrons	6	12	$_6^{12}C$
Carbon-13: 6 protons, 7 neutrons	6	13	$_6^{13}C$
Carbon-14: 6 protons, 8 neutrons	6	14	$_6^{14}C$

106 Detecting radioactivity

Most atomic nuclei go on existing without changing at all—ever! Carbon-12 is one example. But some nuclei don't do this; they break up. These are the **radioactive nuclei**. Carbon-14 is one example; radium is another. When this breakup happens the nucleus emits or gives out **radiation**. This sort of radiation includes particles and very short wavelength electromagnetic waves (p. 95).

There are three fairly simple ways of detecting this radiation. The simplest is to use **photographic film** in the same way that a hospital radiographer working with X-rays does. When the film is developed the parts that received the radiation come out black. So a shadow picture is cast (Fig. 106.1). Film is used in the safety badges worn by people working with radioactive substances.

Fig. 106.1   This shadow of a key was produced by placing it between a piece of photographic film and a radioactive source.

High-flying aircraft may leave vapour trails as they cross the sky so that you see where they have been. These trails are made up of countless water droplets or ice crystals which have formed behind the aircraft as it disturbed the air. Particles from a radioactive substance also disturb any gas they pass through. They may **ionise** it (p. 149). Water or alcohol vapour which may be present condenses to drops on the ions leaving a **track** for you to see. Of course, the conditions have to be just right for this to happen, and this can be done in a **cloud chamber**. Two common ways of getting the right conditions are:

1   To lower the pressure in an **expansion cloud chamber** (Fig. 106.2).
2   To cool the chamber with dry ice in a **diffusion cloud chamber**.

Figure 106.3 shows some tracks from a tiny piece of thorium (the source).

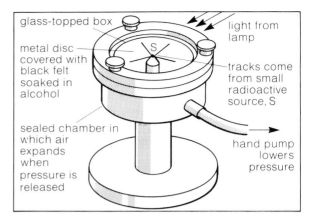

Fig. 106.2   Simple expansion cloud chamber showing four straight tracks. The metal disc and the source are at about + 1 kV and the case is earthed.

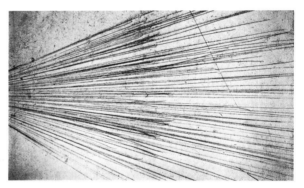

Fig. 106.3   Tracks in a cloud chamber caused by α-particles from a thorium source.

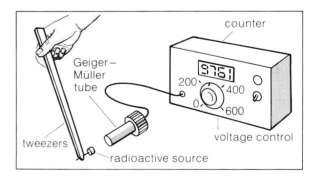

Fig. 106.4   Counting with a Geiger–Müller tube.

A third method uses a special tube called a **Geiger–Müller tube**. Radiation going into the tube ionises some of the gas atoms inside it. This allows a high-voltage pulse to pass for a very short time. These pulses are amplified and can then be counted with an electronic counter (Fig. 106.4).

107 Types of radiation

Experiments show that three kinds of radiation come from radioactive sources (Table 107).

ALPHA-RADIATION

The element americium, Am-241, gives **alpha-(α-) radiation**. You can detect this radiation using a Geiger–Müller tube and counter. The Geiger–Müller tube must be placed close to the source to detect the α-radiation. This radiation will only pass through a few centimetres of air.

Figure 106.3 shows tracks made by α-radiation in a cloud chamber. These tracks are about 7 cm long.

Quite thin paper will stop α-radiation (Fig. 107.1). A very, very strong magnet will deflect it slightly. Passing it between electrically charged plates in a vacuum can also deflect it. The α-radiation moves towards the negatively charged plate.

These and other experiments show that α-radiation is a stream of particles, **alpha-particles**. These particles are positively charged and have a mass number of 4. They are the nuclei of helium atoms. Their mass makes them hard to deflect. They are shot out of the central part, the nucleus, of the americium (and many other) atoms.

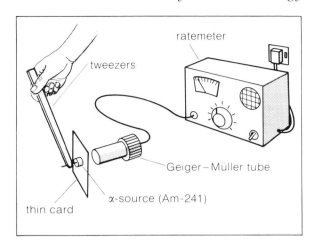

Fig. 107.1 Absorbing α-particles with a sheet of paper.

Table 107 Types of radiation from radioactive isotopes

Type of radiation	What is it?	Deflection by magnetic/electric fields	Typical range in air	Stopped by
Alpha (α)	α-particles/ helium nuclei: mass 4, charge + 2e	A little	A few centimetres	Thin paper, human skin
Beta (β)	β-particles/ electrons: low mass, charge − 1e	A lot	A few metres	Aluminium (5 mm)
Gamma (γ)	γ-rays/ electromagnetic radiation	Not at all	Many metres	Thick lead and concrete

e is the charge on an electron.

BETA-RADIATION

The element strontium-90 gives **beta- (β-) radiation** only. You can detect β-radiation using a Geiger–Müller tube and counter. This radiation can pass through several metres of air. It also passes through paper, card and thin aluminium foil. A 5-mm thick sheet of aluminium will stop it. β-radiation is easily deflected by a magnet (Fig. 107.2). The electric field between two charged plates in a vacuum will deflect β-radiation towards the positively charged plate.

These and other tests show that β-radiation is a stream of fast-moving **beta-particles**. These particles have a negative charge and a low mass (about 1/7000 of the mass of an α-particle). Their low mass makes them easy to deflect. However, as they have a negative charge they are deflected in the opposite direction to α-particles, which have two positive charges, by electric and magnetic fields. They are electrons that are shot out of the nucleus.

GAMMA-RADIATION

The element cobalt-60 gives **gamma- (γ-) radiation** only. γ-radiation can pass through many metres of air. It also goes through paper and aluminium, even through several centimetres of lead. Neither magnets nor electrically charged plates can deflect γ-radiation. γ-radiation is **electromagnetic radiation** (p. 95), not particles. γ-rays are like X-rays, but they have more energy and a shorter wavelength.

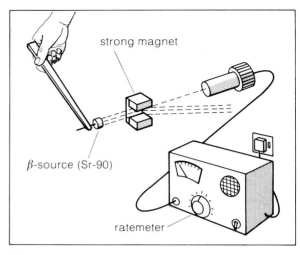

Fig. 107.2 Testing for the deflection of β-particles in a magnetic field.

EVIDENCE FOR THE RUTHERFORD MODEL OF AN ATOM

Physicists use atomic particles as bullets with which to bombard atoms. It was in this way that the model of an atom with a central, massive and positively charged nucleus came about. α-particles were used to bombard thin sheets (foils) of metals. Most of the particles went straight through—it was as though the metal's atoms weren't there. So maybe atoms are largely empty! But a very few bounced right back. Calculations showed that such a particle must have come very close to a small, highly charged particle which repelled it very strongly. That was the nucleus with its positive charge. This theory was proposed by Rutherford.

108 Nuclear reactions—radioactive decay

Carbon isotopes all have six protons in their nucleus, but different numbers of neutrons. Atoms of the carbon-14 isotope split up, or **decay**, spontaneously: Carbon-14 is a **radioactive isotope**, or **radioisotope** (Fig. 108.1).

All types of atoms have some radioactive isotopes. Well-known examples are radium-226, strontium-90 and cobalt-60. It is not possible to stop or slow down the decay of a radioisotope. Nor is there any way of knowing which atom will decay next. Radioactive decay is a **random process**.

HALF-LIFE

Imagine a beaker containing a little radioactive sodium, Na-24. The sodium might be part of some sodium chloride, but it would still decay steadily. As each atom decays it shoots out a β-particle and a γ-ray. You could use a Geiger—Müller tube and counter to find the number of counts per second. As more and more sodium atoms decay there would be fewer left to decay. The counter would show fewer counts per second. After 15 h the counts per second would be only half the value at the start of the experiment. This is because half the sodium atoms have decayed. After another 15 h the counts would have halved again, to a quarter of the first value. This would go on until the count rate was too small to measure accurately (Fig. 108.2).

The time taken for half the atoms in any sample of a radioisotope to decay is called the **half-life** of that isotope. Half-lives differ greatly. Uranium-238 has a half-life of over 4000 million years. For strontium-90 it is 28 years, and for oxygen-13 it is less than 0.01 s.

Example A laboratory buys 4 mg of strontium-90 with a half-life of 28 years. How much Sr-90 is left after 84 years?

The amount halves every 28 years. Therefore, after 28 years ($\frac{1}{2} \times 4$ mg) $= 2$ mg has decayed, so 2 mg is left. After another 28 years (56 in all), ($\frac{1}{2} \times 2$ mg) $= 1$ mg more has decayed, so 1 mg is left. After yet another 28 years (84 in all), ($\frac{1}{2} \times 1$ mg) $= 0.5$ mg more has decayed, so 0.5 mg is left. Therefore 0.5 mg of Sr-90 is left after 84 years.

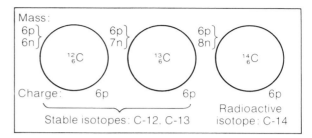

Fig. 108.1 Three different isotopes of carbon (p = proton, n = neutron).

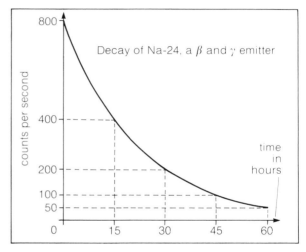

Fig. 108.2 How a radioactive isotope decays during a period of time.

WHAT IS LEFT WHEN DECAY TAKES PLACE?

When uranium, $^{238}_{92}U$, decays it loses an α-particle $^{4}_{2}He$. The atom left after decay is thorium.

$$^{238}_{92}U \rightarrow {}^{234}_{90}Th + {}^{4}_{2}He$$

The thorium atoms stay mixed with the unchanged uranium atoms, and thorium itself decays. The decay goes through several stages until a **stable atom of lead** is formed.

When a carbon-14 nucleus emits a β-particle it changes to a nitrogen nucleus. The β-particle has a mass which is almost zero and a charge of -1. It is an electron. A neutron in the carbon has changed to a proton plus the emitted β-particle. The reaction is written:

$$^{14}_{6}C \rightarrow {}^{14}_{7}N + {}^{0}_{-1}e$$

109 Uses of radioactivity

Some elements are naturally radioactive, for example, radium and uranium. Other types of atom can be made radioactive by putting them inside a nuclear reactor. Natural and artificial radioactive isotopes, or radioisotopes, have many uses. Here are some examples.

WHERE IS IT? RADIOACTIVE TRACING

Plants need phosphates for growth. Biologists using P-32 tracer have found that some plants take in phosphates more readily through their leaves than through their roots. They also measured how quickly the plants took in phosphates and which parts of the plants the phosphates went to. Tests of this type can be done without digging up the plant and killing it.

Engineers use radioisotopes to measure how fast engines wear. The piston of a car or motor-bike engine can go up and down the cylinder 140 times every second. The piston rings rub on the cylinder walls as they go up and down. Tiny pieces of metal wear off the walls and rings and fall into the engine's oil. The rings or cylinder walls can be made of steel containing radioactive iron, Fe-59. The engineers measure the radioactivity in the oil and use this to work out the rate of wear. They can do this without taking the engine to pieces, so this type of testing is quick, easy and cheap to do.

Finding obstructions in oil, gas or water pipes is easy using radioactive isotopes. A rubber ball with a radioactive isotope inside is put into the pipeline. It rolls or floats along until the obstruction stops it. The engineers, using a detector and counter outside the pipe, then know where the obstruction is.

Fig. 109.1 Preparing a bone specimen for radioactive dating with carbon-14.

HOW OLD IS IT? RADIOACTIVE DATING

Radioactive atoms decay. We know their half-lives. The half-life of carbon-14 is 5730 years. All living things contain carbon. While they are living they take in carbon dioxide present in the air. This carbon dioxide contains a little carbon-14. Once they die, no more carbon-14 is taken in. The carbon-14 in their bodies decays.

So, if we find an old piece of wood, say, it is possible to find out how many years have passed since the tree from which it came died. This is done simply by measuring the amount of carbon-14 left. Archaeologists and historians use radioactive carbon dating (Fig. 109.1).

IS IT JUST RIGHT? PRODUCTION CONTROL

It is often necessary in industry to know exactly how thick something is. Is the steel plate to make a tin can too thick or too thin? Steel plate absorbs β-radiation. How much gets through the plate depends on how thick the plate is.

One way to control the thickness is to use a source of β-radiation on one side of the plate and a detector on the other. The readings of the detector can also be used to adjust the rolling mill to give steel of just the right thickness (Fig. 109.2).

CAN WE HELP YOU? MEDICAL USES

There are many medical uses of radioactive substances.

1 A radioactive tracer in the bloodstream can be used to detect blood clots before they become dangerous. Then treatment can be applied in good time.
2 Sources containing cobalt-60 or other radioisotopes are used to treat some types of cancer (Fig. 109.3).
3 A heart pacemaker contains plutonium-238. As this decays it produces heat, which makes electricity by the thermoelectric effect. The electricity gives the heart a series of tiny electric shocks, which keep the heart going for as long as the pacemaker works—this is about 10 years. After this time a new pacemaker has to be fitted.
4 γ-rays are used to **sterilise** bandages, dressings, syringes and other equipment that must be germ free. This method is quicker, more reliable and cheaper than sterilisation by heat.

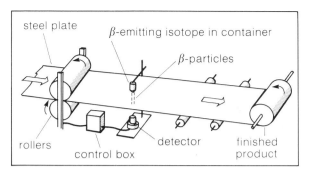

Fig. 109.2 The thickness of the steel plate is measured continuously. This measurement controls the pressure on the rollers so that the thickness doesn't change.

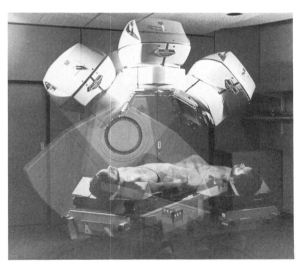

Fig. 109.3 Computer-controlled tracking machine using a Co-60 source.

110 Caution—radioactivity

Radioactive substances are useful but they can be harmful to health (Fig. 110.1). Mild radiation doses may create skin burns. Larger doses can lead to uncontrolled bleeding, eye cataracts, loss of resistance to infection, cancer and death.

BACKGROUND RADIATION

No one can escape radiation. Some comes from outer space, some from natural radioactive elements in the earth. All glass, for example, contains a little radioactive potassium, K-40. This small but continuous radiation is called **background radiation**, or sometimes just **background**. If you switch on a Geiger—Müller tube anywhere it shows about 30 counts per minute even with no source near it. This is the **background count**. It is very small compared to the counts from radioisotopes used in industry and for experiments. But it is there, every day. Users of radioactive sources can't avoid background, but they must avoid direct radiation from sources, and contact with the substances themselves.

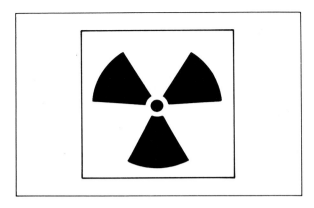

Fig. 110.1 Warning: Radioactivity. This is the take care sign used to remind people of the three types of radiation that can come from a radioisotope.

DIRECT RADIATION

α-particles are easily stopped. Air, paper, cloth and skin absorb them, so they don't usually get far enough to damage people. β-particles and γ-rays go farther but they get weaker as they go. Some of the β-particles are absorbed in the air. The γ-radiation spreads out like light from a lamp. So, the amount falling on a unit area gets less. The further you are from any radioactive material, the safer you are. **Distance** is the best safeguard.

Table 107 on p. 199 shows what stops α-, β- and γ-radiation. Lead and concrete are good **absorbers** (stoppers). Powerful sources are used behind thick lead or concrete walls. Experiments using moderate sources are done behind walls of lead bricks.

When radioactive sources are moved they are carried in lead containers. The more powerful the source, the thicker the lead walls must be. Putting sources behind walls to stop or reduce radiation escape is called **shielding**.

Fig. 110.2 Remote handling of a nuclear fuel rod.

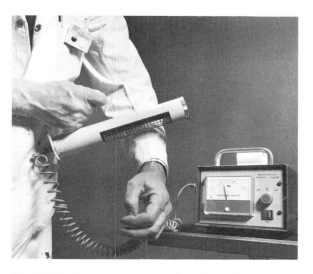

Fig. 110.3 How many methods of monitoring for radioactive contamination can you see?

DON'T TOUCH

Never touch a radioactive substance, breathe it or swallow it. It might go on affecting you for years if your body absorbs it. Even the weak sources allowed in schools are **sealed** to keep the radioisotopes in. These sources are lifted with long tweezers. Workers handle more powerful sources by **remote control** (Fig. 110.2). By moving levers they can unscrew a bottle top, lift the bottle and pour liquid from it into a test-tube. They watch this on closed circuit TV or through thick windows made from glass containing lead. The radioactive substances stay safely shielded behind thick walls.

Anyone who has to deal directly with radioisotopes wears special outer clothing. This is taken off afterwards, and the experimenter is checked with a radiation detector before leaving the laboratory. This checking is called **monitoring**. As an extra check each worker wears a badge with a photographic film in it (Fig. 110.3). Radiation darkens the film. If the film darkens, doctors carefully check the health of the worker.

111 Nuclear fission and fusion

In radioactive decay a particle is shot out of a nucleus of a radioisotope. This is called a **nuclear reaction**. There are other sorts of nuclear reaction. Nuclear fission is one. In **nuclear fission** a nucleus splits into two fragments which are of roughly the same mass. At the same time one or more neutrons are emitted.

The radioisotope uranium-235 is able to do this. It is **fissile**. If a neutron hits a U-235 nucleus at the right speed, the nucleus breaks up into fragments. There are usually two large fragments of about the same mass and some neutrons. One possible reaction is:

$$\text{neutron} + \text{U-235} \xrightarrow{\text{fission}} \begin{array}{c} \text{barium-144} \\ + \\ \text{krypton-90} \\ + \\ \text{2 neutrons} \end{array}$$

Suppose each of these two neutrons hits a U-235 nucleus and the same reaction takes place again. Then you get four neutrons. And so on. This is a **chain reaction** (Fig. 111.1). This reaction can go on just as long as there are neutrons to hit the U-235 nuclei.

The two fission fragments are positively charged nuclei and are very close together. They repel one another with very large electric forces and so fly apart at high speed. They bump into the atoms round them and make them move quickly too. The temperature of the material goes up and a lot of heat is produced. Imagine a 1-cm cube of U-235. If you could use all its energy in an engine it could run the most powerful motor bike flat out for eight months. This would take 20 000 gallons (90 000 litres) of petrol!

HOW BIG MUST THE LUMP OF URANIUM BE?

Big enough! If the lump of uranium is too small, many of the neutrons will leak out through the sides and the chain reaction stops. But there is a **critical mass** for the reaction to keep going. It is the mass of a lump of uranium about the size of a grapefruit.

Suddenly bringing together two smaller pieces of uranium that make a single piece bigger than the critical mass will cause a **nuclear explosion**. The explosion gives an

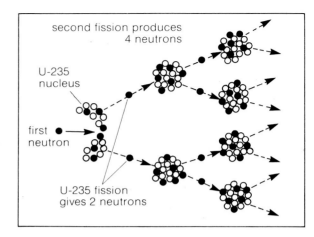

Fig. 111.1 The number of neutrons doubles at each step in this chain reaction.

intense flash. Nearby air expands making a blast wave. There is a powerful burst of γ-rays from the uncontrolled fission and, later, a fallout of harmful radioactive dust. Fission bombs contain either uranium or plutonium.

NUCLEAR REACTORS

The energy from fission can be controlled in a **nuclear reactor**. The **nuclear fuel** is an isotope that is fissile. In the British gas-cooled reactors, this fuel is packed into long cylinders called **fuel rods**. The rods are lowered into the **core** of the reactor, which is a very large block of carbon. The core has vertical channels for the fuel rods and for the cooling gas to flow through. There are also channels for the **control rods**. These are made of a substance that is a good absorber of neutrons. As more fuel rods are put in the number of neutrons flying round the core goes up. Eventually the reactor goes **critical**; that is, the chain reaction starts and continues. The temperature in the core rises and the cooling gas warms up as it carries the heat away. This energy is used to make steam to run a turbine, which drives an electric generator.

The carbon is used to slow the neutrons down. If they move too fast they merely bounce off the uranium nuclei and do not cause fission.

The rate at which the energy is produced is

controlled by the control rods which move up or down inside the vertical channels automatically. If something goes wrong, these control rods fall straight down and shut the reactor down as they do so.

WASTES

In a coal-burning power station the waste products are ash and acid-forming exhaust gases, which pass into the air. In a nuclear power station the waste products are radioactive solids. As the chain reaction continues radioactive fission products build up in the fuel rods. From time to time the rods have to be taken out and reprocessed. This separates the waste products from the unused fuel. It is a difficult and dangerous operation. Some of the radioactive wastes have very long half-lives and must be stored safely for hundreds of years; others decay in a matter of weeks or months to a safe level.

FUSION – THE WAY AHEAD

The sun and other stars get energy from a different sort of nuclear reaction. In a complex and indirect way they squeeze hydrogen nuclei together and produce helium nuclei. This is **nuclear fusion**. The hydrogen nuclei have more mass than the helium nuclei produced, and the mass lost is turned into energy. Although scientists have made a fusion bomb (the hydrogen bomb), they have not so far made a fusion power plant. Sooner or later they will be able to heat hydrogen to temperatures over 1 000 000 K and squeeze it to start controlled fusion. The raw material, hydrogen, will come from water. The fusion product, helium, will be safe and non-radioactive. And we hope the energy produced will be quite cheap.

SUMMARY: RADIOACTIVITY AND NUCLEAR ENERGY

- An atom has a central nucleus with electrons round it.
- The nucleus contains neutrons and protons.
- The atomic or proton number is the number of protons in the nucleus.
- The mass number is the number of protons and neutrons in the nucleus.
- Isotopes of an element have the same number of protons but different numbers of neutrons in the nucleus.
- Radioactive isotopes emit radiation, which can be detected by cloud chambers, Geiger–Müller tubes and counters, or by photographic film.
- α-particles are the nuclei of helium atoms. A sheet of paper stops them.
- β-particles are electrons. A thick sheet of aluminium stops them.
- γ-radiation is part of the electromagnetic spectrum. Its strength is reduced by thick lead.
- α- and β-particles can be deflected by magnetic and electric fields; α-particles have two positive charges, β-particles a single negative charge.
- When a nucleus emits radiation it is said to decay. Radioactive decay is a random process.
- The time taken for half the radioactive atoms in a given sample to decay is the half-life.
- Radioactive isotopes have many uses: for example, tracing, testing, dating and in medicine.
- Radioactive radiation can be harmful to health. No one can escape natural background radiation. Strong radioactive sources are kept behind lead or concrete shielding.
- Certain atoms can split when struck by a neutron. This is called nuclear fission.
- Nuclear fission takes place in nuclear power stations and the atomic bomb.
- Nuclear fission proceeds as a chain reaction as long as the lump of material is big enough.
- Nuclear fusion is the building up of bigger atoms from smaller ones. It is a source of energy which has yet to be developed.

SECTION 24

Electronics

112 Electronic components

A switch, a buzzer and a battery can be connected together to form a simple burglar alarm (Fig. 112.1). But there are many problems with this design. How can we make sure that the burglar presses the button? What happens when the switch is turned off?

To do the job more effectively we need to use an **electronic circuit**. This section tells you something about **electronic components**. You will see how to put them together and how to make them work for you.

RESISTORS

Resistors are used to restrict the flow of electric current in a circuit (p. 151). Resistors used in electronics are usually made from carbon (Fig. 112.2). The coloured bands tell you about the resistance and accuracy of the resistor: the first coloured band represents the first digit; the second coloured band, the second digit; the third coloured band, the number of zeros to be added to the first two digits. The value of the resistance is in ohms (Ω) (p. 152).

Using the colour code shown in Table 112, a 1000-Ω resistor would have a code of:

1st digit	1	brown
2nd digit	0	black
No. of zeros	2	red

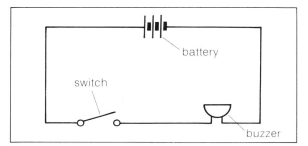

Fig. 112.1 Circuit diagram of a very simple alarm system.

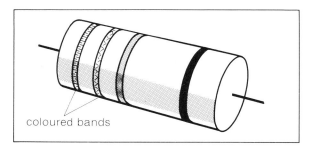

Fig. 112.2 A typical carbon resistor.

Table 112 Colour code for resistors

Colour	1st digit	2nd digit	No. of zeros
Black	0	0	
Brown	1	1	0
Red	2	2	00
Orange	3	3	000
Yellow	4	4	0 000
Green	5	5	00 000
Blue	6	6	000 000
Purple	7	7	
Grey	8	8	
White	9	9	

A 20-Ω resistor would have a code of:

1st digit	2	red
2nd digit	0	black
No. of zeros	0	black

The single band on the right-hand side of the resistor shown in Fig. 112.2 indicates the tolerance of the resistor. If a 100-Ω resistor has a tolerance of 10 per cent (silver band), this means that its actual value could be between 90 and 110 Ω. A tolerance of 1 per cent would mean an actual value between 99 and 101 Ω. For most purposes a tolerance of 5 to 10 per cent is adequate. These resistors are much cheaper than those with a 1 per cent tolerance because they are much easier to manufacture.

A resistor marked yellow, purple, red and silver would, therefore, have a resistance of 4700 Ω (4.7 kΩ) and a tolerance of 10 per cent.

Nowadays a second type of code is being marked on many resistors. In this case a capital letter is used to represent both the units and the position of the decimal point. For example,

1 Ω is written as 1R0, i.e., 1.0 Ω
100 Ω is written as 100R
1 kΩ is written as 1K0, i.e., 1.0 kΩ
10 MΩ is written as 10M

where R represents ohms, K kilo-ohms (1000 Ω) and M mega-ohms (1 000 000 Ω) or megohms.

A final letter represents the tolerance of the resistor, e.g., J represents 5 per cent and K represents 10 per cent. In this second type of code a resistor of 4.7 kΩ and 10 per cent tolerance would be marked as 4K7K.

So far we have looked only at fixed resistors, but on many occasions it is useful to be able to change the value of the resistance, and for this a **variable resistor** is required (p. 151) (Fig. 112.3).

Look carefully at Fig. 112.4. When the slider is near A, the electric current passes through very little resistance. The lamp shines brightly. As the slider is moved downwards, the current meets a larger resistance so that less current flows and the lamp is much dimmer.

An important part of an electronic circuit is the **voltage divider** (Fig. 112.5). If a 400-Ω and 100-Ω resistor are put in series with a 5-V battery, the voltage measured on V_1 will be 4 V, and that on V_2 will be 1 V. If the 100-Ω resistor is changed for a 400-Ω one, both

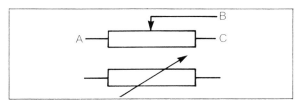

Fig. 112.3 (a) Symbols for a variable resistor.

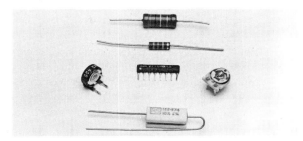

(b) A selection of typical fixed and variable resistors.

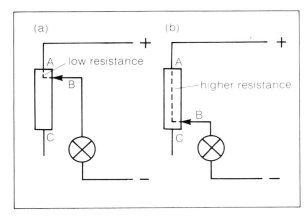

Fig. 112.4 Circuits showing the effect of varying resistance.

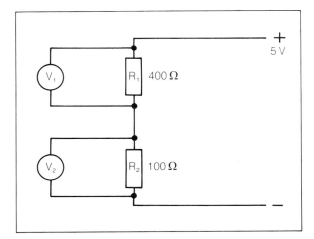

Fig. 112.5 Voltage-divider circuit.

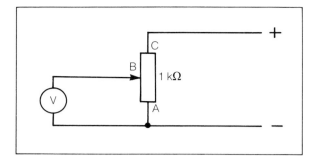

Fig. 112.6 Voltage-divider circuit using a variable resistor.

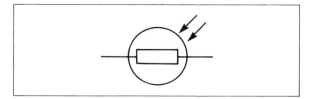

Fig. 112.7 Symbol for a light-dependent resistor.

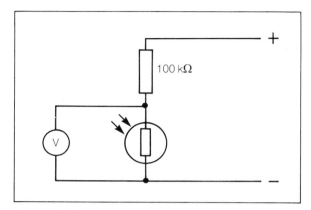

Fig. 112.8 Circuit to show the principle behind a photographic exposure meter.

voltmeters would read 2.5 V. In other words the total voltage available from the supply is shared between the two resistors, with the larger resistor taking the larger proportion of the voltage.

A similar experiment can be done with a variable resistor instead of two fixed ones (Fig. 112.6). When the slider is near C the voltmeter will read 5 V. But as the slider moves towards A, the voltage decreases to 0 V when B reaches A.

LIGHT-DEPENDENT RESISTORS

A useful electronic component is the **light-dependent resistor** (**LDR**) which, as its name suggests, is a resistor whose resistance to electric current changes as the amount of light falling on it alters (Fig. 112.7).

In bright light an LDR has a very low resistance, which means that electric current will flow through it easily. In the dark the LDR has a very high resistance, which means that it is very difficult for an electric current to flow through it. An LDR can be set up in a voltage-divider circuit (Fig. 112.8). As more light shines on the LDR its resistance decreases. This means that the voltmeter reading will also decrease. This illustrates the principle behind an exposure meter used in photography, where light intensity is converted to a voltage on a meter (Fig. 112.9).

Fig. 112.9 An exposure meter.

In a circuit containing an LDR and a buzzer, no sound will be heard in the dark because the resistance is so high that only a very small current will flow. When light shines on the LDR the resistance decreases, so current flows through the buzzer and it makes a sound. This could be thought of as a very simple burglar alarm which operates when light from an intruder's torch shines on the LDR in a dark room (Fig. 112.9). However, a very bright light is needed to operate the circuit and the torch would have to shine directly on to the LDR.

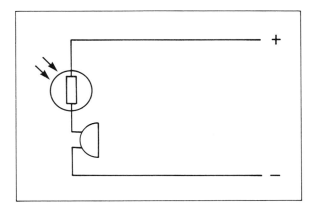

Fig. 112.10 Simple light-operated buzzer circuit.

THERMISTORS

A **thermistor** is a device whose resistance alters when the temperature changes (Fig. 112.11). In the most common type the resistance decreases as the temperature rises.

A simple electronic thermometer can be built using the circuit shown in Fig. 112.12. As the temperature rises the resistance of the thermistor decreases, and so does the reading on the voltmeter. If the thermistor is placed firstly into melting ice and then into the steam above pure boiling water, the voltages corresponding to 0 and 100 °C can be found. It is then possible to convert any other voltage readings to the appropriate temperature.

The advantage of this type of thermometer is that you can take readings at a distance from the place where the temperature is being measured, because you can use a long length of wire to connect the voltmeter to the thermistor. This **remote sensing** is an important aspect of electronics.

Fig. 112.11 Two types of thermistor.

PUSH-SWITCHES

Most switches around your school and home can remain in either an on or off position. The push-switch (Fig. 112.13) is only on when it is pressed. As soon as it is released the switch returns to its normal off position. This type of switch is used a great deal in electronic circuits for sending single bursts or pulses of electric current into a circuit.

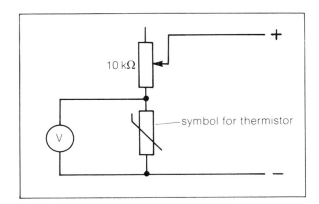

Fig. 112.12 Circuit for an electronic thermometer.

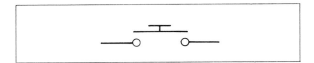

Fig. 112.13 Symbol for a push-switch.

REED SWITCHES

A **reed switch** is controlled by a magnet (p. 139). There are two types of reed switch known as normally open (NO) or normally closed (NC) (Fig. 112.14). This describes the state of the switch contacts when there is no magnet nearby.

A simple demonstration showing one way in which these devices are used in security systems is shown in Fig. 112.15. When the door is closed, the magnet in the door is close to the Normally Closed reed switch. So the contacts are separated and no current can flow. When the door is opened, the magnet moves away and the contacts return to their normally closed position, causing the alarm to sound.

Fig. 112.14   Symbols for reed switches.

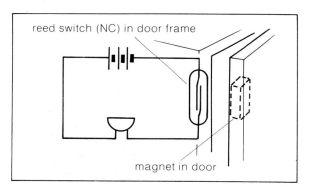

Fig. 112.15   How a reed switch is used in an alarm system.

Fig. 112.16   A reed switch system fitted to a window frame.

CAPACITORS

When a **capacitor** (Figs 112.17 and 112.18) (p. 187) is connected to a battery, electric charge immediately flows into the capacitor until it is full (Fig. 112.19). This takes a fraction of a second. If the capacitor is then connected to an LED (p. 213), a small flash of light is noticed as the electric charge escapes from the capacitor and flows through the LED. When a capacitor is fully charged no more current can flow into it, so it acts as if it were a very high resistance in the circuit.

Fig. 112.17   Symbols for (a) a non-electrolytic capacitor and (b) an electrolytic capacitor.

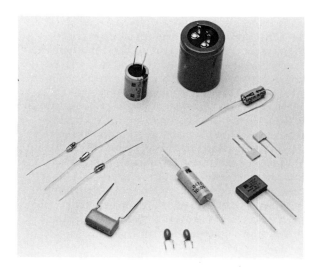

Fig. 112.18   A selection of capacitors.

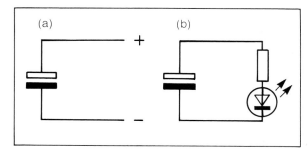

Fig. 112.19   Charging and discharging a capacitor.

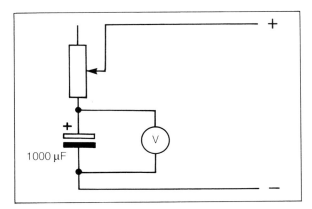

Fig. 112.20 A circuit to investigate the charging of a capacitor.

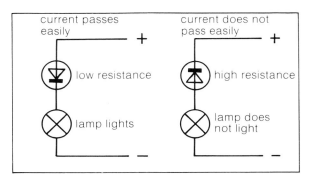

Fig. 112.22 Circuits to show the properties of a diode.

Capacitance is measured in units called **microfarads** (μF). Typical values range from between 0.1 and 1000 μF—the 1000-μF capacitor being able to store more electric charge. The larger value electrolytic capacitors (p. 188) must be connected the right way round in a circuit, but because of the way they are constructed this is not necessary with capacitors of less than 1 μF.

If a capacitor has a resistor in series with it, the charge will enter the capacitor more slowly. The larger the resistance the longer the capacitor will take to become fully charged. This can be investigated using a circuit like that in Fig. 112.20. As the capacitor charges up the voltage across it rises until it is fully charged, at which point the voltmeter should be measuring (very nearly) the supply voltage.

Capacitors are used a great deal in timing circuits. By varying the value of the variable resistor in the circuit in Fig.112.20 the time taken to charge the capacitor fully can be altered. This circuit will be used later as the basis of a timing device (p. 215).

DIODES

A **diode** (Fig. 112.21) is a device that has a very high resistance when connected one way in a circuit, but a very low resistance when connected the other way (p. 193) (Fig. 112.22).

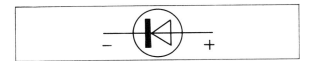

Fig. 112.21 Symbol for a diode.

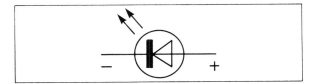

Fig. 112.23 (a) Symbol for a light-emitting diode.

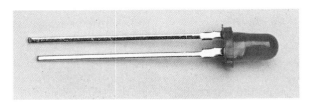

(b) What it actually looks like.

Fig. 112.24 LEDs are used in music centres.

A **light-emitting diode** (**LED**) (Fig. 112.23) operates in the same way as an ordinary diode, but, as its name suggests, it also gives out light when electricity passes through it. LEDs are used in record-players, music centres, video recorders and TV sets as indicator lights because they are small, reliable and only require a very small amount of electric current to make them operate (Fig. 112.24).

As an LED can be easily destroyed if too much current is allowed to pass through it, it is usual to put a resistor (say 330 Ω if using a 5-V power supply) in series with the LED to restrict the size of the current (Fig. 112.25).

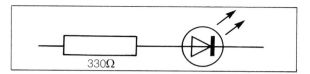

Fig. 112.25   An LED with a series protective resistor.

TRANSISTORS

Transistors (p. 194) can be used either as electronic switches or as amplifiers. They have three terminals – **base, collector** and **emitter** (Figs. 104.2, 112.26). In the n–p–n transistor used here, the collector is made positive and the emitter negative (Fig. 112.26). Current will only flow from plus (+) to minus (−) through the collector and emitter, when there is current flowing through the base. However, the size of the current in the base need only be very small compared with the current flowing in the collector.

As you change the resistance of the variable resistor (Fig. 112.27), the LED should come on or go off. The voltage on the voltmeter should vary between about 5 V and 0 V. When the voltage between the base and emitter is very low the LED does not light up. By gradually altering the resistance the voltage can increase and, at one particular value, the LED will light up. The value of this base/emitter voltage depends on the type of transistor, but it is usually about 0.7 V. Any voltage less than that and the LED will be out, i.e., the transistor is off. Any voltage greater than 0.7 V will ensure that the LED is alight, i.e., the transistor is on.

The transistor switch becomes much more important when it can be operated automatically.

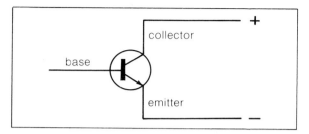

Fig. 112.26   (a) Symbol for a transistor.

(b) What they actually look like.

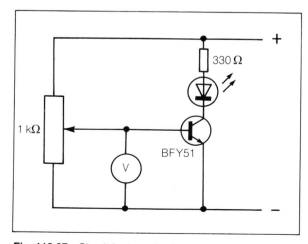

Fig. 112.27   Circuit for investigating the way a transistor operates.

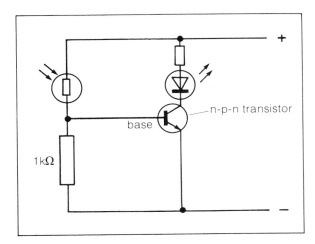

Fig. 112.28 Circuit for a light-operated transistor switch.

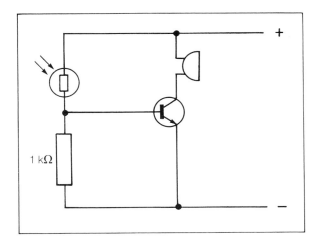

Fig. 112.29 Circuit for a light-operated alarm.

A LIGHT-OPERATED TRANSISTOR SWITCH

In the dark the resistance of the LDR is very high (approaching one million ohms) (Fig. 112.28). This means that there is only a very small voltage between the base and emitter, much less than the 0.7 V needed to switch the transistor on. As the LDR receives more light its resistance becomes less. At the same time the voltage between the base and emitter increases. As soon as it reaches 0.7 V, the transistor switches on and the LED lights. If the 1-KΩ resistor is replaced by a variable resistor of the same value the circuit becomes much more sensitive. By adjusting the resistor the LED can be made to come on at a particular light level.

By replacing the LED with a buzzer, it is possible to make a very sensitive light-operated burglar alarm (Fig. 112.29). When light from the burglar's torch falls upon the LDR, the transistor switches on and the buzzer sounds. Quite a small increase in light level will operate the alarm.

Similar circuits can be built using different detectors, such as a thermistor, or different output devices, such as a motor.

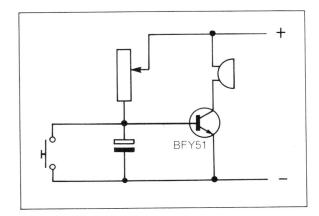

Fig. 112.30 Circuit for an alarm with a time delay.

The use of a capacitor in a transistor circuit can be investigated using the circuit diagram shown in Fig. 112.30. When the switch is pushed there is no voltage difference between the base and emitter (it is a short circuit), so the transistor is off. On releasing the push-switch, current will start to flow into the capacitor and the voltage across it will increase. As soon as the voltage between the base and emitter is 0.7 V the transistor is on and the buzzer will sound. By increasing the size of both resistor and/or capacitor, the time delay can be increased.

113 Electronic logic

Some of the components described in Unit 112 are able to detect changes in their surroundings and convert this information into voltage changes, e.g., LDRs and thermistors. They are called **transducers**. Other components are able to give out information in a visual or audible form, e.g., buzzers and LEDs. These various components can be combined together into a system to do a useful job.

For example, a factory might require a device that will operate a water pump only during daylight hours and only when the temperature of the water in a particular pipe is above 40 °C (Fig. 113.1). So the pump must operate only when the LDR detects light and when the thermistor detects a temperature above 40 °C. The electronic device that can be used to do this is called an **AND** logic gate. It takes in information from the environment, makes a decision based on that information and then gives out a result. The AND gate has two inputs and one output. It could be built from individual transistors and resistors, but it is far more convenient to use a small **integrated circuit** (**IC**), which has all the transistors already connected together on a piece of silicon. The IC is protected by a small plastic case and all the connections are brought out to metal legs on each side of the IC. This format is known as a **dual in-line**, or **DIL** package, and is the most common form for ICs (Fig. 113.2).

The IC shown in Fig. 113.3 contains four (QUAD) AND gates, each having two inputs and one output. Its reference number is TTL 7408; TTL stands for Transistor Transistor Logic, rather than C-MOS which is the other main method of IC manufacture. The IC, or chip, needs a 5-V power supply positive (+) to pin 14 and negative (−) to pin 7. If leads are connected to pins 13 and 12 (inputs), and an LED and protective resistor are connected between pin 11 and pin 7, then an investigation into the properties of an AND gate can be carried out (Fig. 113.4).

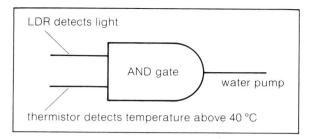

Fig. 113.1 The setup of the system required by the factory.

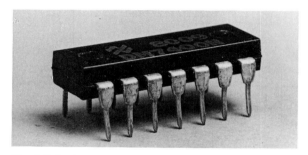

Fig. 113.2 An integrated circuit in a DIL package.

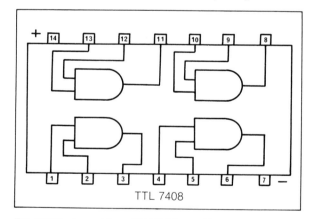

Fig. 113.3 Layout for a QUAD 2 input AND gate IC.

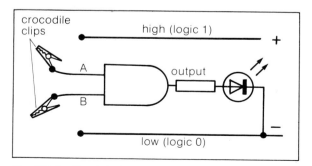

Fig. 113.4 Circuit for investigating an AND gate.

If leads A and B are both connected to negative, i.e., low voltage, known as logic 0, then there is no output. If A is connected to the positive supply, i.e., high voltage, known as logic 1, and B remains at logic 0, then again there is no output (low voltage). If B is at logic 1 and A is at logic 0 there is no output (logic 0). But with both A and B at logic 1 there is a high voltage at the output (logic 1) and the LED lights up. The results can be set out in a **truth table.**

A	B	Output
0	0	0
0	1	0
1	0	0
1	1	1

The only way that the LED at the output will light up, i.e., output is high or logic 1, is when both input A and input B are connected to the positive side of the supply (logic 1); this is why it is known as an AND gate.

Similar experiments can be done with the gates shown in Fig. 113.5 and truth tables set up.

It is possible to build up all of these logic gates using just NAND (that is, NOT AND) gates (Fig. 113.6).

See if you can work out how to make a NOR gate using four NAND gates.

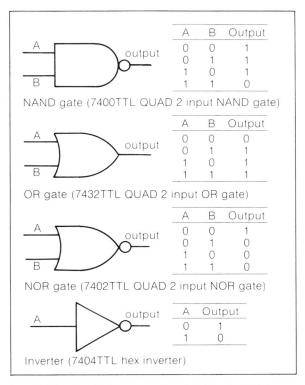

Fig. 113.5 Circuit diagrams and truth tables for NAND, OR, NOR and Inverter gates.

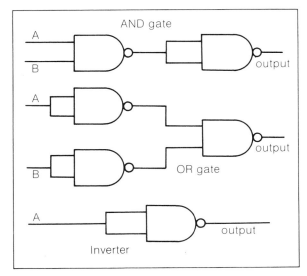

Fig. 113.6 Combining NAND gates to form other types of logic gates.

THE BISTABLE CIRCUIT

A very important circuit in electronics is the **bistable**. It can be made from two NAND gates connected together as in Fig. 113.7. It is used as the basis of counting and memory circuits and plays a role within any microprocessor or microcomputer.

1 When the switches are pushed they make A and D, which are normally high, go low.
2 Suppose gate I has a high output – this means that C is also high. By looking at the truth table you can see that if C and D are both high, then Y will be low.
3 If Y is low then B is low. A is still high and from the truth table this means that X is still high. The circuit is stable and the LED at X is on whereas that at Y is off.
4 If switch R is pressed, D becomes low but C is still high, so Y becomes high and the LED Y lights up.
5 Now B is high and A is high, so X becomes low and the LED X goes out. C is now low and whether D is low (switch pressed) or high (switch released) Y will remain high. This is the second stable state with the LED Y on and the LED X off.
6 The only way to return the circuit to its original state is to press the switch at S. Try to work out for yourself what the logic states would be.

One of the problems with our original burglar alarm was that as soon as the intruder releases the switch or switches the torch off the alarm stops sounding. By using the bistable circuit and a pressure-sensitive mat this problem can be removed. A **pressure-sensitive mat** is like a very large push-switch (Fig. 113.8). When someone treads on it a contact is made, i.e., the switch is on. Moving off the mat breaks the contact, i.e., the switch is off. If a pressure-sensitive mat is put in place of switch S then output X will remain high even when the burglar steps off the mat. It can only be switched off by pressing the reset switch R, which would be hidden somewhere in the house. It is usually operated by a key, rather than a push-switch (Fig. 113.9).

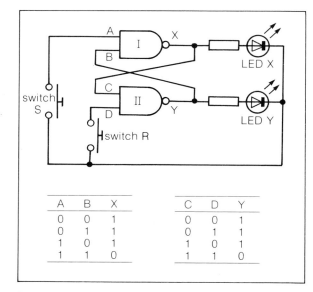

A	B	X		C	D	Y
0	0	1		0	0	1
0	1	1		0	1	1
1	0	1		1	0	1
1	1	0		1	1	0

Fig. 113.7   Circuit diagram and truth table for a bistable circuit. The power supply rails are not shown.

Fig. 113.8   How does this pressure-sensitive mat work?

Fig. 113.9 A key-operated alarm box.

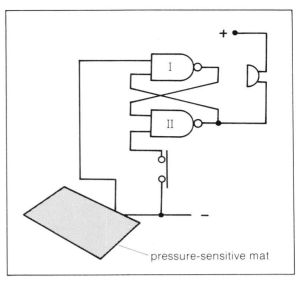

Fig. 113.10 Circuit for a burglar alarm that uses a bistable as a latch.

The circuit diagram in Fig. 113.10 shows how such an alarm could be set up. The position of the buzzer in this circuit may seem to be wrong at first. It is connected to NAND gate II which is normally high but becomes low when someone steps on the pressure-sensitive mat. However, when it is high, both ends of the buzzer are at a high voltage. If electric current is to flow through the buzzer there must be a difference in voltage between the two ends. As there is no voltage difference the buzzer does not work. When the output of gate II is low there is a difference in voltage between the ends of the buzzer and a warning sound is produced. This means that current is flowing from the battery into the gate rather than from the NAND gate into the battery. This is preferable because if too much current is drawn from the output of a logic gate then it can be destroyed.

When a bistable is used in the way shown in this burglar alarm it is known as a **latch**.

114 Some other uses of electronic systems

BAR CODES

Most of the things you buy in supermarkets today have a set of vertical black bars arranged in a rectangle somewhere on the packing (Fig. 114.1). There will be numbers as well. This is a **bar code** and the bars represent the numbers. The code describes the product contained in the packing. It might, for example, stand for 'a 500-g packet of X's corn flakes'.

    The bar code can be scanned with a **light pen**. This makes a tiny spot of light which is moved from left to right across the bar code. The light reflected from the packet is detected by an LDR placed by the side of the tiny light source. The electrical signal that results is a set of longer and shorter pulses, which match the bar code. These pulses are fed to a computer, which uses a machine code that can recognise the sequence. The computer can then deduct the packet you have bought from the stock record; or it can ring up the price you have to pay on the cash till. Some lending libraries use the same system to record all the borrowings of books.

Fig. 114.1 A product bar code.

TV REMOTE CONTROLS

TV sets and video recorders are often fitted with remote controls. These let you change channel and alter the volume of the sound or the brightness of the picture without leaving your chair.

    When you press the button marked, say, BBC 1, the control unit sends out a beam of infra-red radiation which is pulsed. The set of pulses sent out is the one that carries an instruction to the set to change channel to BBC 1. Each button on the control unit sends a message ordering the set to make one change. These message pulses are picked up by a detector in the TV set and the change is made.

SUMMARY: ELECTRONICS

- Resistors restrict the flow of electric current in a circuit.
- A light-dependent resistor (LDR) usually has a low resistance in bright light and a high resistance in the dark.
- A thermistor has a low resistance when hot and a higher resistance when cold.
- A reed switch is a switch that is operated by a magnet.
- Diodes allow electric current to flow through them in only one direction.

- A light-emitting diode (LED) gives out light when electricity is passed through it in the correct direction.
- A transistor can be used as either an electrical switch or as an amplifier.
- A transducer is a component that can detect changes in the environment and convert the information into voltages.
- The simplest logic gates are the AND, OR and NOT gates.
- A bistable circuit is made from two NAND gates connected together.
- A simple burglar alarm can be made from a bistable operating as a latch.

Questions

Section 1 Physicists and physics measurements (pages 8—19)

Questions 1—5 Choose the unit A—E to fit the quantity.

A kilogram B kilogram/metre^3 C metre
D newton E second

1 Length
2 Mass
3 Time
4 Density
5 Force

Questions 6—10 Choose the apparatus A—E used to measure the quantity.

A hydrometer B measuring cylinder
C micrometer D spring balance E stop-watch

6 Length
7 Density
8 Time
9 Weight
10 Volume

Questions 11—12

11 An open spring has a length of 3.6 cm when it has no load hanging from it. When a load of weight 50 N is hung on it, its length becomes 8.6 cm. How long will it be if the weight of the load is changed to 20 N?
12 A metre rule is pivoted at the 50-cm mark. A mass that makes a force of 10 N is hung from the 10-cm mark, a mass that makes a force of 20 N is hung from the 60-cm mark and a mass that makes a force of 5 N is hung from the 90-cm mark.
   (a) Draw a clear diagram of this arrangement.
   (b) Calculate the moment of each force about the pivot.
   (c) State whether each moment is clockwise or anticlockwise.
   (d) Write down the total clockwise moment.
   (e) Write down the total anticlockwise moment.
   (f) Does the rule balance?
   (g) What is the mass in kilograms of each of the three masses used?

Section 2 Force and pressure (pages 20—28)

Questions 1—5 Choose the best word from A—E to fill the gap in the following sentences.

A barometer B capillarity C manometer
D pascal E surface tension

1 The pressure of the laboratory gas supply could be measured by a _____.
2 The _____ is a unit for measuring pressure.
3 When a sponge is placed in water, the water rises into it. This is called _____.
4 The _____ measures atmospheric pressure.
5 A steel needle floating on water shows the action of _____.

Questions 6—7

6 A paving stone 0.5 m by 0.5 m by 5 cm has a mass of 25 kg. What pressure does the stone exert on horizontal ground when (a) it is laid flat and (b) it is stood vertically on one edge. (A mass of 1 kg has a weight of 10 N.)
7 A faulty gas pipe lies at the bottom of a lake 15 m deep. A barometer in a laboratory at the side of the lake gives a reading of 75 cm of mercury. (Density of water is 1000 kg/m^3; density of mercury is 13 600 kg/m^3; a mass of 1 kg has a weight of 10 N.)
   (a) What is the atmospheric pressure (in pascals)?
   (b) What is the water pressure at the bottom of the lake?
   (c) What is the total pressure at the bottom of the lake?
   (d) One of the bubbles coming out of the gas pipe has a volume of 2.0 cm^3. What is the volume of the bubble just before it reaches the water surface?

Section 3 Machines alter forces (pages 29—34)

Questions 1—5 Choose the best word from A—E to fill each gap in the following paragraph.

A efficiency B friction C machine
D mechanical advantage E velocity ratio

There are many devices that help us do a job more easily. Each of these is an example of a _____1_____. If you measure the force you apply to the device and the force it can exert you could calculate its _____2_____. If you also measured the distances moved by these forces you could find the _____3_____. Finally, you could calculate the _____4_____, which is reduced by _____5_____ in the device.

Questions

Questions 6−7

6 Draw a diagram of a pulley system with a velocity ratio of 3.

7 Many years ago, when I was still at school, I visited a working windmill while on holiday. The miller told me to pull a certain rope, which I did. ''Now'', he said, ''go and tell your headmaster that you have lifted a ton.'' Write an account of the conversation that I might have had with my headmaster.

Section 4   Moving along (pages 35−46)

Questions 1−5   Which definition A−E best describes the quantity.

A distance divided by time
B total distance travelled divided by total time taken
C mass multiplied by acceleration due to gravity
D change in velocity divided by the time taken for the change
E the maximum velocity reached when an object falls through a viscous substance

1 Speed
2 Average speed
3 Terminal velocity
4 Weight
5 Acceleration

Questions 6−8

6 Starting from rest, car X can reach a speed of 20 m/s in 8 s while car Y reaches 24 m/s in 12 s. Which car has the higher acceleration?

7 How might you attempt to check the accuracy of the speedometer of a car?

8 Jane is carrying out an experiment in which a trolley is pulling a paper tape through a ticker-timer which makes 100 dots a second. Jane measures the distance of every tenth dot from the beginning of the tape. Here are her results:

Dot	0	10	20	30	40	50	60	70	80
Distance (cm)	5.2	10.3	15.4	20.5	25.6	32.7	41.8	52.9	54.3

(a) Draw (full size) the tape-chart that Jane would get if she cut the tape up into 10-dot lengths.

(b) What could Jane work out from this chart? Give as much detail as possible.

Section 5   Using forces (pages 47−50)

Questions 1−5   Choose the best word from A−E to fill each gap in the following statement.

A equal   B Newton's   C reaction   D recoils
E third

_____1_____ _____2_____ law of motion states that action and _____3_____ are _____4_____ and opposite. This explains why a gun _____5_____ when a bullet is fired from it.

Questions 6−7

6 Why can a rocket work in space whereas a jet engine cannot?

7 A long wooden plank is thrown across a stream 4-m wide to make a bridge. When a man weighing 750 N walks across the plank it bends downwards.
(a) Where will the man be when the bending is a maximum? Explain your answer.
(b) When the man is 1 m from the left-hand end, how large are the forces the bank exerts on the two ends of the plank.

Section 6   Energy and power (pages 51−58)

Questions 1−6

1 A toy car of mass 50 g is travelling at 6 m/s. Its kinetic energy is:
A 0.9 J   B 9 J   C 30 J   D 180 J   E 300 J

2 A box of mass 10 kg is raised through a height of 5.0 m. If $g = 10$ m/s^2, the gain in potential energy is:
A 5 J   B 50 J   C 500 J   D 5 000 J   E 25 000 J

3 A car runs out of control on a steep hill and crashes into a wall at the bottom. Describe the energy changes involved.

4 Joanna has a mass of 40 kg. She runs up a flight of 20 stairs each of height 18 cm. If she takes 6.0 s what power does she develop? Running up stairs, a human body is about 25 per cent efficient. How much power does Joanna develop overall? Where does the extra energy go? ($g = 10$ m/s^2)

5 Explain carefully the energy changes that take place as a mass bobs up and down on the end of a spring.

6 A tube contains a small quantity of mercury and is sealed at each end with a rubber bung. When it is turned upside down the mercury falls through a height of 50 cm. When the tube has been turned 60 times the temperature of the mercury has risen 2.0 °C. ($g = 10$ m/s^2)
(a) If the mass of the mercury is m, how much potential energy is changed into heat every time the tube is turned?
(b) What is the total potential energy converted into heat?
(c) If the specific heat capacity of the mercury is c, how much heat has the mercury gained?
(d) Now calculate c, the specific heat capacity of the mercury.

Section 7 Expanding solids, liquids and gases (pages 59−66)

Questions 1−10 Choose the answer A−J which best fits each description.

A absolute zero B contract C Diesel
D expands E Invar F kelvin G kinetic theory
H thermostat I 4 °C J 373 K

1 Temperature at which water is densest.
2 The normal boiling point of water.
3 Nickel−steel alloy that expands very little when heated.
4 Become smaller.
5 Temperature scale used in calculations on volumes of gases.
6 Idea that solids, liquids and gases consist of tiny moving particles.
7 What water does as it freezes.
8 Type of engine in which compression heats and explodes the fuel.
9 Helps to keep something at constant temperature.
10 The lowest temperature on the Kelvin scale.

Questions 11−14 At which of the temperatures A−D do the following changes take place?

A from 20 to 4 °C B from 4 to 0 °C C 0 °C
D from 0 to −4 °C

11 Water freezes, expanding as it does so.
12 Ice contracts.
13 Liquid water contracts.
14 Liquid water expands.

Questions 15−16

15 A copper pipe 20 m long is heated from 0 °C, by passing steam through it, until it is at a temperature of 100 °C. Work out how much the pipe expands, and thus the length of the pipe when it is hot. (You should refer to Table 30 on p. 60 to do this question.)
16 Sarah invented a gadget to put in her greenhouse to light a lamp if the temperature became too low or too high. The gadget has a bimetallic strip that can touch either of two contacts, 1 or 2.

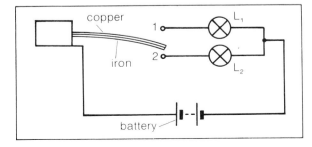

(a) Which lamp lights if the greenhouse is too hot? Explain your answer.
(b) What does it mean when neither lamp is on?
(c) What must Sarah do if the lamp showing that the greenhouse is too cold does not come on until too low a temperature?

Section 8 Measuring temperature (pages 67−71)

Questions 1−10 Choose the answer A−J which best fits each description.

A alcohol B calibrate C capillary
D constriction E heat F ice point G index
H kelvin I temperature J thermocouple

1 Mark a scale on something.
2 Colourless liquid used in thermometers.
3 Something pushed along a thermometer bore to record the maximum or minimum temperature reached.
4 A division of a temperature scale, the same size as a Celsius degree.
5 The temperature of pure melting ice, which is used to mark a place on a thermometer scale.
6 Two wires twisted together, which can develop a voltage.
7 Increase the energy of something.
8 Quantity that tells you how hot something is.
9 Narrow place in the bore of a clinical thermometer.
10 Tube with a very small bore.

Questions 11−12

11 Explain (a) which end of the index of a maximum-recording thermometer shows the highest temperature reached and (b) why a clinical thermometer has a narrow place in its bore.
12 What are the three things you have to do to graduate (or calibrate) an unmarked mercury thermometer?

Questions 13−17 Choose the temperature A−E which best fits each description.

A 273 K B 6000 °C C −39 °C D 78 °C E 37 °C

13 Normal body temperature.
14 Freezing point of mercury.
15 Boiling point of alcohol.
16 Lower fixed point (ice point).
17 Surface of the sun.

Questions

Section 9   Moving and stopping energy (heat) (pages 72−77)

Questions 1−9   Choose the answer A−I which best fits each description.

A calorifier B conduction C conductor
D convection E insulator F direct system
G radiation H reflector I silvering

1 Shiny coating in a vacuum flask that makes the surface a poor radiator.
2 Poor conductor of heat.
3 Substance that readily transmits thermal energy without moving itself.
4 Electromagnetic waves that can carry energy through a vacuum.
5 Heating installation in which water from the boiler mixes with water in the hot-water cylinder.
6 Movement of energy through something that does not move itself.
7 Surface that absorbs very little radiation.
8 Movement of energy through a liquid or gas, which moves with the energy.
9 Coil of pipes in the hot-water cylinder of an indirect water-heating system.

Questions 10−14

10 With the aid of Fig. 40.1 on p. 74 explain what is happening to the water at X which makes the convection current flow.
11 Name two uses of bad conductors of heat. Describe the effect of replacing one of the bad conductors by a good conductor.
12 Why are the tubes in a solar (sun-powered) heater usually made of blackened copper?
13 A glass-fronted box with two holes, A and B, in the lid contains a candle C. How will energy escape from the box if the candle is lit?

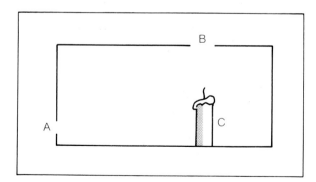

14 A vacuum flask contains ice. Explain why energy from outside the flask takes a long time to melt the ice. Refer to conduction, convection and radiation in your answer.

Section 10   Energy and changes of state (pages 78−87)

Questions 1−12   Choose the answer A−L which best matches each description.

A autoclave B boil C bromine D condensation
E diffusion F evaporate G freeze H fusion
I joules J naphthalene K regelation
L specific heat capacity

1 The number of joules needed to raise the temperature of 1 kg of a substance by 1 °C.
2 Change from liquid to solid by cooling.
3 Change from liquid to vapour at the surface of a liquid.
4 Change from liquid to vapour at any point in a liquid, at a fixed temperature.
5 Mixing of liquids or gases, which takes place without stirring.
6 Unit by which energy, and therefore heat, is measured.
7 Reddish-brown liquid that vaporises easily.
8 White solid that melts at 80 °C.
9 Changing from solid to liquid.
10 Cooling a vapour to make liquid drops.
11 Refreezing of ice after a metal wire has melted its way through.
12 Pressure cooker in which things are sterilised by heating to a high temperature and pressure.

Questions 13−15   These questions are about specific heat capacity, which is the number of joules needed to change the temperature of 1 kg of a substance by 1 °C.

Substance Sp. heat cap. (J/kg °C)	water	aluminium	iron
	4200	840	450

13 The energy needed to raise the temperature of 3 kg of water from 20 to 25 °C is:
  A 15 J B 1400 J C 12.6 kJ D 63 kJ E 252 kJ
14 The energy given out when 10 kg of aluminium cool from 100 to 20 °C is:
  A 800 J B 67.2 kJ C 168 kJ D 672 kJ
  E 840 kJ
15 How many kilograms of iron will need 9 kJ of energy to raise its temperature by 10 °C?

Question 16

16 Copy the following passage about kinetic theory and fill in the blanks.

The _____ of a _____ vibrate more quickly as you heat it. When the solid _____ its molecules escape from their fixed places and move freely in the _____. Some of the faster molecules escape from the surface of the liquid and form a _____.

Section 11   Waves (pages 88–95)

Questions 1–5   Copy the following sentences and fill in the missing words.

1 Waves are repeated vibrations carrying
_____.

2 In longitudinal sound waves the vibrations are _____ the direction the wave is going.

3 In transverse electromagnetic waves the vibrations are _____ the direction the wave is going.

4 A plane wave reflects from a straight barrier as a _____ _____.
Its angle of _____ equals its _____ of _____.

5 The spreading of waves round corners is called _____.

Questions 6–10   Choose the answer A–E which best describes the points or distances labelled 6–10 in the diagram of a transverse wave on water.

A amplitude   B trough   C crest or peak
D wavelength   E average (middle) position of the water surface

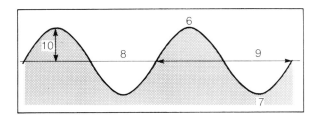

Questions 11–13

11 Find the velocity of a wave of frequency 660 Hz and wavelength 0.5 m.
12 Draw two diagrams to show plane waves crossing a straight boundary into a medium in which their speed is half that in the first: (a) with the lines representing each crest parallel to the boundary; (b) with them at 45° to it. Show their directions of movement and label all clearly.
13 Put the following waves in their correct order of *increasing frequency* (decreasing wavelength), and write under each a use for that wave: ultraviolet, gamma-rays, X-rays, radio, infra-red, light (R,O,Y,G,B,V).

Questions 14–16   Choose the answer A–E which best fits each statement.

A amplitude   B electromagnetic   C interference
D refraction   E speed

14 The bending of the direction a wave travels due to a change of speed at a boundary with a different medium is called
_____.

15 Constructive _____ of two identical waves exactly in step gives a combined wave of double the amplitude of one of them.

16 The crest to trough distance for a wave is equal to twice its _____.

Section 12   Light goes fast and straight (pages 96–104)

Questions 1–4   Copy the following sentences and fill in the missing words.

1 _____ is our name for visible electromagnetic waves. It travels in _____ lines carrying _____.

2 Sources of light are said to be _____. We see some of the light they _____.

3 Most things are _____ luminous. We see them by the light which they _____.

4 The stars are all massive _____ like ours. They just seem _____ because they are at great distances from us.

Questions 5–9   Choose the answer A–E which best fits each statement.

A bright side   B full shadow   C full moon
D penumbra   E total eclipse

5 The umbra where no light arrives is the area of _____.

6 The surrounding part-shadow is called the _____.

7 When you see *all* of the bright *half* of the moon, high in the sky at midnight, the calendar will say it is _____.

8 On the earth during the daytime, we are on its _____.

9 When the moon moves completely into the earth's shadow, we call it a _____.

Questions 10–13

10 Write a few sentences to describe things that rely on the fact that light travels in straight lines.
11 Write a few sentences to explain how a photographic negative shows that light waves carry energy.
12 Write a few sentences to explain what photosynthesis does and why it is so important to everybody.

13 (a) How long does it take radio waves travelling at the speed of light, 3×10^8 m/s, to get from the earth to the moon, a distance of 4×10^8 m?

(b) What then is the shortest possible time between you speaking on earth and you hearing the start of the reply, all by radio, from an astronaut on the moon?

(c) What would be the shortest possible time if you were speaking, by radio, to an astronaut on Proxima Centauri, our nearest star.

Questions 14 – 15 Draw a clearly labelled diagram of the following, and give each one a suitable title.

14 (a) The sun, moon and earth, showing the reflected rays of sunlight by which you see the moon.

(b) Another similar diagram, showing how an astronaut on the moon sees the earth by sunlight.

15 A pin-hole camera, showing on its screen the real image of a tree on a bright day.

Section 13   Light bounces and bends (pages 105–119)

Questions 1–5 Copy the following sentences and fill in the missing words.

1 The image in a plane mirror is the _____ size as the object, and the same _____ _____ as the object is in front.

2 The plane mirror _____ light rays; their angles of _____ equal their _____ of _____.

3 Because no light gets behind a plane mirror, what is seen in it must be a _____ image.

4 Rays of light striking a lens or mirror, and coming from a distant object, are _____.

5 In searchlights the light must be reflected as a parallel beam. So the lamp filament is placed at the _____ of the concave mirror.

Questions 6–8 Choose the answer A–E which best fits each statement.

A inverted   B magnified   C real   D smaller   E virtual

6 A concave mirror or a converging lens can give a real image of a distant, bright object. This image is in colour, smaller and _____.

7 An image that can be seen on a screen is a _____ image.

8 Compared with a plane mirror, a convex car rear-view mirror gives a wider field of view because images seen in it are _____.

Questions 9–11

9 Use the formula and a scientific calculator to work out the angle of refraction, $\angle r$, in a rectangular block of Perspex (refractive index $= 1.5$) for a ray incident from the air at $45°$. Draw a diagram to show your result.

10 Write a few sentences explaining what you have learned about the image of your face in a plane mirror.

11 Write a few sentences comparing the lenses, focusing, apertures, types of image, 'film' surface and shutters of your eye and a camera.

Questions 12–13 Copy the following diagrams, twice size, and continue the light rays, showing them reflected accurately from each mirror. The angle given is from the ray *to normal*.

12 Two rays incident at $30°$ and $80°$, to show equi-angular reflections, from a plane mirror.

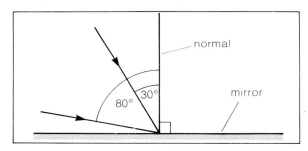

13 A ray incident at $30°$ on one of two mirrors set at right angles to show parallel reflection from a 'corner of mirrors'. Try a ray incident at $60°$.

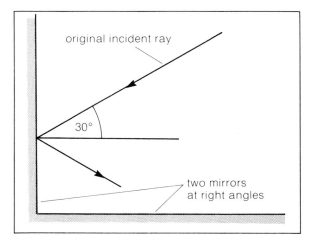

Section 14 Seeing in colour (pages 120−122)

Questions 1−7 Copy the following sentences and fill in the missing words.

1 A red sun early or late in the day is due to the colour _____ in the sunlight being scattered more by the earth's atmosphere than the red.
2 White light can be split into the spectrum of colours: _____,
_____, _____,
_____, _____,
and _____.
3 The spreading out of the colours in white light due to their slightly different speeds through a glass prism is called _____.
4 A green colour filter absorbs all colours except _____.
5 The light energy that a colour filter absorbs _____ it very slightly.
6 A white surface reflects all _____equally.
7 When all the spectral colours (rainbow) are recombined _____ light appears.

Questions 8−11

8 Write a few sentences to explain how thousands of tiny dots of red, green and blue light give all the colours you see on a TV screen.
9 Write a few sentences to explain which jobs someone with red-green colour-blindness should not attempt.
10 Write a few sentences to explain why it is not sensible to check that two colours match under fluorescent lights in a shop, and say what it is best to do.
11 Make a table listing what you see when you look at different coloured objects under (a) filament lamps, (b) sunlight, (c) fluorescent tubes, (d) yellow street lights and (e) blue-green ones.

Question 12

12 Draw a clearly labelled diagram, with a suitable title, showing a ray of white light being bent and split by a triangular glass prism into the spectral colours in order, with red bent the least.

Section 15 Sound (pages 123−131)

Questions 1−4 Copy the following sentences and fill in the missing words.

1 Sound can travel in solids, liquids and gases, but *not* through a _____.
2 The harmonics or overtones made by a musical instrument give the sound its characteristic _____ or _____.

3 High pitch means high _____.
4 Loudness or intensity of sound is measured in units called _____, for which the symbol is _____.

Questions 5−8 Choose the answer A−E which best fits each statement.

A frequency B hertz C longitudinal
D resonance E transverse

5 In air, sound travels as a _____ pressure wave.
6 The number of vibrations in one second is called the _____.
7 Anything that vibrates has its own natural _____.
8 Building up the amplitude of the vibration of a sounding string or pipe by driving it at its natural frequency is called _____.

Questions 9−15

9 (a) To raise the pitch of the fundamental by one octave for a given string under constant (the same) tension, how must its length change?
   (b) To lower it by two octaves, how must its length change?
10 A survey team fire a gun and time the echo, 12 s, from a distant cliff face. Use the speed of sound in air (330 m/s) to work out how far away the cliff is from the team. Round your answer to two significant figures in kilometres.
11 Write a few sentences to explain three different ways by which noise around us is reduced.
12 Explain with sketch diagrams how your ear and brain can tell whether you are hearing noise, speech or a musical instrument.
13 List, with explanations, the three principal ways in which the frequency of a string instrument can be increased or decreased.
14 Draw and label a standing wave pattern with three loops. Show all nodes and antinodes and the wavelength of the waves on the string.
15 Copy and complete the table of matching pairs of terms.

Musicians	Physicists
_____	Frequency of fundamental
Loudness	
Tone, timbre	_____
Quality	Quality
_____	Harmonics
	Twice the frequency
One octave lower	_____

Questions

Section 16 Magnetism (pages 132–139)

Questions 1–4 Choose the answer A–E which best fits each description.

A angle of dip B declination C domain
D induced pole E magnetically soft

1 Part of a magnet in which the atomic magnets all point one way.
2 Temporary magnetic pole which a permanent magnet produces in a magnetic material.
3 Easy to magnetise but loses its magnetism readily.
4 Angle between true and magnetic north.

Questions 5–6 These questions are about permanent magnets. The diagrams A, B and C represent the atomic magnets within the magnet.

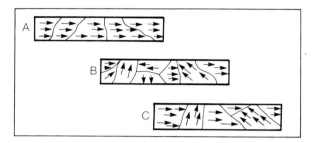

5 Which diagram represents a bar which is (a) unmagnetised, (b) magnetically saturated and (c) partly magnetised?
6 Mention three ways by which you could change the magnet from state A to state B.

Questions 7–10 These questions are about mapping magnetic fields. A card covers part of the apparatus for an experiment. The map of the magnetic field is as shown.

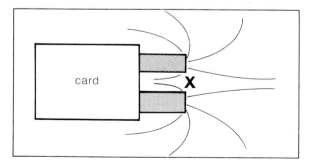

7 Name the curved lines shown in the diagram.
8 What do the curved lines show?
9 What is the name for the point X?
10 Are the shaded parts the ends of two bar magnets or the ends of a horseshoe magnet? Explain your answer.

Section 17 Electrostatics (pages 140–143)

Questions 1–5 Choose the answer A–F which best fits each statement.

A conductor B electrons C insulator
D negative E neutral F positive

1 A conductor with equal numbers of positive and negative charges is _____.
2 A _____ charge will repel a positive charge.
3 A negative charge will _____ a positive charge.
4 A _____ body may be attracted by either a positive or a negative charge.
5 When a charged _____ is made to touch an uncharged one there will be a flow of _____ between them.

Questions 6–8

6 Two of the following are not insulators. Which? Air, nylon, polythene, the human body, rubber, tap water, waxed paper
7 Copy the diagram and add positive (+) and negative (−) signs to show what happens when a conductor is charged by induction.

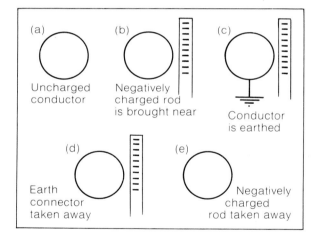

8 How does a lightning conductor work? Use a labelled sketch to explain your answer.

Section 18 Electric circuits and measurement (pages 144–155)

Questions 1–4 Choose the answer A–F which best fits each statement.

A ammeters B battery C cells D current
E parallel F series G voltmeters

1 The current in a _____ circuit is the same wherever it is measured.

228

2 Ammeters are connected in circuits in
_____, voltmeters in
_____.
3 A car battery is made up of several
_____ connected in
_____.
4 _____ are used to measure
currents.

Questions 5−9

5 What are the advantages of connecting lamps in
parallel rather than in series?
6 In the diagram, ammeter A_1 reads 3 A and
ammeter A_2 reads 5 A. What does ammeter A_3
read?

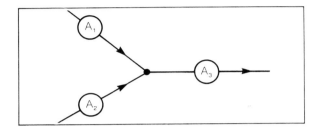

7 A potential difference of 12 V is applied to a
resistance of 3 Ω. The current flowing is:
A 36 A   B 15 A   C 9 A   D 4 A   E 0.25 A

8 Two resistors have resistances of 8 Ω and 4 Ω.
Calculate the effective resistance if they are
connected (a) in series and (b) in parallel.
9 A student connected up a circuit to test whether
Ohm's law applied to a motor car headlamp
bulb.
(a) Draw a circuit diagram to show how the
student connected together the supply
(which could be varied to give any potential
difference from 0 to 12 V), a headlamp bulb,
an ammeter and a voltmeter.
(b) The student recorded the following readings:

p.d. (V)	0	2	4	6	8	10	12
current (A)	0	0.7	1.4	2.1	2.6	2.8	3.0

Draw a graph to illustrate these results. Explain
whether Ohm's law may be applied to this lamp.

Section 19   Using electricity (pages 156−167)

Questions 1−4   Choose the answer A−G which
best fits each statement.

A anode   B cathode   C chemical   D heating
E longer   F magnetic   G shorter

1 Electric currents always have
_____ fields around them.

2 When an electric current passes through a
filament lamp, the lamp gives out light because
of the _____ effect of the
current.
3 In electroplating, the object to be plated is made
the _____ in a circuit.
4 To get a thicker layer of electroplate, the current
is passed for a _____ time.

Questions 5−9   Choose the unit A−E to fit the
quantity.

A ampere   B coulomb   C kilowatt-hour   D volt
E watt

5 Potential difference
6 Electric charge
7 Energy
8 Electric current
9 The power of a lamp

Questions 10−15

10 (a) Why are fuses put into mains and car
circuits? How do they work?
(b) There are two places in the home where you
may find a fuse. Where are they?
11 Mains-operated appliances, such as electric irons
and kettles, always have an earth connection.
What is an earth connection? How does it protect
(a) the user of the appliance from harm and
(b) the wiring of the power circuit to which the
appliance is connected?
12 What is the power rating of a lamp that carries a
current of 3 A when it is connected to a potential
difference of 12 V?
13 (a) What current will flow through a 3-kW
heater connected to a 250-V supply?
(b) Which fuse would be best for this heater
circuit?
A 3 A   B 5 A   C 10 A   D 13 A   E 30 A
14 If electrical energy costs 6p per kWh (unit),
calculate the cost of using a 200-W electric
blanket for one hour every night for five weeks.
15 Calculate the readings you would expect to get
on the four meters in the following circuit.

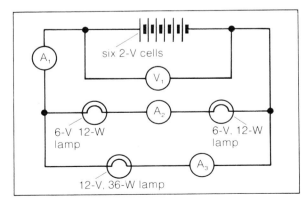

six 2-V cells

6-V 12-W lamp

6-V, 12-W lamp

12-V, 36-W lamp

Section 20   Magnetism from electricity
(pages 168−174)

Questions 1−5   Choose the answer A-E which best fits each statement.

A circular   B parallel   C similar   D solenoid
E stronger

1 The magnetic field lines round a long straight wire carrying a current are _____ in shape.

2 A _____ is a long coil with many turns of wire.

3 The magnetic field lines inside a solenoid are _____ and straight.

.4 The magnetic field outside a solenoid is _____ to the field of a bar magnet.

5 If a solenoid is wound on an iron former the magnetic field is much _____

Questions 6−9

6 How could you make an electromagnet from an iron bar and a long length of insulated wire? What else would you need to make the electromagnet work?

7 How do relays and reed switches work? Make suitable sketches to illustrate your answers.

8 How does a moving-coil loudspeaker work? Illustrate your answer with a labelled diagram.

9 Make a list of at least five things you have seen today that use an electric motor.

Section 21   Electricity from magnetism
(pages 175−186)

Questions 1−5   Choose the best word from A−E to fill each gap in the following paragraph.

A electromagnetic   B generator   C induced
D reverse   E quickly

When a magnetic field through a coil connected to a galvanometer is changed an _____1_____ current will flow. Reversing the direction of the field will _____2_____ the direction of the current. Making the change more _____3_____ increases the current. The name of this process is _____4_____ induction. It is used in a _____5_____ of mains electricity.

Questions 6−9

6 A transformer has a primary coil of 2000 turns and a secondary coil of 500 turns. If the input voltage is 240 V the output voltage will be:
   A 2000 V   B 960 V   C 500 V   D 240 V   E 60 V

7 Outline the energy changes at a coal-fired power station. Say what happens at each stage and the form or forms of energy involved.

8 Why is electrical energy generated as alternating current (a.c.)? Explain why electrical energy is transmitted through the National Grid at such high voltages.

9 A power station alternator with an output power of 660 MW produces alternating current at 3300 V. The rotor of the alternator rotates at 3000 revolutions a minute. What is the supply frequency?
   The current from the alternator is led to a transformer where the voltage is stepped up to 132 kV. How many turns are there on the secondary coil compared with the number on the primary coil?
   What is the current in the overhead transmission line when the system is working at full power?

Section 22   The electron (pages 187−195)

Questions 1−5   Choose the best word A−F to fill each gap in the following paragraph.

A accelerate   B conductors   C electric   D mass
E negative   F positive

Electrons are very small _____1_____ particles. They also have a very small _____2_____. It is therefore very easy to _____3_____ them to high speeds in _____4_____ fields. They also move very easily through _____5_____.

Questions 6−10

6 What does thermionic emission mean? How does an electron gun work? Where would you find such a gun?

7 A cathode ray oscilloscope will have controls labelled (a) brightness, (b) focus, (c) X-shift and (d) time-base speed. What do each of these controls do to the beam of electrons in the cathode ray tube?

8 Here are some sketches of the patterns seen on the screen of a cathode ray oscilloscope. Describe the input to the oscilloscope in each case.

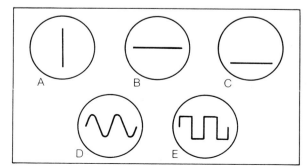

9 What is meant by rectification? Name one device that makes use of rectification. Sketch a graph to show a full-wave rectified current. How would you attempt to smooth the output of a rectifier?

10 What are the differences between a transistor, an integrated circuit and a chip?

Section 23   Radioactivity and nuclear energy (pages 196–207)

Questions 1–8   Choose the answer A–H which best fits each description.

A atomic number   B background radiation
C critical   D fission   E ionise   F isotopes
G proton   H radioisotope

1 Turn into a charged form.
2 Radiation that is always present from natural sources.
3 Splitting of a nucleus into two main parts, roughly equal in mass.
4 Positively charged particle in the nucleus of an atom.
5 Number of protons in an atom.
6 State of a reactor in which a chain reaction starts and can go on.
7 Unstable form of an atom that splits giving rays and/or particles.
8 Forms of an atom with equal numbers of protons, but different numbers of neutrons.

Question 9

9 Radioactive substances can be used as tracers. Explain what this means and describe briefly two uses of tracers.

Questions 10–12   These questions are about the radioactive decay of uranium-238. U-238 decays forming thorium:

$$^{238}_{92}U \rightarrow {}^{4}_{2}He + {}^{234}_{90}Th$$

10 238 is the mass number of the uranium. What does this mean?
11 What does the equation tell you about the alpha-particle emitted?
12 U-238 has a half-life of 4.5×10^9 years. Explain what this means.

Question 13

13 **Fill in the blanks in the table.**

Question 14

14 Copy the passage, filling in the blanks.

A Geiger–Müller tube produces pulses that are counted by a _____. The rays or _____ from the _____ substance ionise the argon in the tube.

Section 24   Electronics (pages 208–220)

Questions 1–4   Choose the answer A–F which best fits each statement.

A capacitor   B LED   C LDR   D resistor
E thermistor   F transducer

1 The resistance of an _____ changes with the amount of light falling on it, but the resistance of a _____ changes with its temperature.
2 When a current passes through the _____ in a calculator it lights up.
3 A microphone is an example of a_____.
4 Small amounts of electric charge can be stored in a _____.

Questions 5–9

5 Integrated circuits are usually packaged in the form called DIL. What does DIL stand for? What is the usual abbreviation for integrated circuit?
6 Copy and complete the following truth table for an AND gate. What do A and B stand for? Why is it called the truth table for an AND gate?

A	B	Output
0	—	0
—	1	0
1	0	—
1	—	1

7 Write out the truth table for a NAND gate. (Remember NAND = NOT AND.)
8 What is a pressure-sensitive mat?
9 A problem with the simple burglar alarm is that it only makes a noise when the torch is on or when the mat is stepped on. What electronic component can be used to make sure that the buzzer continues to sound once it has started?

Radiation	What it is	Charge	Deflected by magnet	Penetrates aluminium foil
α-particle	Helium nucleus	2 +	_____	_____
β-particle	_____	– ve	Easily	_____
	_____	0	_____	Yes

A short physics dictionary

Absolute zero   The lowest possible temperature, approximately $-273\,°C$ (or 0 K).

Acceleration   The rate of increase of speed, equal to the change in speed divided by the time taken for the change. It is measured in metres per second squared (m/s^2).

Acceleration due to gravity   The constant acceleration of an object falling freely. It is given the special symbol g and is about $10\,m/s^2$ near the surface of the earth.

Accommodation   The ability of the eye to see objects at different distances by changing the shape of the eye lens.

Alpha-particles   The nuclei of helium atoms. They are emitted by certain radioactive nuclei, are positively charged and have a short range.

Alternating current   A current that continually changes size and reverses direction regularly.

Ampere   The SI unit of electric current.

Amplifier   Makes electrical signals bigger.

Amplitude   The distance of a wave crest or trough from the middle position.

Anomalous expansion of water   If liquid water is warmed above $4\,°C$ or cooled below $4\,°C$ it expands.

Anode   **1** The electrode connected to the positive of the supply. **2** The electrode at which the negative ions arrive.

Archimedes' principle   The upthrust on a solid immersed in a liquid or gas is equal to the weight of the liquid or gas pushed out of the way by the solid.

Atmospheric pressure   The pressure due to the air round us. It is measured by a barometer and is about 760 mm of mercury or 100 000 Pa.

Atom   The smallest particle of an element.

Atomic number   The number of protons in the nucleus of an atom. Also called proton number.

Background radiation   The natural radioactive radiation that is always present.

Battery   A collection of cells.

Bernoulli's principle   When a fluid is flowing smoothly, an increase in speed means a decrease in pressure.

Beta-particles   Electrons emitted from certain radioactive nuclei.

Bistable circuit   A device, usually electronic, that has two stable states, logic 0 or 1. Any change will 'flip' the circuit from the state it is in to the other.

Boiling point   The temperature at which a liquid boils. It is raised by impurities or increased pressure.

Boyle's law   When a fixed mass of gas is kept at the same temperature, the product of the pressure and volume of the gas does not change.

Brownian motion   The random zigzag motion of very small particles due to bombardment by fast-moving molecules.

Capacitance   Measures the ability of a capacitor to store electric charge. It is often measured in microfarads (μF).

Capacitor   Stores charge and electrical energy. Two plates are separated by an insulator.

Capillarity   The movement of a liquid that occurs in narrow tubes or channels because of surface tension.

Cathode   **1** The electrode connected to the negative of the supply. **2** The electrode at which positive ions arrive.

Celsius scale   The scale of temperature on which the melting point of pure ice is $0\,°C$ and the boiling point of pure water is $100\,°C$, both at standard atmospheric pressure. It used to be called the Centigrade scale.

Centre of gravity   The one point in an object where the whole weight seems to act.

Centripetal force   Acts inwards on an object to make it go round in a circle.

Chain reaction   Repeated nuclear fission in which the released neutrons cause further fission and so on.

Charge   When a Perspex or polythene rod has been rubbed on a woollen cloth it can attract small pieces of paper, as a result of becoming charged. Charges can be positive or negative depending on whether electrons have been lost or gained.

Circuit   A complete path round which an electric current can flow.

Concave mirror   A mirror having the same shape as the inside of a sphere or cylinder. Also called a converging mirror.

Conductor   A material that allows heat or electricity to flow easily through it.

Contraction   The decrease in size of an object when it is cooled. Water also contracts when it is heated from 0 to $4\,°C$.

Convection   The flow of a fluid or gas carrying thermal energy with it.

Converging lens   Makes parallel rays of light come together. Also called a convex lens.

Convex mirror   A mirror having the same shape as the outside of a sphere or cylinder. Also called a diverging mirror.

Coulomb   The SI unit of electric charge, equal to one ampere-second.

Critical angle   The angle of incidence inside water, glass or Perspex for which the angle of refraction in the air outside is $90°$. The sine of the critical angle equals one divided by the refractive index.

Declination, angle of The angle between the direction of true, geographical north and magnetic north.

Density Mass divided by volume. It is measured in kilograms per cubic metre (kg/m^3) or grams per cubic centimetre (g/cm^3).

Diffraction The spreading of a wave through a narrow hole or by a small object.

Diffusion The spread of a gas or liquid into all the space available.

Diode Only allows current to flow one way through it. A rectifier is a diode.

Dip, angle of The angle at which a freely pivoted magnet points below the horizontal.

Direct current A current that is always in the same direction.

Diverging lens Makes parallel rays of light spread out. Also called a concave lens.

Earth wire The third wire in a domestic electrical system. It is connected to the earth and acts as a safety device.

Echo A reflected sound.

Eclipse of the moon Occurs when the earth comes between the sun and the moon. Its shadow forms areas of darkness on the moon.

Eclipse of the sun Occurs when the moon comes between the earth and the sun. Its shadow forms areas of darkness on the earth.

Eddy currents Wasteful currents induced in the core of a transformer, for example.

Efficiency The ratio of the useful energy got out of a machine to that put in, usually given as a percentage.

Elastic limit The greatest force that can be applied to a spring for it still to obey Hooke's law.

Electric current The rate of flow of electric charge. It is measured in amperes (A).

Electrode The metal (or carbon) plate leading electricity into or out of a cell, electrolysis vessel or electronic device.

Electrolysis Chemical action caused by an electric current.

Electromagnet A coil of wire on an iron frame that becomes a magnet when a current flows.

Electromagnetic induction, Laws of **1** The size of the induced potential difference and current depends on the rate at which the magnetic field changes in the circuit (Faraday's law). **2** The induced potential difference or current will be in a direction that opposes the change causing it (Lenz's law).

Electromagnetic waves The family of related waves—radio, infra-red, visible light, ultraviolet, X-rays and gamma-rays—that all travel at the same speed in a vacuum (300 000 km/s).

Electrons The very small particles that surround the nucleus of an atom. Each electron has one unit of negative charge, the smallest amount of charge known.

Electrostatic attraction and repulsion Like charges repel, unlike charges attract.

Energy It exists in many forms—kinetic, potential, chemical, thermal (heat), wave, electrical and nuclear. The total energy always remains constant (the law of conservation of energy). A useful job can be done when energy changes from one form to another. It is measured in joules (J) or newton metres (N m).

Equilibrium If an object is not moving when several forces act on it, it is in equilibrium.

Evaporation The change from liquid to vapour at temperatures lower than the boiling point of the liquid. Evaporation will result in cooling of the liquid if extra energy is not supplied to it.

Expansion The increase in size of an object when it is heated.

Faraday's law of electrolysis The change in mass of an electrode is proportional to the product of current and time.

Fleming's left-hand rule Hold the left hand with the thumb, first and second fingers at right angles. Point the first finger in the direction of the magnetic field, the second finger in the direction of the current and then the thumb shows the direction of the force.

Fleming's right-hand rule Uses the right hand to find the direction of the voltage induced when the directions of the force and the field are known.

Fluorescence Some substances fluoresce (give out light) when energy is given to them. This energy may come from light of a different wavelength or from the impact of a fast-moving electron.

Focal length The distance from the mirror or lens to its principal focus.

Force A push or a pull. It is measured in newtons (N), often by a spring balance.

Freezing point The temperature at which a liquid turns to a solid. See also melting point.

Frequency The number of repeated events happening in one second.

Friction The force opposing motion.

Fuse A thin piece of wire that melts if too much current flows.

Gamma-radiation Electromagnetic radiation of very short wavelength emitted from certain radioactive nuclei.

Gravity The force of attraction that one mass exerts on another. The earth's gravity provides the centripetal force that keeps the moon in orbit.

Half-life The time taken for half the atoms in any sample of a radioactive isotope to decay.

Harmonics The frequencies heard when a musical note is played.

Hertz The SI unit of frequency, equal to one complete event per second.

Hooke's law The extension of a spring is proportional to the force.

Image The picture of an object formed by a lens or mirror.

Incidence, angle of The angle between the incident ray and the normal.

Induced current The current produced in a circuit containing a coil when a magnet is moved into or out of the coil or when the magnetic field changes.

Inertia Massive objects require larger forces to reach a particular acceleration than less massive ones. They have more inertia.

Infra-red radiation Part of the electromagnetic spectrum with wavelengths greater than that of light.

Insulator A material that does not allow heat or electricity to flow easily through it.

Integrated circuit Contains large numbers of electronic components in a very small space.

Interference Pattern of reinforcement and cancellation formed where two similar waves cross.

Ion A charged particle formed when an atom gains (negative ion) or loses (positive ion) electrons.

Isotopes The different species of an element having different numbers of neutrons in the nucleus.

Joule The SI unit of energy or work: one joule (J) is one newton metre (N m).

Kelvin scale The scale of temperature that starts at absolute zero and uses the same sized divisions as the Celsius scale. Also called the absolute scale.

Kilogram The SI unit of mass.

Kilowatt-hour A unit of electrical energy equal to 3 600 000 joules. Electrical energy is sold in these units (kWh).

Kinetic energy Energy due to movement. It is equal to half the mass of an object multiplied by the square of its velocity.

Kinetic theory The explanation of the way matter behaves based on the idea that matter is made of molecules that can move in different ways depending on whether it is a solid, liquid or gas.

Lens A piece of glass or transparent plastic with curved surfaces. If it is thicker in the middle than at the edges it is a convex or converging lens. If it is thinner in the middle than at the edges it is a concave or diverging lens.

Light-dependent resistor (LDR) A resistor whose resistance changes as the amount of light falling on it alters.

Light-emitting diode (LED) A diode that gives out light when electricity passes through it.

Lines of magnetic force The lines used to show the pattern and direction of a magnetic field. Also called magnetic field lines.

Logic gates Electronic devices that respond to various combinations of inputs according to definite rules.

Longitudinal wave A wave in which the vibrations move in the same direction as that in which the wave is travelling.

Loudness A loud sound has a larger amplitude and carries more energy. Loudness, or intensity, is measured in decibels (dB).

Magnetic attraction and repulsion Like poles repel, unlike poles attract.

Magnetic domains A large group of atoms in a magnetic material with all the atomic magnets pointing the same way.

Magnetic field The space round a magnet in which you can detect its magnetic effect. It can be mapped with iron filings or a plotting compass.

Magnetic induction When a magnet is placed near a piece of iron the iron becomes a temporary (induced) magnet.

Magnetic north pole The point on the earth to which the north-seeking pole of a compass needle points.

Mass number The number of protons and neutrons in the nucleus of an atom.

Maxwell's corkscrew rule The direction of the lines of force round a current is the same as the direction in which you would turn an ordinary screw to move it forwards in the direction of the current.

Mechanical advantage The load lifted by a machine divided by the effort that has to be used to raise the load.

Melting point The temperature at which a solid turns to a liquid. It is lowered by impurities or increased pressure.

Meniscus The curved surface at the top of a liquid in a tube.

Metre The SI unit of length.

Moment of a force Its turning effect about a pivot. It may be clockwise or anticlockwise. The moment is equal to the force multiplied by the distance from the pivot (measured at right angles to the force).

Moments, principle of If a system is in equilibrium the sum of the clockwise moments about any point equals the sum of the anticlockwise moments about that point.

Neutron A particle of about the same mass as a proton but with no charge. It is found in every nucleus except that of hydrogen.

Newton The SI unit of force. A newton will give a mass of one kilogram an acceleration of one metre per second squared.

Newton's laws of motion 1 A body continues at rest or in uniform motion along a straight line unless a force acts on it. 2 Force is the product of the mass and the acceleration ($F = ma$). 3 Action and reaction are equal and opposite and act on different bodies.

North (seeking) pole   If a magnet is freely suspended it will point approximately north−south. The end pointing to the north is called the north (seeking) pole.

Nuclear fission   A nucleus, struck by a neutron, splits into two large fragments and two or three more neutrons. Energy is released.

Nuclear fusion   The building up of helium from hydrogen. This releases a great deal of energy.

Nuclear reactor   Uses a controlled chain reaction as a source of energy.

Nucleus   The central part of an atom which is made up of protons and neutrons. It carries a positive charge and most of the mass of the atom.

Ohm   The SI unit of electrical resistance.

Ohm's law   The resistance of a metal wire is constant providing its temperature is constant.

Opaque   An object that does not allow light to pass through it.

Parallel connection   Parts of an electric circuit that are joined side by side.

Pascal   The SI unit of pressure. It is equal to one newton per square metre.

Pitch   The musician's word for frequency.

Plane mirror   A mirror having a flat surface.

Pole of a magnet   The region in a magnet where the magnetic effect is strongest.

Potential difference   Electrons flow in a complete circuit because they are repelled by the charge on the negative pole and attracted by the positive pole of the generator. As the current flows through any component in the circuit, energy is transformed. The amount of energy transformed by each coulomb of charge is the potential difference across the component. It is measured in volts (V) and is often called the voltage.

Potential energy   The energy an object has due to its position. When an object is lifted it gains gravitational potential energy, which is equal to its weight multiplied by the height it is raised.

Power   1 The rate of doing work or of converting energy from one form to another. 2 Power in an electric circuit is the product of the potential difference and the current. 3 Power is measured in watts (1 W = 1 J/s).

Pressure   Force divided by area. It is measured in newtons per square metre (N/m^2) or pascals (Pa). In a liquid, pressure is given by the product of depth, density and g (10 m/s^2).

Primary colours   The three colours of light (red, blue and green) that can be added together to give white light.

Principal focus   The point at which a beam of rays parallel to the axis of a curved mirror or lens converge, or from which they appear to diverge,

after reflection in the mirror or passing through the lens.

Proton   The nucleus of a hydrogen atom and a part of the nucleus of every other atom. It has a positive charge equal in amount to that on an electron.

Radiation   1 The transfer of energy by electromagnetic waves. 2 Emission from radioactive materials.

Radioactive decay   The breakdown of a radioactive nucleus by the emission of alpha-, beta- or gamma-radiation.

Radioisotope   A radioactive isotope of an element.

Real image   An image that can be caught on a screen.

Recharging   The process of returning a secondary cell to its original condition by passing a small, steady, direct current through it.

Rectifier   A one-way device for electricity.

Reflection, angle of   The angle between the normal and the reflected ray.

Reflection, laws of   1 The incident ray, the reflected ray and the normal are all in the same plane. 2 The angle of incidence is equal to the angle of reflection.

Refraction   The bending of waves as they pass from one substance to another.

Refraction, angle of   The angle between the refracted ray and the normal.

Refraction, laws of   1 The incident ray, the refracted ray and the normal are all in the same plane. 2 The sine of the angle of incidence divided by the sine of the angle of refraction is always the same for the same two materials. This ratio is called the refractive index.

Resistance   The opposition of a circuit or part of a circuit to the flow of an electric current. It is equal to the voltage divided by the current and is measured in ohms (Ω).

Resistor   An electrical component with resistance.

Resonance   The large amplitude that occurs if a naturally vibrating system is driven at its own natural frequency.

Rheostat   A variable resistor.

Second   The SI unit of time.

Semiconductor   A material with conductivity between that of a conductor and an insulator.

Series connection   Each part of the electric circuit is joined end to end. The current is the same throughout such a circuit.

Shadow   The dark area behind an opaque object in the path of light.

Short circuit   A fault in an electric circuit when two bare wires touch and too large an electric current flows.

SI units   The International System of units used in all scientific measurements.

Specific heat capacity   The energy needed to raise

the temperature of one kilogram of a substance through one degree Celsius or one kelvin. It is measured in joules per kilogram kelvin. To raise the temperature of a mass of a substance requires energy equal to (mass × specific heat capacity × temperature rise).

Specific latent heat   The amount of energy needed to change one kilogram of solid into liquid (fusion) or liquid into vapour (vaporisation) at constant temperature. It is measured in joules per kilogram. The energy supplied is (mass × specific latent heat).

Spectrum   The colours red, orange, yellow, green, blue and violet seen when white light is split up in a rainbow or by a prism.

Speed   The distance travelled by an object divided by the time taken. It is measured in metres per second (m/s) or kilometres per hour (km/h).

States of matter   Most substances can exist either as a solid, liquid or vapour (gas). A change of state is a change from one of these states to another.

Surface tension   The force found in the surface of a liquid.

Temperature   A measure of how hot something is. It is measured by a thermometer in degrees Celsius (°C) or kelvin (K).

Thermionic emission   The escape of electrons from a very hot metal.

Thermistor   A device whose resistance alters when the temperature changes.

Thermocouple   A junction of two metal wires that produces an electrical potential difference when it is heated. It forms a common type of thermometer.

Thermometer   An instrument that measures temperature. Common types have mercury or alcohol in a bulb at one end of a very fine (capillary) tube.

Thermostat   A device that keeps the temperature constant.

Total internal reflection   When light, travelling in water, glass or Perspex, reaches a boundary with air it is totally reflected if the angle of incidence is greater than the critical angle.

Transducer   A device that detects a change in, say, temperature and converts the change into some other form—perhaps a change in voltage.

Transformer   Two coils on an iron core that can efficiently alter the voltage of an alternating current supply. If the voltage is increased it is a step-up transformer, but if it is decreased then it is a step-down transformer.

Transistor   An electronic component that can be used either as a switch or an amplifier.

Translucent   An object that allows light to pass through it but you cannot see clearly through it.

Transparent   objects allow light to pass through them and you can see clearly through them.

Transverse wave   A wave in which the vibrations move across the direction in which the wave is travelling.

Ultraviolet radiation   Part of the electromagnetic spectrum with wavelengths less than that of visible light.

Velocity   Speed in a given direction.

Velocity ratio   The distance moved by the effort divided by the distance moved by the load.

Virtual image   An image that cannot be caught on a screen; the light only appears to come from it.

Volt   The SI unit of potential difference: one volt (V) is one joule per coulomb.

Voltage   Another name for potential difference.

Voltage divider   A circuit or component in which only part of the supply voltage is passed on.

Watt   The SI unit of power, equal to one joule per second.

Wave   A repeated vibration carrying energy as it travels.

Wavelength   The distance from one wave crest to the next.

Wave speed   The speed of travel of any wave crest. Wave speed is the product of frequency and wavelength.

Weight   The pull of the earth on an object. It is the product of the object's mass and the acceleration due to gravity. Weight is a force and so is measured in newtons (N).

Work   Product of a force and the distance through which it moves. It is measured in joules (J).

X-rays   Very short wavelength electromagnetic waves that can penetrate many substances that light cannot.

Index